A History of Europe

VOLUME I

HENRI PIRENNE was born in Belgium in 1862. He lectured at the University of Liége, and in 1886 became a professor of medieval and Belgian history at the University of Ghent. During World War I, while teaching at the University of Ghent, he was arrested and deported to Germany as one of the leaders of Belgium's passive resistance. In 1922 he was invited to deliver a series of lectures in America. *Medieval Cities,* which appears in the Anchor series, grew from these lectures. At the time of his death in 1935 Pirenne was professor emeritus at the University of Ghent.

His works include: *History of Belgium,* 7 volumes; *Belgium Democracy: Its Early History; An Economic and Social History of Medieval Europe;* and *Mohammed and Charlemagne.*

A History of Europe

VOLUME I

From the End of the Roman World

in the West to the Beginnings

of the Western States

Henri Pirenne

With an Introduction by
Dr. Jan-Albert Goris

DOUBLEDAY ANCHOR BOOKS
DOUBLEDAY & COMPANY, INC.
GARDEN CITY, NEW YORK

Translated by Bernard Miall

A HISTORY OF EUROPE was published by University Books Inc. in 1956. The Anchor Books edition is published by arrangement with University Books Inc.

Anchor Books edition: 1958

The picture used on the cover is from the Portail Royal of Chartres Cathedral: the figure is of Aristotle, xiith century. Cover design by Leonard Baskin. Typography by Edward Gorey.

CONTENTS

BOOK ONE

The End of the Roman World in the West
To the Musulman Invasions

BOOK TWO

The Carolingian Epoch

BOOK THREE

Feudal Europe

BOOK FOUR

The War of Investitures and the Crusade

CONTENTS

BOOK FIVE
The Formation of the Bourgeoisie

BOOK SIX
The Beginnings of the Western States

Introduction

No country in Western Europe has had such a tormented, complicated and dramatic history as Belgium. Wedged in between France, Germany and England, she constantly suffered from the political pressure these large powers exerted on her while, at the same time, deriving profit from their cultural influences. Constantly solicited by her neighbors when not under actual military attack by them, the country succeeded in keeping its own character and nationality. As a borderland and sometimes a buffer state, its history is intimately connected with all the conflicts, political as well as ideological, that have divided Europe in the past. Until it reached its complete independence in 1830, it had been a pawn in power politics in Western Europe for over three centuries.

In the 19th century a great number of historians had delved into its archives and into those of the other European countries with which its fate had been linked; many workers had devoted themselves to the careful reconstruction of the history of the cities and the principalities of the country. But no one had undertaken to write the history of Belgium on a national plan. When those who were tempted to do so looked at the material confronting them, they saw a building-yard in utter confusion. Unending patience and devotion, honest scholarship of hundreds of local investigators had prepared the bricks of which history is built but none of them had had the vision and the audacity to erect out of that material a building that could stand criticism and that would prove to have solid foundations. A few had tried to write a preliminary synthesis but their efforts were clumsy and what they produced was, at best, a readable essay which often expressed far more what the author thought Belgium's history must have been, than what it had been in fact. To all of them, the labor required to disentangle purely Belgian facts from the history of France, England, Germany, Spain and Austria, seemed an herculean task that discouraged them from the outset. Therefore they satisfied themselves by endlessly writing valuable, solidly documented monographs on every aspect of the country's past. It was Henri Pirenne's first great achievement to conceive and write a *Histoire de Belgique* that, although begun more than a quarter of a century ago, still stands unequalled, solid in its conception and scarcely dated in its details. That this monumental work was not only of local interest is best proved by the fact that the initial volumes were first published in German translation from the original manuscript which was put out in French two years later.

Pirenne's *Histoire de Belgique* was immediately recognized as a work of national significance and his fundamental thesis exerted a considerable influence on political thinking in Belgium; it bolstered national unity and national pride in a country that is even more a political paradox than Switzerland, since it has no natural borders. But Pirenne himself disclaimed any patriotic inspiration or purpose for his work. With every appearance of reason he maintained that his intentions had been purely scientific. When the patriotic significance of his work was extolled, he declared impishly: "I have written the history of Belgium as I would have written the history of the Etruscans, without sentiment or patriotism." This statement, which at the time surprised and even slightly shocked those who used his thesis for political purposes, was the declaration of an honest craftsman and a true historian *sine ira et studio*. In a country where ideological and linguistic oppositions are lively, no one ever cast a doubt on his scientific objectivity. His position as the national historian has never been seriously challenged.

What explains such exceptional success? The solution

may be found in the appreciation one of his colleagues gave of his talent: "He is an architect, not a carpenter." It should be added however, that before being an architect, Pirenne had been an excellent carpenter, by which is meant that he knew and had practiced the most humble aspects of his profession: the exasperating research in archives, the boring labors of the bibliographer, the painstaking study of a number of purely local problems and the exacting scientific demands of text publications. He was indeed a complete historian, familiar with all the disciplines of his craft, before he set out on his great venture of synthesis for which he was eminently suited.[1]

Born in Verviers, in 1862, the son of a cloth manufacturer, he studied history at the University of Liége, where he had Godefroid Kurth as a master. From there he went to Germany where he took courses at the Universities of Berlin and Leipzig, and where he familiarized himself with the work of Karl Lamprecht. German historical science was then at the height of its prestige and it is doubtless that Pirenne profited a great deal from his experience in Germany. He was impressed by the Germanic thoroughness of his masters but he objected to their conscious and subconscious tendency to make history into a handmaiden of political reasoning. In 1920, he devoted his address, at the opening of the University of Ghent, to the theme: "Ce qu'il faut désapprendre de l'Allemagne," what we should "unlearn" from Germany.[1]

From Germany he went to France where he spent some time at the Ecole des Chartes and at the Ecole des Hautes Etudes.

For a year, he taught paleography and diplomatics at Liége and in 1886 he was appointed Professor of Medieval History at the University of Ghent, a post he kept without interruption—except for his imprisonment in Germany during the first World War, the details of which are told with great eloquence and feeling in the preface of this book. In 1930, Pirenne retired.

[1] The reader will note that Ghent is of course also (in French) Gand and that the latter spelling is used in other places in this book—Editor's Note.

On May 28, 1935, he died in his home, at Uccle, having finished a few days before the first draft of one of his major works: *Mohammed and Charlemagne.*

It is the general consensus that Pirenne was not only a good historian but a great historian. Which are the qualities required to make a great historian? First of all, a complete command of all the available facts, then a gift for synthesis which is essential, and also a feeling for style which is no less important. There was a time, not so long ago, when the writing of history was merely a form of literary endeavor, when facts counted little and when the synthesis presented by the author was always strongly inspired by a desire to prove either a point of national pride or a religious thesis. History has tried very hard indeed to become a science. It will probably never be an exact science but it has more and more been compelled and inclined to accept the discipline and the morality of other sciences.

The first requirement now for the historian is that he be dispassionate, although this demand may impose on him a more or less superhuman restraint. He may not bend the facts to his thesis and he has to respect them and to present all of them.

As to his style: in that field also, he has to live up to certain restrictions. He should not write *too* well, which means that he should not, like the novelist or the poet are wont to do, employ all the artifices of language and style in order to make his point, or to prejudice the reader in favor of his views. The success of historical vulgarization in our time depends largely on stylistic qualities. Several famous writers have become popular historians: their books are eminently readable, but one could scarcely find a paragraph in their daring synthetic views, which does not insult the knowledge of the reader familiar with the historical material.

Pirenne had an encyclopedic knowledge of history, no major work in the European languages had escaped him.

Although of Walloon origin, he had none of the Walloon's alleged traditional reluctance and incapacity to learn Germanic languages. Transplanted in Flanders, he devoted himself, in the early part of his career, to the publication of a corpus of documents relating to the important clothing industry of medieval Flanders. Trained both in Germany and France, he personally experienced the role his country had fulfilled in European history: to fuse and harmonize whatever was valuable in Germanic and Latin science and thinking. He was alert to every occasion for enlarging his knowledge. In the years of his captivity in Germany, he learned Russian and thus became one of the very few European historians of his time, if not the only one, to become familiar with Russian historians.

It has been remarked that in Book VIII of the *History of Europe,* his familiarity with the Russian historians made it possible for him "to write about the Slav states with more authority than any other European historian." Even in small details, he succeeded in using his knowledge of Russian. When he explains that the Avars were practically exterminated by Charlemagne, he makes this event come to life by referring to the Russian proverb: "He vanished like the Avars."

As for his gift of synthesis, when one examines his extensive list of works, it is apparent that he possessed this primary requirement for the historian to an exceptional degree from the outset of his career; but the urge to apply it on an ever increasing scale grew in him with the years. His first works were labors of scholarship requiring perfect knowledge of all the subsidiary sciences of history which he applied for the first time in a synthetic view when writing his *Histoire de Belgique.* It is remarkable to note that his very last article was devoted to a minute historical detail which had required great patience to elucidate. "The final goal of history," he used to say, "is to write the history of mankind." He wrote the history of his own country in such a way that it threw light on the history of Europe; he elucidated the origin of the medieval towns and proceeded from there to revise our concepts about the end of the Roman Empire and the beginning of the Middle Ages. In his final work, he opposed Mohammed and Charlemagne in a broad conception that impresses us as a daring and entirely new vision of European history. Thus the scope of his work was constantly enlarged and through the years the "magic perceptiveness of his orderly, synthetic mind" became more and more visible.

I ventured to say, above, that an historian should not write *too* well. The beauty of his style should not detract the attention from what he says and cloud the judgment of the reader. It is quite certain, for instance, that Winston Churchill's majestically beautiful prose will be submitted, a hundred years from now, to severe scrutiny as to its contents. Pirenne repeatedly pointed out that we cannot resign ourselves to the logic of history because we look too much at the events and the situations from the angle of our passion, our interests as persons or as individuals belonging to a class. These impediments to good scientific historical writing appear clearly in a style that is too personal. Pirenne wrote well, with precision and clarity, and it is noticeable that he restrained himself all the time, not wanting to indulge in *beautiful* writing. His French is elegant, limpid, and impeccable. It translates easily. That is probably due to the fact that he believed one should never use a word that Voltaire had not used. The rapid portraits he drew of some historical personages are exceedingly well done but he never succumbed to the temptation of interpreting their secret thoughts or of reconstructing their psychology: he sticks obstinately to the facts. Even in *Mohammed and Charlemagne,* the picture he draws of Charlemagne is very sober, although legend and literature gave him abundant material to indulge in artificial reconstruction. He was altogether too conscientious a scientist to believe in the providential action of one man when history is known to be the result of many diverse forces which the function of the "great man" is but to catalyze.

One felt that he constantly refrained from the temptation of coining phrases and writing striking formulas which, however fortunate they may be, nearly always lead to a distorted view of the subject. He did not aim at brilliancy for brilliancy's sake.

Buffon has taught European writers that: "The style is the man himself." "The man himself" had a magnetic personality. One of his German critics who, under the Nazi regime, critized him severely, was forced to recognize that:

"Er erzaehlt nicht, er erklaert." He does not tell the story, he explains it. Those who had the privilege of having Pirenne as a professor testify that he had no equal. One of his American pupils declared: "One understands him only by watching his hands." He formed a whole generation of excellent historians who held him in such high esteem that on the day he gave his last lecture at Ghent, he found them all sitting on the school benches in their former alma mater, in order to be present at his adieux.

All his life he remained a student. He delighted in meeting his friends in cafés, tossing around ideas that had come to him and forcing his friends to contradiction and discussion. For him a synthetic view, however daring, was always an hypothesis which had to be checked by facts. As to his character, his affability, his natural charm and gentleness did not exclude a firm attitude on occasion.

When teaching at the University of Ghent was stopped in 1914, the German governor of Belgium, General von Bissing, asked Pirenne to resume his courses. The conversation was conducted in French, a language von Bissing handled with great difficulty. Finally he asked Pirenne: "You speak German, don't you?" Pirenne answered: "I used to know it but I have forgotten it since August 3, 1914." The next day, he was shipped to Germany.

On two occasions only did I approach Henri Pirenne and each time I was impressed by his humility and his kindness. The first time was a rather formidable one for me: I had to appear before a three man committee which was to decide if the Belgian government would grant me a travel fellowship on the merits of my thesis. Pirenne presided and startled me from the outset by asking me to state in five minutes what my book contained. I had worked on it for three years, seriously undermined my health in the process, and ruined my eyesight for over nine months. His question sounded like an insult. I stuttered and proceeded to give a short outline of the first chapters. In the midst of a sentence I stopped and told Pirenne that the 704 pages of my work were but a commentary and elucidation of *Guicciardini's Discours on the Merchants of Antwerp, their*

Traffic and Commerce, which in a sense was true. The great man stopped me right there. He had written brilliant chapters on the economic history of Antwerp in the 16th century. Had I discovered anything that contradicted his synthesis? I had, and I developed with local pride that, contrary to his opinion, the burghers of my home town had not been essentially intermediaries between the Spanish, Italian and Portuguese merchants and financiers, but that they had played a respectable role in the economic development of the city. Soon we were arguing back and forth on this point and I noticed that the half hour normally allotted for the examination was largely exceeded. After an hour, Pirenne abruptly ended our discussion which had become quite lively, saying: "Young man, you're probably right but you have a tendency to become emotional about your home town. An historian may not do that—not too much anyway."

My second encounter with Pirenne occurred a few years later. I had, by chance, unearthed a satirical version of the Battle of the Golden Spurs, the great glory of Flanders in which the Flemish town militia defeated the pick of the French aristocracy in Kortrijk, in 1302. A monk in some English monastery had amused himself by telling the story of the French defeat in terms of the Gospel. I sent a copy of my article to Pirenne and while I was having lunch in a modest Brussels restaurant, he swooped down on me, recognizing the trembling examinandus of a few years before, put his hands on my shoulders and said: "Young man, you have taught me something I did not know." He recited part of the Latin text to me and gave far better comments on the document than I had been able to provide. Praise from Caesar, I thought. The Nobel Prize could not have given me greater pleasure at the moment.

To sum up his contribution to history, limiting this survey to his written work, one can say that he discovered and clearly outlined the basic forces which related Belgium's history to the development of Europe in general. He revolutionized the conceptions which were generally held of Belgian history and taught the Belgians that their country had in fact originated at the time of the Treaty of Verdun. While former historians had been blinded by the diversity of the tendencies in the history of the country, by the excessive individuality of the cities and by the constantly changing panorama of the loyalties within the country, Pirenne pointed to the enduring elements in the country's history that had drawn together the Provinces through their economic interests and through their ideas and their traditions.

He understood that Belgium had been, through the ages, a microcosm of history and that its unity did not depend on language nor on the existence of a monarchy, but on the cohesion derived from a unity of social level.

By so doing, he rendered his country and his countrymen a great service; while they have at times a tendency to stress what divides them, he showed them with dispassionate clarity what holds them together.

He also performed the remarkable feat of showing—the first to do so—how the Burgundian state originated. This event in European history has more than local importance: even if the Burgundian state did not fulfill its magnificent dream, at least it was for a short time one of the most impressive political constructions of Western Europe and, at the same time, one of the most powerful and original cultural centers of the civilized world.

One of his main contributions to historic writing was that he introduced the economic and social phenomena in history which had been neglected for a long time but, by drawing attention to these factors, he did not fall into the trap where so many German historians had lost their objectivity. He did not feel that history should only be explained through economic and social elements. He saw the development of history as a constant flow and was never fascinated by those figures which, through distance and legend, have acquired gigantic proportions. In his *History of Europe* he says: "Like all men who have changed history, Charlemagne did no more than accelerate the evolution which social and political needs had imposed upon his time." When the German translation of his *History of*

Europe appeared, such utterances were criticized by German scholars as proof that Pirenne did not understand the importance of the "Fuehrer prinzip" and, indeed, in all his writings he proved that he had a catholic interest in man in every station high or low.

A sizable part of his work is devoted to the study of the medieval town democracies, to the origins of trade and to the formation of the Flemish towns. With regard to the origin and the development of urban and communal life, his research had a pioneer quality. He was the first to explain clearly the birth of the cities through the economic and social elements. His book on medieval cities remains a model of insight and of precise historical writing.

Still enlarging the scope of his studies and his vision he then discovered that the chronology and the division into periods of European history which has been accepted in modern times had no foundation. It was believed that Roman influence had ceased abruptly when the Byzantine Empire fell and when the Barbarians had infiltrated the Roman territory, settled down and organized their own kingdoms. Pirenne proved that the influence of the Roman institutions continued far later than the third century; that economic activity throughout the Mediterranean continued as before, that city life remained active, that trade between East and West was not affected and that Rome survived through the form of its administration and through its cultural prestige. To him the Merovingian period was but a prolongation of Rome and he discovered that the real break in history happened only in the seventh or eighth century. Only then was Gaul forced to fall back on its own means of existence. When trade with the Mediterranean became impossible, when the Mediterranean became a *Moslem lake*, economy in Western Europe had to strive for self-sufficiency.

Pirenne first outlined this theory in this book, which he wrote under the particular circumstances described in the Preface by his son Jacques. It is, of course, quite irrelevant to the scientific value of the *History of Europe*, that it was written under those difficult circumstances.

In a certain sense, Pirenne's imprisonment in Germany was fortunate insofar as it gave him the occasion to make up an inventory of what he had studied and found out for about 35 years, and to organize it in a brilliant construction.

Professor Gray Cowan Boyce evaluated it as follows:

"Standing in a class by itself, the *History of Europe* is unique in plan, unique in origin and in the conditions under which it was composed; unique in the fact that it lay untouched for twenty years before again seeing the light of day. Unique too in that Pirenne considered that, in the long run, it might prove to be his most enduring and important contribution to historic scholarship."

It was hailed as a model of descriptive and objective commentary: the balance of the book, its lucidity and its bold and penetrating judgment was praised and it was said that it stood out head and shoulders above all other outlines on the same scale.

The portentous effect produced on Europe by the advent and the spreading of Moslem power continued to fascinate Pirenne for many years. He first outlined his theory about the opposition between Mohammed and Charlemagne in a short article published in 1922, and from then on he developed it in many lectures until 1933. A few weeks before his death, he finally wrote it down and the book appeared posthumously. Charlemagne, he wrote, would not have been without Mohammed, the one conditioned the other. It is quite certain that Pirenne's thesis provoked an increase of interest in the origins of our Middle Ages and forced historians to revise their opinions and to undertake new research in fields which they had neglected or scarcely exploited until then. Not only did he affect the Byzantinists and open the door to the knowledge of Russian historiography but he also made it clear that European history would gain by a greater familiarity with the Arabic and Moslem writers.

When one has summed up his achievements and discovered how harmoniously his genius as an historian developed, widening all the time the scope of his vision and the depth of his understanding, one has to agree that he fulfilled the noblest and most ambitious life program a man of science can set for himself, to be like Socrates was, a "midwife of ideas."

JAN-ALBERT GORIS

New York
August, 1955

Preface

On March 18th, 1916, about nine o'clock in the morning, a German officer of the Army of Occupation called at the house in which my father, M. Henri Pirenne, was then living (in the Rue Neuve Saint-Pierre, in Gand) and requested him to follow him to the "Kommandantur." There he was received by a major, who informed him that he was to leave for Germany immediately. When my father asked him why he had been arrested, the officer confined himself to replying: "I don't know; it's an order."

My mother was allowed to come and bid her husband farewell in the presence of an officer; but his son Robert, who was then in school, was not able to come and kiss his father good-bye, for an hour after his arrest M. Pirenne was already on his way to the Crefeld Camp.

Suddenly torn from his family and friends, and obliged to leave my mother alone in a country occupied by the enemy (her health had already been shaken by the death of her son Pierre, killed on the Yser on November 3rd, 1914), my father, on his arrival at the officers' camp at Crefeld, having resolved that he would not give way to dejection, immediately set to work. As a number of Russian officers were interned in the camp, he began, with the help of one of them, to study the Russian language.

My father's internment at Crefeld was provisional only, as was that of his friend and colleague Paul Fredericq at Gütersloh, whither he had been deported on the day of my father's arrest. The German authorities had hoped, by thus arresting them, to intimidate the professors of the University

of Gand, and to induce them to resume their lectures, as
they had been requested. The result disappointed their ex-
pectations. The University refused to re-open its doors during the alien occupation. The consequence of this resistance
was not long delayed. On May 12th, 1916, the order
reached Crefeld to transfer my father to the camp at Holzminden. His internment there influenced him profoundly.

The camp, as he describes it in his *Souvenirs de Captivité*,
"contained at this time from eight thousand to ten thousand
prisoners, divided among eighty-four great wooden barracks, arranged in rows in a space of some ten acres. The
central avenue, 'Avenue Joffre,' as the prisoners called it,
was thronged from morning to evening by a heterogeneous
crowd in which all national types and all social classes were
represented, and in which every language was spoken, excepting English, for there was not a single Englishman at
Holzminden.

"In the centre of the camp ten barracks enclosed by a
wire trellis sheltered the women and children. Every day,
between noon and three o'clock, the women were allowed
to leave this enclosure. As for the children, of whom there
were a certain number in the camp, one could see them, of
a morning, going to the schools which certain good people
had somehow managed to provide for them.

"Naturally, the bulk of this heterogeneous population
consisted of men of the people. Holzminden was the recep-
tacle into which Germany poured, pell-mell, undesirable or
inconvenient persons from all the occupied countries. A barrack near that which I occupied sheltered the inmates of
the prison of Loos, near Lille, among whom were a certain
number of convicted murderers. With a few exceptions, all
these men endured their fate with a resignation that was
truly admirable. Many, in the long run, were physically de-
bilitated; there were sick men, and neurasthenics, and a few
cases of insanity; but in nearly all the mental and moral
faculties remained intact. Yet many of them had already
been there for two years. For that matter, these were the
most resolute. They had known the miseries of the first
months of the war, suffered the brutality of the sentries, endured the cold of winter in unheated barracks, and wit-

nessed the agony of the unhappy citizens of Louvain who were thrown into the camp in September 1914. Little by little they had organized themselves. Thanks to the consignments of food from the committees in all parts of Europe which watched over the welfare of the prisoners, and to the parcels received from friends and relatives, the alimentary conditions had become tolerable. Clothing had been received, medicines, and books. Private initiative had got to work in a thousand ways. Some French students had had a small barrack built at their own expense, 'the University,' in which professors and engineers gave lectures, and which contained a library, whose volumes were bound by a bookbinder from Brussels. Benevolent societies were organized, and schools established for the children. Cafés and even restaurants were opened. Some Catholic priests had installed a chapel in the barracks. Some Belgians had fitted up an empty space for ball games: there was a skittle alley too, and a bowling green, much frequented by players from the North of France. Not many, however, indulged in athletic sports; there was too little room, and all were weakened by captivity and lack of exercise.

"We seldom came into contact with the Germans. The General in command of the camp was hardly ever visible; he left things to his subordinate, a harsh and brutal reserve officer. The organization of the camp, which was under his supervision, was simple enough, the officials being recruited from among the prisoners themselves. There was a *chef de camp*, a *chef de district* and a *chef de baraque*, who were responsible for the discipline of the camp; and it was with them that the prisoners came into contact. Every evening a bulletin appeared, containing the orders and regulations for the following day. Only police duties were left to the soldiers and the noncommissioned officers; and they performed these duties without amenity. The barracks were constantly searched; letters were seized, and the 'guilty' persons were sent to the cells for one or more days' solitary confinement. Such punishments were an everyday matter; one would often see a notice affixed to the door of 'the University': 'Professor X—— will not lecture to-day, as he is in prison.'"[1]

My father found his place immediately in this strange environment. As director of the benevolent society he came into contact with the most unfortunate of the prisoners, whose miseries he endeavoured to alleviate. But he devoted himself above all to the work of sustaining the morale of his companions in misfortune, by organizing two courses of lectures. "For my own part," he writes, "I delivered two courses of lectures, one on economic history for two or three hundred Russian students who were captured at Liége in August 1914, and another in which I related to my fellow-countrymen the history of their native country. I never had more attentive pupils, nor did I ever teach with such pleasure. The lectures on the history of Belgium presented a really striking spectacle. The listeners were jammed together, some perched on the palliasses which were piled up in one corner of the barrack that served as lecture-hall, others crowded together on the benches, or standing up against the boarded partitions. Some were gathered outside under the open window. Inside a suffocating heat was radiated from the tarred paper roof. Thousands of fleas were jumping all over the place, leaping in the sunlight like the drops of a very fine spray. Sometimes I fancied I could hear them, so profound was the silence of all these men, who listened while a fellow-Belgian spoke to them of their native country, recalling all the catastrophes which it had suffered and overcome. No doubt the size of my audience made the 'Kommandantur' uneasy. One day I received an order to the effect that I must discontinue my lectures. I naturally protested against a measure which was directed against myself alone among all the teachers in the camp. I sent the General a note which he promised to forward to Berlin, and this was the beginning of an interminable correspondence. For a whole fortnight I had to furnish notes and reports and explanations of every kind. At last I received permission to resume my lectures. But I had

[1] Henri Pirenne, *Souvenirs de Captivité en Allemagne*, 1921, pp. 31–35. These reminiscences appeared also in the *Revue des Deux Mondes*, February 1st and 15th, 1920.

to pledge myself to deliver every night, at the *bureau du camp*, a summary of the next day's lecture, and I had to put up with the presence, among my audience, of two or three soldiers who understood French."[2]

And while he was devoting himself to teaching others, my father continued, under the guidance of a student, the study of the Russian language which he had begun at Crefeld.

The course of lectures on economic history which he was delivering to an audience of students led him to consider a plan which he had already been cherishing for some years: that of writing a general history of Europe; and by degrees, even in the depressing atmosphere of the camp, deprived of all comfort, and all possibility of research, he elaborated in his mind the plan of the vast synthesis of which he dreamed. He managed to obtain some of the works of certain Russian historians, the study of which was to open new horizons, and to enable him to produce a work that no historian had ever attempted to undertake unaided —a general history of Europe, expounded on the lines followed in his *Histoire de Belgique*.

My father's arrest and internment had called forth many attempts at intervention; the Academy of Amsterdam proposed that he should be interned in Holland; American professors begged that he might be sent to the University of Princeton; President Wilson, King Alfonso XIII, and the Pope had endeavoured to persuade the German Government to release him.

Eleven months before his arrest—on April 6th, 1915—the Swedish Academy had conferred upon him the title of Associate Member, though it was only in the Holzminden camp that he received the official notification of his nomination; and finally a pamphlet published by Professor Christian Nyrop of Copenhagen, on *L'Arrestation des professeurs belges et l'Université de Gand*, had moved the scholars and scientists of all the neutral countries. The German Government wished to respond to these manifestations by an act

[2] Henri Pirenne, *Souvenirs de Captivité en Allemagne*, 1921, pp. 38–39.

of clemency. In June 1916, it made my father an offer: he could choose, as his place of residence, one of the University cities of Germany. As he refused to leave the camp, he was transferred to Jena on August 24th, 1916.

There he found his friend Paul Fredericq, and for some months he was able to make use of the University library, and to devote himself methodically to the study of the Russian historians. But the German "clemency" proved to be ephemeral indeed. On January 24th, 1917, the rooms of the exiles were suddenly searched, and their letters and papers seized. Brought before a colonel, the burgomaster, and the *Bezirksdirektor*, they were reproached with having abused the "hospitality of Germany." A few days later, while M. Fredericq was sent to Burgel, my father was deported to Kreuzburg on the Werra, a little Thuringian town of two thousand inhabitants, a few miles from Eisenach.

Described as "extremely dangerous," he was refused a room in the best hotel. He was installed in the "Gasthof zum Stern," where they consented to give him lodging. "It was a large house in the market-place, opposite the church and the Rathaus, with a big tiled roof, a wide *porte cochère*, and, at the back, a courtyard enclosed by a stable, a barn and a dairy."[3]

My father was able to go about as he pleased, but once every day he had to present himself before the burgomaster and give in his correspondence, which had to be censored at the *Bezirksdirektion* of Eisenach.

It was then that the work took shape of which he had elaborated the plan in the barracks of Holzminden. My father has himself described the circumstances under which it was written: "I decided immediately that I could never hold out against the monotony of my detention unless I forced myself to undertake some definite occupation, with every hour of the day reserved for its special task. I continued the study of the Russian language. . . . Every afternoon, from two o'clock to five, I went for a walk. At five o'clock I set to work on the draft of a book of which I had

[3] Henri Pirenne, *Souvenirs de Captivité en Allemagne*, 1921, p. 64.

often thought before the war, and of which I carried the plan in my head. This occupied me until supper-time. I read the newspaper, and the day was done, and on the following day I observed the same timetable. I never departed from this regimen, whatever the weather or season. It offered me the inestimable advantage of knowing, in the morning, what I had to do until the evening. It set a barrier to my vagrant imaginings, calmed my anxieties and banished boredom. In the end I became really interested in my work. I thought about it during my solitary walks in the fields and woods. There was nothing there to recall the war, and I forced myself to forget it. I used to talk to myself. Having no duties to perform, no work to do, and being free from all mundane or social obligations in my solitude, I tasted the charms of meditation, of the slow and progressive elaboration of the ideas that one carries in one's mind, the ideas with which one lives, and in which one finally becomes absorbed.

"In short, I understand, or at least I think I did understand, the voluntary seclusion of Descartes in his 'room with a Dutch stove.' I too was living in 'a room with a stove,' and if I was living there despite myself, there were moments when I managed to forget this. . . . Every morning, about ten o'clock, I interrupted my work to call on the burgomaster, whom I found on the first floor of the Rathaus. This was the most exciting moment of the day. Should I find there some of those letters which were the sole distraction and the only solace of my exile? . . .

"One by one I made the acquaintance of the aristocracy of the village, the *Honoratioren,* to employ the consecrated term. The most important and also the most cultivated of these gentlemen was the Superintendant.[4] We used to exchange a few words whenever we met, and at times I was able to get him to speak of the war. He was a good talker, and he was fond of talking. He certainly had no idea of the pleasure I felt on hearing him expatiate on a subject with which I had long been familiar, thanks to my talks at Jena. Race and its historic influence was constantly recur-

[4] Crefeld is the seat of a Lutheran "superintendance."

ring in his conversation. Romanism, Germanism! For him, these were everything. Romanism was the Catholic Church, where form had precedence over content, convention and tradition over liberty of thought and the individual conscience. Apart from this he ascribed the history of the world to Protestantism and Protestantism to Germanism.—'But, after all, Calvin!' I protested, one day.—'Calvin!' he said, 'is Luther adapted to the Roman spirit . . .'

"On another occasion we spoke of political freedom. This too was the appanage of the Germans. Luther had announced the true formula—a formula, of course, not to be understood by foreigners.—'After all,' I suggested, 'the truth is, very probably, that this notion of liberty is characteristic of a people whose own liberty is of recent date. With us, serfdom was abolished in the 13th century; but it still existed in Germany at the beginning of the 19th century. For people who have been accustomed to liberty for the last six hundred years, and for those whose grandfather perhaps was liable to render "ban service" to his lord, and was *adscriptus glebae,* words have not the same meaning, and they find it hard to agree.'—The Superintendant gazed at me in astonishment. He was doubtless asking himself if I was really in earnest. . . . The more I learned of Germany the more obvious it seemed to me that her discipline, her spirit of obedience, her militarism, and her lack of political ability and understanding, were largely explained by the renaissance of serfdom that occurred in the 16th century. In these respects there is a profound and radical difference between Germany and the Occidental countries. But for the almost universal serfdom of the rural populations to the east of the Elbe, could Lutheranism ever have spread as it did, and could the organization of the Prussian State have been conceivable?"

It was in this solitude, a solitude occupied with meditation, and interrupted by conversations which often opened wide horizons, that my father wrote his *History of Europe.*

When he first set to work, a few days after he was installed in the Thuringian inn, he had no books at his disposal other than a little historical manual which was used in the local school. To begin with, he reduced to writing, in small school exercise-books, the plan which he "carried in his head." On March 23rd, 1917, he began the first draft. The dates which he noted every day in the margin of his manuscript enable us to follow the progress of the work. Written without interruption and almost without erasure, consisting of short chapters, themselves divided into paragraphs, we feel that we have here the expression of a mind which had indeed reached the zenith of its development. In the midst of the most dramatic episodes the author's self-restraint was such that he preserved the most perfect objectivity. Yet he was not living in a hermetic cell, and the proof of this is in his work. If I have recalled certain conversations to which he draws attention in his *Souvenirs,* it was simply because one feels that they were clearly related to the pages which he was then writing; the eagerness of the official German scholarship to explain everything by race inspired several observations which show us the utter falsity of this historical theory, which is born of political necessity, and the character of the population in whose midst he was living evidently inspired certain social explanations which are among the most striking passages in the book. Deprived of any access to sources, unable to refer to details or to verify dates, my father was obliged to confine himself to the study of historical aspects; social history, economic evolution, and the great religious and political movements absorbed his attention, the historical data serving, after all, merely as the supporting basis of the great fresco which he painted with broad strokes, embracing East and West in a single perspective.

The reader may perhaps be surprised to find that so many dates are cited in parentheses. In the manuscript they were nearly all absent; the parentheses were there to be filled in later, and I thought it best, in publishing this history, to add the dates as my father would have done.

The *History of Europe* ends abruptly about 1550. Yet the plan which the manuscript follows, page by page, is continued down to 1914. Events interrupted the full elaboration of the plan. The arrival at Kreuzberg on August 8th,

1918, of my mother and my younger brother Robert, who, after more than two years, had at last obtained permission to share my father's exile, caused only a few days' interruption. It was the armistice that set a term to the work.

Returning to Belgium, my father was chiefly preoccupied with the continuation of his *Histoire de Belgique*, and the *History of Europe* was laid aside. Yet *Les Villes du Moyen Âge*, *La Civilisation occidental en Moyen Âge*, and his last work, which my father completed only a few months before his death, *Mahomet et Charlemagne*, are merely partial developments of the *History of Europe*.

How often we have spoken of this work, which I for my part consider to be his masterpiece! It was his intention to complete it one day. But I must publish it—he told me—if he did not live to finish it. In offering it now to the public I am performing a pious duty.

Yet on reading the *History of Europe* one must not forget that the author was unable to give it its definitive form. It is published as it came from his pen; he did not even re-read it; so that it may seem, here and there, a little unpolished as to its style, but all the more attractive in the vigour and boldness of its thought, still untarnished by careful considerations of form. My father wrote the *History of Europe* for himself. The book that he would have given to the public, had he lived, would doubtless have been illustrated by a greater number of data and references and quotations, and its style would have been more chiselled. It could not have been more vital, more compressed, more pregnant with thought. The author has poured himself into the mould of his book. At the time of writing it he had already built up the great synthesis of which the books which he published after the war were merely the development.

The *History of Europe* is the outcome of all the research which my father had undertaken during the thirty-five years which he had devoted to history before 1914; it is the synthesis of all his knowledge, ripened in meditation at a time when, being deprived of access to books, he could confront that knowledge only with his own thought.

It is this thought, in which the whole man lives again,

that my mother and I have felt we must offer, in all its
spontaneity, to those who seek in history the fundamental
explanation of the great historical movements which have
given birth to our own age.

JACQUES PIRENNE

Author's Preface

I am alone here with my thoughts, and if I cannot succeed in controlling them, they will end by allowing themselves to be controlled by my sorrow,[1] my ennui, and my anxieties for my dear ones, and will drive me into neurasthenia and despair. I absolutely must react against my fate. "There are people," my dear wife writes to me, "who allow themselves to be prostrated by misfortune, and others who are tempered by it. One must resolve to be of these latter." I shall try, for her sake and my own.

At Holzminden the Russian students for whom I improvised a course of economic history expressed the desire, and I could see that it was sincere, that I should publish my lectures. Why should I not attempt to sketch here, in its broad outlines, what might be a *History of Europe?* The lack of books cannot prove a great handicap, since this is a question of a broad sketch only. I had already thought of it at Jena, and I made some notes for it. It seems to me that I saw certain relations unravelling themselves. In any case, this would be an occupation. It seems to me that I am no longer thinking very clearly, and my memory has certainly deteriorated. But perhaps the effort will do me some good. The essential thing is to kill time and not allow oneself to be killed by it.

I dedicate my work to the memory of my beloved Pierre, to my dear wife, and to my dear sons.

H. PIRENNE

Kreuzburg A.D. Werra
  Gasthof zum Stern
January 31st, 1917

[1] The writer had lost his son Pierre, who had enlisted as a volunteer in the Belgian Army, and was killed at the age of nineteen, on November 3rd, 1914, in the course of the Battle of the Yser.

BOOK ONE

The End of the Roman World
in the West

To the Musulman Invasions

becoming accommodating with his animus. They were no

CHAPTER I

The Barbarian Kingdoms in the
Roman Empire

1. *The Occupation of the Empire*

It would be a great error to imagine that the Germans who
established themselves in the Empire in the 5th century
were like those whom Tacitus has described. Their contact
with Rome had taught them many things. The Empire, too,
which appeared less formidable once they had crossed the
frontier, was becoming more familiar to them; they were
growing accustomed to it now that it was no longer inaccessible to them. And the Empire, in its turn, since it could
no longer treat them with arrogance, was beginning to be
more accommodating. Julian, in 358, allowed the Franks
to settle in Taxandria, in return for military service, and
through these Franks how much Roman influence must
have crossed the Rhine!

At the other extremity of the Empire, on the banks of the
Danube, the contact was still closer. The Goth Ulfila had
brought Christianity from Byzantium, and had spread it
among his compatriots. To be exact, this Christianity was
that of the Arians, who were then predominant in the East.
But the consequences of this fact would not appear until
a later period. The essential thing was that even before they
entered the Roman world, the Goths, the most powerful of
the Germanic peoples, had abandoned their paganism, and

with it had lost the great safeguard of their national individuality.

The Empire itself was swarming with Barbarians who
had come to take service in the legions, and on whom fortune had smiled. Stilicho was a Barbarian; and Aetius; the
two last great warriors of Western antiquity. And we can
imagine how many of their compatriots would find their
way, under the protection of such men, into the civil as
well as the military administration. Even in Rome, or at the
Imperial court, the sons of northern kings were found, who
had gone thither to learn the Latin tongue, or to be initiated
into the Latin civilization. So, little by little, the Empire was
becoming accustomed to the Barbarians. They were no
longer strangers. The danger still existed, but it was less
urgent.

But with the invasion of Europe by the Huns (372) the
peril recurred in all its gravity. The Goths, who were established on both banks of the Dniester—the Ostrogoths, as
their name indicates, to the east of the river, the Visigoths
to the west—did not attempt to resist the Mongol horsemen,
the very aspect of whom filled them with terror. Before
them the Ostrogoths retreated in disorder; the Visigoths,
pressed by this retreat, found themselves driven against the
Danube frontier. They demanded the right to cross it. The
danger had come so suddenly that they had not been able
to take measures to cope with it. Nothing of the kind had
been foreseen. The very terror of the Visigoths made it clear
that they would not hesitate to use force if their request
were refused. They were given permission to pass, and they
continued to pass for many days before the wondering gaze
of the Roman outposts: men, women, children and cattle,
on rafts and in canoes, some clinging to planks, and others
to inflated skins or barrels. An entire people was migrating,
led by its king.

And it was in this very fact that the peril of the situation
lay. What was to be done with these newcomers? It was
impossible to disperse them among the provinces. The Romans had to deal with a whole nation, which had left its
own territory in order to occupy another country. And they
would have to find a country for it within the Empire. A

people which would retain its own institutions and its own king would have to be admitted to the Empire, and allowed to live under the Roman suzerainty. It was the first time that such a problem had presented itself. The Romans tried to circumvent the problem by a subtle manœuvre. The king of the Visigoths was proclaimed a Roman general, so that without ceasing to be the national leader of his people he had his place in the Imperial administration; a fantastic and equivocal solution of a contingency no less equivocal and fantastic.

The first consequence of this solution was to give the revolt of the Visigoths, which broke out a little later (A.D. 378),[1] a very disconcerting character. It was actually the insurrection of an alien people, which was asking for territory and the right of permanent settlement in the very heart of the Empire. But it could also be regarded as a military mutiny, and this made it possible to negotiate with the enemy. In order to prevent the pillage of Thrace, the Emperor Arcadius, reigning in the East, ordered the Visigoths to occupy Illyria, which he claimed his brother Honorius, reigning in the West, was holding in defiance of his rights. The rebels asked nothing better than to profit by this "order." They conscientiously occupied Illyria. But this rugged country was not what they were looking for. Italy was close at hand. The Germanic peril, which had hitherto menaced both halves of the Empire at once, now definitely turned away from the East and concentrated itself upon the West. The Greek world was to have no further contact with the Germans.[2]

To save Italy from this menace the West mustered all its forces in one supreme effort. Stilicho recalled from Gaul and Noricum and Rhaetia the legions which were defending the passage of the Rhine and the Danube. He defied the Barbarians in two great battles, at Pollanzo and Verona,

[1] On August 9th, 379, Valens was defeated at Adrianople. The peace of Theodosius enabled the Goths to establish themselves in Mesia. There was a fresh revolt under Alaric in 395.

[2] Three-quarters of a century later Byzantium was once more to feel the pressure of the two Theodorics, and of the Ostrogoths, but once again she contrived to divert their attention to Italy.

and drove them back into Friuli. Flatterers were not lacking
to compare him with Marius. A poem in his honour which
has come down to us fills the reader with melancholy surprise; it still expresses such enthusiasm for the majesty of
Rome, and is so convinced of the immortality of the Empire.

But the Empire, alas, was ruined. Its exhausted finances
no longer enabled it to maintain on its frontiers the compact armies which might have contained at any point the
thrust of the Germans driven back by Attila, whose hordes
were still triumphantly advancing towards the West, over-
throwing, as they came, people after people. Stilicho saved
Italy only by leaving undefended all the Transalpine provinces. The result could not be long delayed.

The Vandals crossed the Rhine with bands of Suevi,
passed downwards through Gaul, pillaging as they went,
crossed the Pyrenees, and halted only by the shores of the
Mediterranean, where they installed themselves in the south
of Spain and on the coast of Africa. The Burgundi followed
the course of the Rhone and spread through its basin as
far as the Gulf of Lyons. Less adventuresome, the Alamanni
contented themselves with colonizing Alsace, the Ripuarian
Franks the neighbourhood of Cologne as far as the Meuse,
and the Salic Franks the plains of the Scheldt and the Lys.

At the same time a second attack was made upon Italy.
Some bands of Germans crossing from Noricum and Rhaetia crossed the Alps under the leadership of Radagaisus,
ravaging the Cisalpine territories and marching upon Rome,
demanding land. A second time Stilicho stayed the flood.
The invaders were cut to pieces and massacred under the
walls of Florence (405). Then the victor himself perished
(408). Thereupon the Visigoths took it upon themselves to
avenge him. Under the pretext of punishing his assassins
they resumed their march upon Rome. Stilicho's army was
still in being; but as might have been expected of an army
of mercenaries, it did not care to oppose the avengers of its
leader. There was no resistance. Honorius shut himself up
in Ravenna while Alaric entered Rome. This was the first
time Barbarians had entered the gates of the Eternal City
since the invasion of the Gauls in 380 B.C. True Barbarians
as they were, they contented themselves with wrenching off

the ornaments of gold and silver that glittered in the Forum and on the pediments of the public buildings. They had no hatred of Rome and they did not maltreat the population. What they wanted was land, and the charm of the country growing upon them as they marched southwards, they continued on their way through the enchanting landscape of Campania. Alaric would have led them into Sicily, but he died suddenly not far from Cosenza (410). His companions gave him a funeral of epic majesty. They dug the warrior's grave in the bed of the Busento, whose stream was diverted from its course. Then the river was allowed to return to its bed, and to flow above his last resting-place. The slaves who had dammed the river and dug the grave were slain, that the position of the grave, which is still inviolate, might for ever remain a secret.

The Visigoths acknowledged Athaulf, the brother of Alaric, as his successor. We may judge of the progressive Romanization of the Barbarians from the fact that he was passionately desirous of alliance with the Imperial family. In order to get rid of him, Honorius resigned himself to giving him in marriage his sister Galla Placidia. The nuptials were celebrated with great pomp, to the accompaniment of the inevitable epithalamium inviting Venus and Cupid to shower their gifts upon the spouses. Athaulf was evidently anxious that the Romans, and his wife, should pardon his origin. He asked nothing better, he said, than to place the forces of his Barbarians at the service of the Empire. He was asked to employ them in expelling the Vandals who were still infesting the south of Gaul. He led them into Aquitaine, and there they settled, and also in the north of Spain.

But was the Empire to become the property of the Germans? Or would Germans and Romans share the same fate and fall beneath the Tartar yoke? For the first time the Yellow Peril was menacing the whole of Europe. Attila was continuing his advance, and conquering the Germanic populations, or driving them before him. Already he was crossing the Rhine, and his hordes, veering towards the south-west, were invading the north of Gaul. It was there, near Chalons-sur-Marne, that the last warrior of antiquity,

Aetius, came forward to offer him the decisive battle. The
Franks, the Burgundi and the Visigoths had sent him reinforcements, and the army which he commanded was really
a microcosm of that Empire which, though submerged by
the Germans, refused to disappear. Before it perished it did
humanity a supreme service in repulsing the Hun invasion.
The superior tactics which Aetius owed to the civilization
for which he was fighting saved that civilization from inundation by the Barbarians. After two days of battle Attila
decamped, and turned back to Germany. This retreat was
not yet a rout, and in the following year the "Scourge of
God" ravaged upper Italy. But once again he withdrew,
and in the year 453 he died, suddenly, in the midst of an
orgy.

The Empire of this predecessor of Jenghiz Khan crumbled as rapidly as that of his follower eight hundred years
later, leaving nothing to mark its existence but ruins, and
a lasting memory of terror in popular tradition.

Aetius, the conqueror of Attila, was assassinated by order
of the Emperor Valentinian III. With him vanished, says a
contemporary chronicler, "the salvation of the Western
State." Rome was taken and pillaged by the Vandals in
455; and the noble Majorian was unable to avenge the
insult. But more and more the power was passing into the
hands of the German chieftains: Ricimer, Orestes and
Odoacer placed themselves, in succession, at the head of
the German soldiers and adventurers who had been pouring
into Italy since the Hunnish catastrophe, and who were
eager to obtain land.

The last Emperors were deposed; the last of all, Romulus
Augustulus, the son of Orestes, was banished to Campania,
and the Barbarian Odoacer, not venturing to call himself
Emperor, conferred upon himself the only title at the disposal of the Germans: that of king.

It was in the midst of this lamentable disorder that another king, Theodoric, followed by a whole people, descended on Italy from the Alps. The Ostrogoths who followed him, and who had been driven back from the
Dniester toward the Upper Danube by Attila, and then
subjected by him, profited by their release to claim their

share of Italy. Between them and the disorganized horde that recognized Odoacer fortune was not long in the balance. The Herulian adventurer, defeated in open battle (488), took refuge in Ravenna. Unable to reduce the city by siege, Theodoric invited him, under a sworn safe-conduct, to an interview, and slew him with his own hand (493). Henceforth Italy was his.

This was the last war of the widespread invasion. In the West, the whole Empire was now submerged by it. A medley of kingdoms covered all its provinces: Anglo-Saxon kingdoms in Britain, a Frank kingdom in the north of Gaul, a Burgundian kingdom in Provence, a Visigoth kingdom in Aquitaine and in Spain, a Vandal kingdom in Africa and the islands of the Mediterranean, and lastly, an Ostrogoth kingdom in Italy. As a matter of fact, this Empire, whose territory was thus dismembered, had not ceded an inch of soil to its invaders. In law, they were only occupiers of the soil, and their royal titles meant nothing save to the peoples they had brought with them. This is so true that, even though each of them reigned over a far greater number of Romans than of Germans, they did not call themselves King of Gaul, or King of Italy, but King of the Franks, King of the Ostrogoths, etc. But what followed? There was no longer an Emperor. And the Empire, one may say, disappeared in virtue of this adage of Roman law, that "in the matter of possession, occupation is equivalent to title."

2. *The New States*

If we compare a map of the Roman Empire in the West with a linguistic chart of modern Europe, we see that the domain of the Germanic languages has undergone very little expansion, although the whole Empire was in the hands of the Germans. There are only five frontier provinces in the whole or part of which a Germanic language is spoken, apart from the British Isles: the second Belgium, in which Flemish is spoken, and the two Germanies (the Rhenish province, Alsace), Rhaetia, and Noricum (Switzerland, Basle, Württemberg, Southern Bavaria, Austria), which are German by language. Everywhere else the Latin tongue has survived into our own days, in the form which it has assumed in the various Romance languages: French, Provençal, Spanish, Portuguese, Romansh, Italian. It was only on the extreme frontier of the Empire that the Germans descended *en masse*, submerging the Latinized population, which, of course, in these constantly threatened regions, must have been extremely sparse. Everywhere else the contrary phenomenon was observed. The Germans who penetrated farther into the Empire, being there in the minority, were absorbed by the provincials. After two or three generations their language had disappeared; and intermarriage did the rest. The number of French or Provençal words of Germanic origin hardly exceeds five hundred. We should seek in vain to-day among the populations of Provence, Spain and Italy for the fair hair and the blue eyes of the invaders of the 5th century—and if we did find them, should we not attribute them to the Gauls? The Germanic manners and customs resisted no better. For example, the monuments of Visigothic law that have been preserved show how superficial the Germanization of the Empire was in actual fact. It is not correct to say that the Roman world became Germanized. It became "barbarized," which is not at all the same thing.

With the exception of the Anglo-Saxons of Britain, the Germanic peoples did not import their political institutions into the Empire. The exception confirms the rule: for in Britain the provincials retreated before the invaders, and the latter, finding themselves alone, naturally continued to govern themselves as they had done in their old home. But everywhere else the Roman population not only remained in its place, but continued to live under almost the same conditions as before the conquest. There was, of course, a great deal of pillage and massacre, and there were individual acts of violence, but there was no systematic spoliation; still less was there any enslavement of the people. Nor was any rational resistance offered by the provincials (with honourable exceptions in Gaul and Britain), nor were the Germans hostile to them. Perhaps there was a little contempt on the one side, a little respect on the other. For that matter, the people could not be quite sure that the Germans were not soldiers of the Empire.

Moreover, the Germans, like the Romans, were Christians; and while they entered the Empire as conquerors, they submitted themselves to the Church, which, under her authority, merged the Germans with the Romans.

The Christianity which they professed was certainly one of the essential causes of their immediate rapprochement to the populations of the conquered countries, and there seems to be no doubt that the readiness with which the Barbarians abandoned their national tongues was explained by the fact that the language of the Church was Latin.

The Germans, for that matter, did not attempt to superimpose themselves upon the Roman populations; they settled down beside them. In the south of Gaul the Visigoths established themselves on the principles in force for the billeting of the Roman armies (the *tertia*), according to which one-third of the inhabitant's dwelling had to be placed at the disposal of the soldiers. The measure was extended to the land, the German occupation being now permanent, and a sort of peaceful penetration took place, concerning which, however, we have very little information. In the north of Gaul the newcomers were settled on the domains of the treasury or on unoccupied land. As for the juridical status of the person, this remained, on either side, what it had been. Germans and Romans continued to live in conformity with their national laws, each retaining their special customs in respect of property and the family and inheritance. The "territoriality" of the law was replaced by its "personality," and this "territoriality" made its reappearance only during the 9th century, when the fusion of the two peoples had become complete.

This intermingling of two distinct but equal nationalities obviously excluded the possibility of applying to the more numerous and more civilized people the political institutions of the other. Moreover, these institutions, applicable to Barbarian life, were no longer so to the new conditions to which the Germans had just been introduced. They fell into desuetude of themselves, and no one thought of reviving them.

Nothing illustrates more clearly the transformation which had occurred in this respect in the 5th and 6th centuries than a glance at the situation of royalty.

The Germans, we know, had kings. But with them the royal power was completely subordinated to the assembly of the people, who conferred it on whom they pleased, since it was elective. But there was nothing of this after the conquest. Set high above his fellows by the power which conquest had conferred upon him, the king was henceforth possessed of absolute authority. There was now only one power in the State—the king's; the constitution was reduced to the simple exercise of personal government. The king had shed all vestiges of his primitive origin. He no longer bore any resemblance to his Germanic ancestors; but only to the Roman Emperor. At all events, the irresponsibility and the autocratic power of the Emperor were his.

However, he willingly proclaimed himself the lieutenant of the Emperor. While for his Germanic subjects he was a national king, for the Romans he was merely a general of the Empire, and the titles which he assumed or demanded of the Emperor enabled the latter to regard him as the representative of the Imperial authority.

Installed in Ravenna after the Goths had established themselves in the north of Italy, Theodoric continued the Roman traditions and was recognized by the population, and by the Church, as the representative of legality. Genseric himself, after he and his Vandals had conquered Africa, the richest and most prosperous of the Western provinces, had all the appearance, despite his rupture with Rome, of a Romanized king, whose absolutism was manifested in the bloody repression of any leanings toward independence on the part of the Germanic aristocracy, and found expression within the framework of Roman institutions. The court of the Visigoths—first at Toulouse, then at Toledo—was also completely Roman. The population of the old, conquered provinces retained its Roman institutions and officials, adopted by the new rulers, and its Roman judges, and continued to pay its taxes. The Germanic army, installed in the midst of the conquered population in accordance with principles of "hospitality," had blended with it so completely in less than a century that it had lost all its old national institutions, its language, and even its military organization.

The ephemeral Burgundian kingdom, which from 534 onwards was to become merged in the Merovingian Francia, effected, with the greatest ease, the fusion of the victors and the vanquished, under the absolute rule of a Barbarian king who had the greatest respect for the Roman Empire in whose name he ruled, and whose municipal institutions he left intact, both in Lyons and in Vienne.

Only the Franks, in the north of Gaul, were to retain their customs, their language and their institutions. But being far removed from the capital of their kings, who had suddenly become the masters of the immense Gallo-Roman kingdom, they exercised no influence over the destinies of Francia before the Carolingian epoch. Of all the Barbarian kings, the Frankish were the most remote from the Roman conception of power. They regarded the kingdom as their patrimonial estate, and they applied to the succession to the throne the principles which regulated the succession to real estate, under the Salic law: that is, on the death of the king his sons divided the kingdom into equal shares. Here we find a crude ideal of despotic royalty, departing no less completely from the Germanic customs than from the absolutism of the Empire. Yet the king, like the Emperor, was the supreme military commander, and the sovereign justiciary of the kingdom; and it was incumbent on him to ensure that peace reigned within his frontiers.

However, the Frankish kings were quickly becoming Romanized. As a matter of fact, from the time of their installation in the Empire they had to assume a definitely defensive attitude in respect of Germania—so much so that they tended to forget those of their people who were segregated in the extreme north, and even allowed them to retain their pagan religion until far into the 7th century. On the other hand, the old Imperial administration which they found in Gaul was bound to impress upon them the Roman conception of the State.

It is true that the Frankish king employed the officers of his court to administer his property and his kingdom.

The court was composed of various dignitaries whose titles show that they were once borne by slaves, as was the case with all dignitaries of Germanic origin: the marshal (the horse-slave), the seneschal (the senior slave), the major-domo (the chief domestic servant), the butler (the cellar slave). But these servants, these household officers, shared in their master's fortunes, and naturally enough, since what was royal was public, they became his ministers. In addition to these ministers there was an official of the Roman type, the referendary, at the head of the scribes taken over from the Imperial bureaucracy, who despatched the royal precepts or diplomas.

While the administration of the country was falling into a state of decadence in so far as it was separated from Rome—that is, from the central government, on which the whole administrative machinery was dependent—it continued to work after a fashion.

The king confided the government of the provinces, which coincided almost everywhere with the old Roman "cities," to paid officers—counts (*comites*), dukes (*duces*) and prefects (*praefecti*)—the great majority of whom were Gallo-Roman; but they were commonly favourites of the king, and sometimes of the lowest origin. They were subject to no supervision, no control. All that was required of them was that they should furnish certain sums of money to the treasury every year: for the rest, they could oppress the people unchecked, and they did not fail to do so. One must read Gregory of Tours to realize the brutality and cruelty of the Merovingian counts. In their demoralization and their arbitrary use of power they merely followed the example of the court.

Perhaps there has never been a more depressing spectacle than that which was offered by the Western world during the two centuries that followed the Germanic invasions. Brought too suddenly into contact with civilization, the Barbarians, in their haste to enjoy its advantages, adopted its vices, and the Romans, no longer restrained by the strong hand of the State, acquired the brutality of the Barbarians. There was a general unleashing of the crudest passions and the basest appetites, with their inevitable accompaniment of perfidy and cruelty.

But decadent and semi-barbaric though it was, the administration was none the less Roman. Only in the north shall we find royal officers with Germanic names: *grafio, tunginus, rachimburgi*.

The financial system too was still Roman. The king's private fortune was clearly separated from the public treasury. The monetary system and the impost were still the foundation of the royal power. The gold solidus was still current everywhere. Moreover, gold was still being coined. The State, it is true, was no longer able to regulate the minting of money, nor to guarantee a standard. The Frankish king even left the minting of money to private enterprise, without troubling himself about the debasement of the currency which was the natural consequence.

Thus all the Barbarian kingdoms which divided the Western Empire between them presented a number of common characteristics, by virtue of which they were not barbaric States, but "barbarized" Roman kingdoms. All had abandoned their national tongue and their pagan religion. Being Christian, they had by that very fact become the faithful subjects of the Church, which was completely imbued with the Roman civilization. And yet, like the Empire, these kingdoms were essentially secular. The bishops, in theory appointed by the clergy, were actually nominated by the king; their influence, however great, was confined to the religious domain; no bishop filled a public office before the advent of the Carolingians. The king, moreover, held his power in his own right, without the intervention of the Church. Like the Emperor, he was an absolute sovereign, free from all popular tutelage; for although the Germanic armies were occasionally assembled in *conventus*, this did not in any way resemble the ancient Assembly of the people.

Lastly, the new States—and this is an essential point— had preserved a fiscal organization and a considerable treasury. The public fisc or treasury had immense resources: the Imperial domain with its villas, its forests, its mines, its ports, and its highways, its treasure in minted gold, and the revenue from taxes, which, although it was dwindling from day to day, was still, for a long time to come, considerable.

The financial administration, with its offices and its books, was still staffed by scholars, and was still able—though with increasing difficulty—to recruit its personnel from laymen who had been educated on Roman lines.

Down to the time of the Merovingian decadence the financial resources of the Barbarian kings were very much greater than those of any other Western State would be until the close of the 13th century.

These kingdoms were not Roman merely because the Roman civilization had furnished them with the framework within which, and thanks to which, they had succeeded in organizing themselves, but also because they *wished* to be Roman. The king spoke of his *palatium,* of his *fiscus,* gave his officials titles which were borrowed from the Constantinian hierarchy, and made his chancellery imitate the formula and the style of the Imperial edicts. Theodoric, in Italy, took Cassidorus for his prime minister, was for a time the patron of Boetius, rebuilt the aqueducts of the Roman Campagna, organized games in the circus, and at Ravenna built, in a purely Byzantine style, Sant' Apollinare and San Vitale. The Vandal and Visigoth kings did their best to follow his example, and there was not one of them, even to the sons of Clovis, who was not proud to confer his patronage on the poor poet Venantius Fortunatus, when he came to seek his fortune at his court.

On the other hand, there was a cultivated class, and they were Roman jurists who codified, for the Barbarian kings, the Germanic and Roman laws of their subjects. Of course, the standard of the lay schools sank to a very low level; indeed, except in Italy, only a few lingered on. They were replaced, to some extent, by the religious schools which sprang up beside the churches, and, before long, in conjunction with the monasteries.

However this may be, and however deplorable the decadence of culture and learning under the Merovingian kings, the latter always had literate officials at their service.

The aspect of the civilized world, as it existed after the

invasions, presented the spectacle, not of youth, but of the decadence of the Imperial civilization; and Gregory of Tours, who lived in this world, and was horrified by it, sorrowfully summed up his impression of it in these discouraged words: *Mundus senescit* (the world grows old).

Justinian—the Lombards

1. *Justinian*

The Visigoth peril once averted, the eastern provinces of the Empire had nothing further to fear from the Germans. Attila, in pushing the latter westward, had, at least for the moment, driven them away from the frontiers of the Empire. But in the 6th century other Barbarians—the Slavs—began to appear on the left bank of the Danube. Being much nearer to Constantinople than the Germans to Rome, they were conscious at once of the attractive power of the great city. They flocked thither in ever-increasing numbers, taking service there as labourers or as soldiers, and more than one achieved a position of wealth and influence.

It is usual to date the latter period of the history of the Roman Empire, which is quite properly known as the Byzantine period, from the reign of Justinian. Yet it was Constantine, in imitation of Diocletian, whose residence was in Nicomedia, who made Byzantium the capital of the Imperial government of the East. Henceforth, while Rome was abandoned for Milan or Ravenna by the successors of Theodosius, Byzantium was always, until in 1453 it fell into the hands of the Turks, the residence of the Emperors, the city of the Tsars, the *Tarsagrad* of the Russians. Favoured from the first by its incomparable geographical situation, the privilege of sheltering the court, and with it the central government, soon had the result of making it the chief city of the East. We may even say that from the time of the Moslem conquests it was to become the one great city of the Christian world. While after the Moslem invasions all the urban centres of the West became depopulated and fell into ruin, Byzantium retained a population of several hundreds of thousands, whose alimentary needs placed under requisition all the territories bordering on the Black Sea, the Aegean, and the Adriatic. It was Byzantium that promoted the trade and the navigation of the Empire, and the attractive force which it exerted on the whole of the Empire was the surest guarantee of its unity. Thanks to this force, the Byzantine Empire presented, so to speak, an urban character, in a much greater degree than the old Roman Empire. For Rome had merely attracted to herself the exports of the provinces, but had given them nothing in return; she restricted herself to the rôle of consumer. Byzantium, on the contrary, both consumed and produced. The city was not only an Imperial residence; it was a trading centre of the first order, into which were poured the products of Europe and Asia, and it was also a very active industrial city.

By language it remained a Greek city, but a Greek city more than half Orientalized. Incomparably richer, more thriving, and more populous than Thrace or Greece proper, the provinces of Asia Minor exercised an irresistible ascendancy. Syria, the most active of the provinces, exerted a preponderant influence on the capital. Byzantine art is really a Hellenic art transformed through the medium of the art of Syria.

But of Greek thought and Greek science only as much survived as Christianity had seen fit to spare; and this was little enough. Justinian, as we know, closed the school of Athens, where a faint echo of the ancient philosophers might still be heard. But the dogmas and mysteries of religion provided an abundance of material for the passionate love of dialectic which had for so many centuries characterized Hellenic thought. No sooner did Christianity appear than the East began to teem with heresies: there were pitched battles in the great cities, Council attacked Council, and the three Patriarchs of Byzantium, Antioch and Alexandria engaged in conflict. Naturally, all these heresies had their repercussions in the capital, and in every conflict the Emperor had to take sides, for the old conception that made him the religious leader, as well as the head of the State, had been perpetuated in Constantinople. In the capital every theological debate became a governmental affair. The parties pulled what wires they could at court, each seeking to obtain the all-powerful support of the sovereign. Turn and turn about, orthodoxy or heresy, according to the choice he made between them, became the religion of the State.

With all this the Empire, though confined to the East, was, nevertheless, the Roman Empire. From the 9th century onwards the title of Βασιλεὺς τῶν Ρωμαίων was actually the official title of the Byzantine Emperor. From the reign of Diocletian the government of the Empire was often divided between two Emperors, but this division of power did not destroy the unity of the Empire.

To speak, as we do for convenience' sake, of the Empire of the West and the Empire of the East, is to employ an inaccurate description. In actual fact, although for administrative purposes it was divided into an eastern and a western portion, the Empire was nevertheless a single organism. If the ruler of one of these two halves disappeared, it passed, by this very fact, under the power of the other ruler. And this is precisely what happened at the time of the invasions. The Emperor of the West having disappeared, the Emperor of the East found himself henceforth the sole Emperor. And as we have seen, he did not cede any portion of the Empire; his right to the possession of the whole remained intact. Even after the conquest the memory of his supremacy lingered. The Germanic kings recognized that he exercised a sort of primacy over them; it was not clearly defined, but they betrayed their feeling by the respect which they paid to the Emperor. For the Pope, he remained the legitimate sovereign, and the pontifical chancellery continued to date its Bulls from the year of the Consulate—that is, from the accession of the Byzantine Emperor. Moreover, in the Church the tradition persisted that the Empire was both necessary and eternal. Did not

Tertullian and St. Augustine proclaim its providential nature?

The Romans had yet another reason to regret the Empire. Their new masters, the Germanic kings, were not orthodox. Apart from the King of the Franks, who was converted to Catholicism at the beginning of the conquest of Gaul by Clovis, the others—Visigoths, Ostrogoths and Vandals—were Arians by profession. To the Arian heresy, which had been so formidable in the 4th century, and which had caused so much bloodshed in the East, the Germans obstinately adhered. In actual fact it was not very dangerous. The Arian Church was making no proselytes in the heart of the Roman population, and there is reason to believe that as the Barbarians became absorbed by the latter the number of its adherents was progressively decreasing. But enraged by its very impotence, and confident of the favour of the kings, it was aggressive and intolerant in its treatment of the Catholic clergy. And the quarrels of the priests embittered and exasperated the orthodox population. In Italy the conflict became so acute that the Pope, in his despair, having invoked the intervention of the Emperor, Theodoric flung him into prison, to the great scandal of the faithful.

All this was known in Byzantium; it was known also that the strength of the new kingdoms was not very alarming. In all of them the dynasty was destroying itself by intestine quarrels and domestic murder. In the Visigoth and Ostrogoth kingdoms the various competitors for the crown begged the Emperor to come to their assistance. In the Ostrogoth kingdom, after the death of Theodoric, Theodatus had his wife Amalasontha, the daughter of the late king, assassinated, in order that he might reign alone. What with religious persecution and political scandals, there were plenty of pretexts for intervention!

Justinian (527–565) did not fail to profit by them. He had restored peace in his States, reorganized the finances, and renovated the army and the fleet; he now employed them to reconstitute the Roman Empire. The first blow was struck at the Vandals. In the year 533, five hundred ships landed in Africa 15,000 men, led by Belisarius. The campaign was as brief as it was brilliant. Within a few months the Vandal kingdom was completely conquered, and its king sent to Byzantium to figure in the Emperor's triumph. The Visigoths, who had stood aside indifferently while their neighbours were being defeated, now suffered the same fate. The whole maritime region was occupied and subdued without difficulty; the Byzantines did not trouble to pursue the king, who had fled to the mountains. The Ostrogoth kingdom held out longer. Only after eighteen years of warfare was its fate decided by the bloody defeat of its last forces on the slopes of Vesuvius (553).

The Mediterranean had once more become a Roman, or should we say, was becoming a Byzantine lake. On every side the Byzantine dukes and exarchs were organizing the administration of the reconquered provinces. Rome was once again part of the Empire, and, as in the good old days, the Emperor's orders ran as far as the Pillars of Hercules.

It might well have seemed that the Byzantine civilization, after performing such brilliant services, would become the European civilization, and that Constantinople, where Justinian was building the basilica of St. Sophia in lieu of a triumphal arch, was destined to draw the entire West into its orbit.

2. *The Lombards*

But these successes were brilliant rather than lasting. When he died, in the year 565, Justinian left the Empire oppressed by crushing taxation and incapable of further effort. And yet the task was not completed. Even now, if the Empire wished to assure itself of the mastery of the Mediterranean, it must fight the one independent State that bordered its shores—the Frankish kingdom. For the coast of Provence had been spared by Justinian's armies. To complete and consolidate the task which had been begun, this omission must be made good. But once Provence was subdued it would evidently be necessary to go further, and, in order to assure its conquest, to revive the policy of Caesar, and annex Gaul. Then, defended once more by the Alps and by the Rhine, the Roman world, centred on the

Mediterranean, would be, as of old, protected against all invasion. But in the Franks the Empire had to deal with an enemy far more formidable than any it had yet encountered.

How could Justinian's successor, his nephew Justin II (565–578), have dreamed of such an enterprise? Not only were his finances in confusion, but new enemies had just appeared on the Danube. Advancing in the East, coming from the Russian steppes, whence they had driven the Slavs toward the Carpathians and southwards, were the furious Avars; and in the West two Germanic peoples, the Gepidae and the Lombards, were occupying the middle course of the river. At the other extremity of the Empire, in Asia Minor, the Persians were assuming a menacing attitude on the frontier. Far from making preparations for distant enterprises, the Empire had to apply itself to the task of defence.

Justin thought he had struck a masterly blow by inciting the Lombards and the Avars against the Gepidae. This unhappy people was annihilated, but the Avars immediately occupied its territory, and the Lombards, feeling that they were the weaker, made way for them. Like the Ostrogoths a hundred years earlier, they marched upon Italy, and invaded Cisalpine Gaul, which thenceforth bore their name (568). The Lombard conquests continued until the reign of Rotharis (636–652), who conquered Genoa and the Ligurian coast.

The Byzantines, surprised by the attack, did not attempt to resist, but took refuge in the cities, which fell one after another. They succeeded in retaining only the coast of Istria, the country about Ravenna, Pentapolis, the region surrounding Rome, and that part of the peninsula that lies to the south of Spoleto and Benevento.

This epilogue to the Germanic invasions—the descent of the Lombards into Italy—was of great significance.

The newcomers, by interposing themselves between the Byzantine Empire and the Frankish kingdom, rendered impossible the conflict which must have occurred had the two States remained in contact. On the other hand, their arrival on the south of the Alps was to determine the fate of Italy even down to the 19th century. This was the end of the unity of that country which had created the unity of the civilized world. The struggle of the Lombards and the Byzantines for its possession was only the first chapter of its tragic history, in the course of which the land was invaded, occupied, and dismembered by the Germans, the Normans, the Spaniards, the French, and the Austrians, until the day when it at length shook off the alien yoke, realized the secular longing of its patriots, and accomplished its *risorgimento*. The Italian question which in different forms intruded itself into every chapter of European history had its beginning in the Lombard invasion. At the moment which we are now considering, the solution provided by the success of the invaders must still have seemed extremely precarious. Byzantium had retreated, but had not renounced the struggle, and might still hope for the success of a counter-offensive. In spite of all that had happened, her position in the West, where she possessed a good part of Italy, Sicily, Africa, and the coasts of Spain, permitted her to reckon on the future. But a new upheaval, the most profound and the most violent that Europe had ever experienced, was about to decide otherwise.

CHAPTER III

The Musulman Invasion

1. *The Invasion*

In the whole history of the world there has been nothing comparable, in the universal and immediate nature of its consequences, with the expansion of Islam in the 7th century.

The overwhelming rapidity of its propagation was no less surprising than the immensity of its conquests. It took only seventy years from the death of Mohammed (632) to spread from the Indian Ocean to the Atlantic. Nothing could stand before it. At the first blow it overthrew the Persian Empire (637–644); then it deprived the Byzantine Empire, one by one, of each of the provinces which it attacked: Syria (634–636), Egypt (640–642), Africa (698), and Spain (711). The Visigoths had retaken Spain from the Byzantines, and their last king, Roderick, fell in the battle of Cadiz (711).

The onward march of the invaders was checked only at the beginning of the 8th century, when the great movement by which they were threatening Europe from both sides at once was halted beneath the walls of Constantinople (717) and by the soldiers of Charles Martel on the plain of Poitiers (732). It was checked; its first expansive energy was exhausted; but it had sufficed to change the face of the globe. Wherever it had passed the ancient States, which were deeply rooted in the centuries, were overturned as by a cyclone; the traditional order of history was overthrown. This was the end of the old Persian Empire, the heir of Assyria and Babylon; of the Hellenized regions of Asia which had constituted the Empire of Alexander the Great, and had thereafter continued to gravitate in the orbit of Europe; of the ancient Egypt, whose past was still living beneath the Greek veneer that had covered it since the days of the Ptolemies; and of the African provinces which Rome had won from Carthage. Henceforth all these regions were subject, in religion and political obedience, to the most powerful potentate who had ever existed, the Caliph of Baghdad.

And all this was the work of a nomadic people which had hitherto lived almost unknown in its rock-strewn deserts, which were disdained by all the conquerors, and numbered infinitely fewer inhabitants than Germany. But this people had just been converted by a prophet who had issued from its womb. It had shattered all its old idols, and had suddenly adopted the purest monotheism, and its conception of its duty to God had a formidable simplicity: it was, to obey Allah and compel the infidels to obey Him. The Holy War became a moral obligation, and its own reward. Warriors who fell with their weapons in their hands enjoyed the beatitudes of Paradise. For the rest, the booty of the rich traders who surrounded poverty-stricken Arabia on every side would be the lawful prize of the military apostolate.

There can be no doubt that it was fanaticism—or if you will, religious enthusiasm—that launched the Musulmans on the world. Between the invasions of these sectaries, who surged onward invoking Allah, and those of the Germans, who left their country only to acquire more fertile soil, the moral difference is impressive. Yet the social constitution of the Arabs fitted them admirably for their rôle. Nomads and poor, they were fully prepared to obey the command of God. They had only to saddle their horses and set off. They were not, as the Germans were, emigrants dragging behind them women and children, slaves and cattle; they were horsemen, accustomed from childhood to cattle-raids, and now Allah had laid upon them the duty of raiding the world in His name.

It must be admitted, however, that the weakness of their

adversaries very greatly facilitated their task. Neither the Byzantine nor the Persian Empire, surprised by the unexpectedness of the attack, was in a condition to resist it. After Justin II the government of Constantinople had grown continually weaker, and nowhere, from Syria to Spain, did the invaders find armies before them. Their fiery onset encountered only disorder. Of the conquests of Justinian nothing was left, after 698, but Italy. Christianity, which had reigned on all the shores of the Mediterranean, now held only the northern shore. Three-fourths of the littoral of this sea, hitherto the common centre of European civilization, now belonged to Islam.

And they belonged to it not only by occupation, but also by virtue of religious and political absorption. The Arabs did not, like the Germans, respect the *status quo* in the conquered territories. They could not. While the Germans, on abandoning their religion for Christianity, immediately fraternized with the Romans, the Musulmans appeared as the propagandists of a new faith, an exclusive and intolerant faith to which all had to submit. Religion, wherever they ruled, was the basis of political society; or rather, the religious organization and the political organization were for them identical; Church and State forming a single unity. The infidels could continue the practice of their cult only as simple subjects, deprived of all rights whatsoever. Everything was transformed, from top to bottom, in accordance with the principles of the Koran. Of the entire administration—justice, finance, the army—nothing was left. Kadis and emirs replaced the exarchs of the country. The Musulman law replaced the Roman law, and the Greek and Latin languages, before which the old national idioms of the coasts of Syria, Africa and Spain had long ago disappeared, were ousted in their turn by the Arabic tongue.

These two elements—religion and language—constitute the Arab's contribution to the Musulman civilization. This civilization, despite its brilliant achievements during the first few centuries of Islam, can boast of little that is original. The conquered peoples were all more refined than their nomad conquerors, and the latter borrowed from them in a wholesale fashion. The Arabs translated the works of their scholars and philosophers, drew inspiration from their art, and adopted their agricultural, commercial and industrial methods. The extent and diversity of the countries and the nations upon which they imposed their rule subjected them to a quantity of influences, which blended together, giving the Musulman civilization an aspect of great variety, but little depth. Of these influences, that of Hellenism rivalled that of Persia. This should not surprise us, when we reflect that the Arabs occupied the richest and most populous sections of the contemporary Greek world—Egypt and Syria.

Their architecture gives us a fairly precise idea of the variety and the relative importance of their borrowings. We see in its decoration characteristics which are evidently of Persian or Indian origin, but the general conception, and the essential members of the buildings, reveal an obvious relationship with Byzantine architecture. The predominance of Greek thought is even more plainly evident. Aristotle was the master of the Arab philosophers, who added nothing essential to his philosophy. On the whole, in the intellectual domain, the Musulman civilization did not greatly influence the European peoples. The explanation is simple: there was much in it that was artificial, and the sources upon which it drew most freely were, for the most part, European sources.

But the case is different in respect of the economic domain. Here, thanks to their contact with the West and the far East, the Arabs were valuable intermediaries. From India they imported sugar-cane into Sicily and Africa, rice into Sicily and Spain (whence the Spaniards took it to Italy in the 15th and 16th centuries), and cotton into Sicily and Africa; they acclimatized in Asia the manufacture of silk, which they learned from the Chinese; and from the Chinese also they learned the use and manufacture of paper, without which the invention of printing would have been valueless, or would not have been made; and from China they imported the magnetic compass. But it was a long while before these innovations—with many more—became the property of the European peoples. At first they only helped to make Islam a more formidable enemy to its European neighbours, as being both richer and more perfectly equipped. From the 7th to the 11th century Islam was incontestably the master of the Mediterranean. The ports which the Arabs constructed—Cairo, which succeeded to Alexandria, Tunis, and Kairouan—were the *étapes* of a commerce which circulated from the Straits of Gibraltar to the Indian Ocean, through the Egyptian ports, which were in communication with the Red Sea, and the Syrian ports, which gave access to the caravan route to Baghdad and the Persian Gulf. The navigation of the Christian peoples was restricted to a timid coastwise trade along the shores of the Adriatic and southern Italy, and among the islands of the Archipelago.

2. *The Consequences of the Invasion*

An unforeseen event is always followed by a catastrophe in proportion to its importance. It flings itself, so to speak, across the current of historic life, interrupting the series of causes and effects of which this current is constituted, damming them up in some sort, and by their unexpected repercussions overturning the natural order of things. This was what happened at the time of the Musulman invasion. For centuries Europe had gravitated about the Mediterranean. It was by means of the Mediterranean that civilization had extended itself; by means of the Mediterranean the various parts of the civilized world had communicated one with another. On all its shores social life was the same in its fundamental characteristics; religion was the same; manners and customs and ideas were the same, or very nearly so. The Germanic invasion had not changed the situation in any essential respect. In spite of all that had happened, we may say that in the middle of the 7th century Europe still constituted, as in the time of the Roman Empire, a Mediterranean unity.

Now, under the sudden impact of Islam, this unity was abruptly shattered. The greater portion of this familiar sea —which the Romans had called "our sea," *mare nostrum*— became alien and hostile. The intercourse between the West and the East, which had hitherto been carried on by means of this sea, was interrupted. The East and the West were suddenly separated. The community in which they had lived so long was destroyed for centuries to come, and even to-day Europe is still suffering from the consequences of its destruction.

Obliged to meet the menace from the East, the Empire could no longer stand firm on the Danube. The Bulgars, Serbs and Croats spread through the Balkans, and only the cities remained Greek. The invaders did not mingle with the population, as the Germans had done. The Byzantine Empire ceased to be universal; it became a Greek State.

The Bulgars, in 677, subdued the Slav tribes, and became merged with them in Mesia. In the middle of the 9th century their prince, Boris, was converted by Methodius and took the name of Michael.

The Byzantine Empire, henceforth confined between the coast of Illyria and the Upper Euphrates, devoted the bulk of its forces to withstanding the pressure of Islam. In its long history, down to the day when it finally succumbed, in the middle of the 15th century, under the blows of the Turks, it was still to know some moments of splendour, and was to witness the development of a civilization whose originality consisted in the blending of ancient traditions with orthodox Christianity and an increasing Orientalization. But this history, most of the time, was alien to that of Western Europe. Venice alone kept in touch with Byzantium, and found, in her rôle of intermediary between East and West, the beginning of her future greatness. For the rest, although Byzantium had ceased to intervene in the West, she none the less continued to exercise an influence which was to outlive her by many centuries. It was Byzantium that Christianized the Slavs of the South and East— the Serbs, Bulgars and Russians—and it was the people of the Empire who, after bearing the Turkish yoke for 400 years, reconstituted the Greek nationality in the 20th century.

As for the West, its separation from Byzantium confronted it with a completely novel situation. This separation seemed to exclude it from civilization, since from the beginning of the ages all the forms of civilized life and all social progress had come to it from the East. True, with the Arabs established in Spain and on the coast of Africa the East was at its door. But in spite of material contact, the difference of religious faith prevented any moral contact between its Christian population and this Musulman Orient. For the first time since the formation of the Roman Empire, Western Europe was isolated from the rest of the world. The Mediterranean by which it had hitherto kept in touch with civilization was closed to it. This, perhaps, was the most important result, as regards the history of the world, of the expansion of Islam.[1] For the Christianity of the West, when its traditional lines of communication were cut, became a world apart, able to count only on itself, and in respect of its further development it was thrown upon its own resources. Driven off the Mediterranean, it turned to the still barbarous regions beyond the Rhine and the shores of the North Sea. European society, continuously expanding, crossed the ancient frontiers of the Roman Empire. A new Europe was created with the rise of the Frankish Empire, in which was elaborated the Western civilization which was one day to become that of the whole world.

[1] See Henri Pirenne, *Mohammed and Charlemagne* (in preparation).

BOOK TWO

The Carolingian Epoch

CHAPTER I

The Church

1. *The Atony of the Fifth to the Seventh Century*

During the vicissitudes of the 5th, 6th and 7th centuries, while Europe was torn by the conflicts of the Germans, the Empire, and Islam, what became of the Catholic Church, the great force of the near future? It contented itself with continuing to exist, or rather to vegetate. Its influence upon the course of events was negligible; its moral influence over society was imperceptible. And yet, amidst the ruins of the Empire, it remained intact. It had saved its organization, its hierarchy, its incalculable wealth in land. And it had no enemies. The Germans no less than the Romans were its dutiful children. The Arian heresy, as we have seen, was only ephemeral, and never gave it real anxiety.

The apathy of the Church, however, is very simply explained. Something had happened to it which had happened, though in a greater degree, to the whole of society after the invasions: it had become barbarized. The Latin literature of Christendom, which was still so vigorous in the 4th century, the century of St. Augustine, had nothing to show in the 5th century but epigoni of the type of Salvian. After this the life of the mind became dormant; the vein opened by the Fathers of the Church was exhausted. A few clerks continued to write biographical or historical narratives, but the world had to wait for Gregory the Great before the study of theology and religious and moral philosophy was revived, though in quite a new spirit. More striking still was the inertia of the Church in the face of the pagan or grossly heretical Barbarians who had lately made their way into the Empire, and were living within reach of it. When they did become converted they merely followed the example of their kings, who, for reasons of political interest, or in imitation of Roman manners, had adopted Christianity: as the Franks were converted after the baptism of Clovis. As for the Germans, who in the north of Gaul and beyond the Rhine had preserved their old national cult, the Church made no attempt to bring them into the fold. The apostles to the Salic Franks, St. Amand and St. Remaculus, were inspired by personal enthusiasm. The kings supported their efforts, but we do not find that they received any backing from the ecclesiastical authorities. The latter, indeed, were so far from taking any interest in the apostolate that they left the work which was incumbent upon themselves to foreigners. Introduced into Ireland in the 4th century, Christianity had rapidly spread through the country. In this remote isle, which had no communication with the Continent, it created for itself an original organization, in which the great monastic colonies were the centres of a most ardent religious life. In these centres there were large numbers of ascetics and proselytes, who, from the 6th century onwards, began to leave their native country, some to seek, in distant lands, inaccessible solitudes, and others, souls to be converted. When the Norsemen discovered Iceland in the 9th century they were astonished to find that the only inhabitants of its misty shores were monks who had come from Ireland. They were Irishmen, too, who devoted themselves with such enthusiasm to the conversion of Northern Gaul and Germany. The hagiography of the Merovingian period is teeming with saints to whom are attributed the foundations of a host of monasteries in Northern France and Belgium. St. Columban and St. Gall are the most celebrated representatives of this tribe of missionaries, whose intellectual culture, disinterestedness and enthusiasm found a sad contrast in the boorishness of the Merovingian clergy. They could not, however, rouse the clerics from their apathy. The bishops,

nominated by the clergy of the diocese, but really appointed
by the kings, rarely owed their sees to anything but the
favour of the sovereign. One must have read the portraits
which Gregory of Tours has traced of some of his colleagues
to form any idea of the state of their knowledge and their
morals. Many of them could hardly read, and indulged
without concealment in drunkenness and debauchery. The
honest Gregory is indignant with such behaviour, yet it is
evident, from what he says, that his indignation was but
faintly echoed. And what an example he furnishes in his
own person—greatly superior though he certainly was to the
majority of his colleagues—of the decadence of the Church!
The Latin which he writes—as he is well aware—is a barbarous idiom, taking strange liberties with grammar, syntax
and the vocabulary; and his morality—but this, unhappily,
he does not realize—is capable of very irregular indulgences
and very surprising judgements. And after his time things
were even worse. At the close of the 7th century and the
beginning of the 8th not only the language but the very
thought was like that of a paralytic. The so-called Chronicle
of Fredegarius, and certain Lives of Saints of this period,
are incomparable examples of the inability to express the
simplest notions.

Nevertheless, decadent though it was, the Church was
the great civilizing force of the period; indeed, we may say
the only civilizing force. It was through the Church that
the Roman tradition was perpetuated; it was the Church
that prevented Europe from relapsing into barbarism. The
lay power, left to its own devices, would have been incapable of preserving this precious heritage. Despite the
good intentions of the kings, their crude and clumsy administration was quite unequal to the task which they
wished to perform. Now, the Church possessed the personnel which the State lacked. As it was formed and developed
under the Empire, so it continued after the invasions. The
hierarchy was still intact, and, moulded as it was on the
pattern of the administrative organization of Rome, it retained its firm and simple structure in the midst of the
growing disorder. The metropolitan sees established at the
capital of each province, the episcopal sees instituted at

the capital of each "city," disappeared, for a time, only in the northern regions. Everywhere else they were spared or respected by the conquerors. While the civil administration lapsed into decadence, the ecclesiastical administration remained unshaken, with the same structure, the same dignitaries, the same principles, the same law, the same language as in the days of the Empire. In the midst of the surrounding anarchy, the Church remained intact, in spite of its temporary decadence; the clergy were protected by the mighty edifice that sheltered them, and by the discipline imposed upon them. Ignorant, negligent and immoral though some of the bishops may have been, they could not absolve themselves from the essential duties of their functions. They were obliged to maintain, in connection with their Cathedral, a school for the education of young scholars. While lay education disappeared, and the State was reduced to employing illiterate servants, the Church continued, by a necessity inherent in its very existence, to train a body of pupils of whom each member was at all events able to read and write Latin. By this very fact it exercised a preponderant influence over secular society; it possessed, without having sought or desired it, the monopoly of knowledge. Its schools, but for rare exceptions, were the only schools, its books the only books. Writing, without which no civilization is possible, appertained so exclusively to the Church from the end of the Merovingian period that even to this day the word that describes the ecclesiastic also describes the scribe: *clerc* in French, *clerk* in English, *klerk* in Flemish and Old German, *diaca* in Old Russian. During the 8th century intellectual culture was confined to a sacerdotal class; so that the Catholic clergy acquired a position which had never been allotted to any other clergy before them. Not only were the clergy venerated because of their religious character; not only did they possess, in the eyes of laymen, the prestige which knowledge enjoys in an ignorant community, but they were also an indispensable auxiliary to civil society. The State could not dispense with their services. In the Carolingian period, when the last traces of lay education had disappeared, it was from the clergy that the State was obliged to borrow its staff of scribes, the heads of its chancellery, and all those agents or counsellors in whom a certain degree of intellectual culture was essential. The State became clericalized, because it could not do otherwise, under penalty of relapsing into barbarism; because it could not find elsewhere than in the Church men capable of understanding and accomplishing the political tasks which were incumbent upon it. And if it could find them only in the Church, this was not because their character as the apostles of Christ made them peculiarly fit to serve it. The servants of Him who has said that His kingdom is not of this world had not learned from Him the conduct of secular affairs. If they had the requisite knowledge it was because they had acquired it from Rome; because the Church to which they belonged had survived the ruin of the ancient world, and because this world was perpetuated in it for the education of the new world. In short, it was not because it was Christian, but because it was Roman that the Church acquired and maintained for centuries its control over society; or, if you will, it exercised a preponderant influence over modern society for so long merely because it was the depositary of a more ancient and more advanced civilization. It goes without saying that the Church profited by this situation to realize its religious ideal, and to bend to its will the State which had called upon its services as auxiliary. The inevitable collaboration between Church and State, which was presently established, bore within it the germ of formidable conflicts, which no one could have foreseen in the beginning.

On entering the service of the State, the Church did not submit itself to its employer. Whatever the concessions which it may have made, at certain moments, of its own free will, or under compulsion, it still remained, with regard to the State, an independent power. It claimed and enjoyed, in Western Europe, a liberty which it did not enjoy in the Roman or the Byzantine Empire. This was not so much because the Western sovereigns never exerted a power comparable to that of the Emperors, as because the Church was from the first in an economic situation which enabled it to live and develop itself on its own resources. And here again we see in the Church the heir of Rome.

The immense fortune in real estate which lay at its disposal it owed to Constantine and his successors, who transferred to it the wealth of the pagan temples. They not only made the Church the greatest landed proprietor in the world; they also made it a privileged proprietor, by exempting its members from the poll tax and its property from the land tax. Both property and privileges were respected by the Barbarian kings, so that at the time when the history of the modern peoples begins the Church was in possession of incomparable wealth. This explains how it was able to pass through the crises of the invasions without becoming enfeebled; how it could safeguard its organization and recruit and maintain its clergy in a time of political and social turmoil.

Thus, from whatever angle we examine it, we see that the Church, despite its decadence in the 5th, 6th and 7th centuries, was still powerful and capable of future development. The cause of its decline was not in itself but in the circumstances of the moment. Moreover, when we speak of its decadence we are thinking only of the official Church, of the secular clergy, the only clergy visible as yet; in addition to whom, in a state of gradual development, were the clergy whom we do not yet perceive, but who were gradually making a place for themselves, and obscurely rehearsing the part which they would presently play: the regular clergy, the monks.

2. The Monks and the Papacy

The asceticism which necessarily springs from an exclusive conception of Christianity had undergone rapid development, from the 2nd century onwards, in the Eastern provinces of the Roman Empire. For a long while its adepts were simply laymen who renounced the activities and the goods of this world in order to devote themselves in solitude to the salvation of their souls. These solitaries were the first monks (μοναχος, μονος). St. Pacomus (348) conceived the notion of imposing a rule upon them, and, for this purpose, of organizing them in a community. The monks who adopted this new kind of life grouped themselves in enclosures formed by cells built around a central chapel. To distinguish them from the solitaries the inhabitants of these pious colonies were given the name of cenobites. To this cenobitic institution belonged the Western monasteries, of which the first was founded in the 6th century, on Monte Cassino, near Naples, by St. Benedict. The originality and also the importance of Benedict's achievement (*c.* 543) was that he withdrew the monk from secular life, making of him a religious bound to his vocation by the three perpetual vows of obedience, poverty and chastity, and imposing upon him the obligation of priesthood. Side by side with the secular clergy, whose origins go back to the constitution of the primitive Church, a new clergy makes its appearance, emerging from asceticism, and unfolding to those who wish to realize it in this world the ideal of the Christian life. Its rule—to which it owes its name of *regular*—is not merely a rule of prayer and of pious exercises: it also requires the monk to honour God by labour—whether by manual work or by study.

The diffusion of the monasteries proceeded rather slowly at the outset. They gradually spread through Italy, and reached the south of Gaul, and then, thanks to the apostolate of the Irish, they established themselves in considerable numbers in the north of the Frankish kingdom during the 7th and 8th centuries.[1] But so far they had no mutual relations, and no influence over the outer world, and it seems that they were by no means favourably regarded by the diocesan bishops, who hardly knew what to do with these newcomers.

It was reserved for the Papacy to utilize this great force, unconscious of its own strength, and to make it serve the State, constituting—so to speak—a permanent reserve army at the disposal of the State. It was the first of the great Popes, Gregory the Great (590–604), who was responsible for this stroke of genius.

Until the reign of Gregory the pre-eminence of the Pa-

---

[1] The monasteries of Ireland were very different from the Benedictine monasteries. But the monasteries which the Irish missionaries founded on the Continent were organized in conformity with the Benedictine communities.

pacy was ill-defined; it had little basis beyond the twofold quality of the Pope as the successor of St. Peter and the Bishop of Rome. It was manifested rather by the respect which was paid to him than by the authority which he exercised. In the various kingdoms the bishops appointed by the kings paid him deference at the most: their relations with the Papacy went no farther. The Pope himself was regarded by the Patriarchs of Alexandria, Antioch, Jerusalem and Constantinople as an equal merely. The Emperor of Byzantium, indeed, reserved to himself the right to ratify the nomination of the Pope, no less than the nomination of the Patriarchs, or, after Justinian, to have it ratified in his name by the Exarch of Ravenna. The situation of Italy, and especially the position of Rome, since the turmoil of the invasions, restricted the activity of the Popes, or directed it to tasks which had nothing to do with the government of the Church. Since the Emperor no longer resided in the "city," the Pope had actually become its most important personage. It was incumbent on him—in the absence of lay authorities—to negotiate with the invaders, and to supervise the administration, the revictualling and the fortification of the city: and this, as Rome became depopulated and impoverished, rendered more and more arduous the task of keeping its enormous area and its monuments in some sort of order and repair. After the invasion of the Lombards in particular the Popes had to contend against difficulties and dangers with which they could cope only by forcible measures; for the Emperor, engrossed in the defence of the Syrian and Danubian frontiers, left it to the Popes to resist the new enemies, who were obstinately bent on the conquest of Rome. At the most he sent the Popes, from time to time, a few troops, and a few subsidies, both equally inadequate. The Exarch of Ravenna, who was himself threatened, was in no position to furnish effective collaboration. At the moment when Gregory the Great, in 590, ascended the throne of St. Peter, he evidently despaired of the future, comparing Rome to a ship battered by the tempest and on the point of foundering.

Gregory the Great may be regarded as the first interpreter of religious thought after the Fathers of the Church.

But he did not continue the work of the Fathers. He was not interested in questions of dogma: for him they had been finally answered. He was concerned rather with drawing the moral consequences from the dogmas, with organizing the Christian life in respect of its aim—in respect of "last things" which were summed up in the terrifying dilemma of Heaven and Hell. His vision, so to speak, was fixed upon the Beyond, and the pictures which he drew of the life to come were enormously effective in helping to give medi-aeval religiosity that gloomy and agonized cast, that preoc-cupation with terror, that obsession with eternal torments, which found their immortal expression in the "Divine Com-edy." The Church being the instrument of eternal salvation, its power over men's souls must be augmented in order that they might be saved from the abyss. And here, in Gregory, as in other great mystics—in St. Bernard, for example, and Loyola—that practical genius revealed itself, which, in order to attain the supraterrestrial end that it had proposed to it-self, excelled in organizing the affairs of the pressing world which it held in disdain. Perhaps his origin—he came of an ancient family of Roman patricians who had by tradition played their part in the administration of the city—was not without its influence on this side of his character. One can hardly believe on reading his letters, that they were written by the author of the *Moralia* and the *Dialogus miracu-lorum*. They show him at work restoring the patrimony of St. Peter—that is, the enormous domains of the Roman Church—scattered all over Italy and the coasts of Illyria and Sicily, which the disorders of the invasions had dismem-bered, ruined, and disorganized. We see him laying claim to lands that had been alienated or invaded, appointing in-tendants, laying down the rules which they were to follow, and enforcing the measures necessary for the collection and centralization of the revenues. He therefore merits the two-fold and singular honour of being regarded as at once the earliest mystic and the earliest economist of the Middle Ages. For the rest, his economic activity was entirely im-pregnated with Roman practices, and he did much toward preserving and diffusing, by the intermediary of the Church, the domainal institutions of the Empire. In a few years the task upon which he had embarked was completed. The Papacy found itself in possession of a regular income and abundant resources. It had become the first financial power of its time.

To this first source of strength Gregory added a second, by associating the monks with the Papacy. He was impelled to take this step no less by his leanings to asceticism than by his lucid grasp of realities. He perceived very clearly what an ascendancy the Papacy would acquire from those monasteries which were scattered all over Europe by constituting itself their protector. He did not confine himself to founding new monasteries in the Eternal City; he also conferred upon a number of them privileges of exemption which placed them under the direct authority of the Holy See. Since the days of St. Benedict the monks had formed part of the Church; and from the days of Gregory the Great we may say that they were associated in its activities.

It was, in fact, to the monks directed and organized by him that Gregory confided the great achievement of his pontificate, the evangelization of the Anglo-Saxons.[2] But this would have been impossible if he had not had at his disposal the funds required for its realization; so that the two great reforms of his reign—the reconstitution of the patrimony of St. Peter and the alliance with monasticism—contributed harmoniously to an enterprise which was itself in perfect harmony with the religious ideal and the practical abilities of its initiator.

The conversion of England was a masterpiece of tact, reason and method. After long preparation for their task by the Pope, St. Augustine of Canterbury and his companions went to work in accordance with instructions which were the fruit of ripe meditation, and inspired throughout by charity, indulgence, toleration and common sense. Nothing could be more unlike the rash and enthusiastic attitude of the Celtic missionaries than the patient and prudent behaviour of the missionaries of Gregory. They arrived in England only after they had studied its language, customs and religion. They were careful not to offend the

[2] St. Augustine landed in England in 596: the work of Christianization was completed in 655.

prejudices of the English: they did not try to obtain premature results, and they even renounced their ambition to achieve martyrdom. They won men's confidence before they won their souls: and so they won them completely. Sixty years later the Anglo-Saxons were not only Christians, but were already on the point of furnishing the Church with missionaries worthy of those who had converted them. One hundred and twenty years after the landing of St. Augustine on Hastings beach (596) St. Boniface embarked upon the evangelization of pagan trans-Rhenian Germany (716).

The conversion of England marks a decisive stage in the history of the Papacy. The direct foundation of the Pope, the Anglo-Saxon Church, was subject from the beginning to the immediate control and direction of Rome. It was in no sense a national Church; it was apostolic in the full meaning of the term. And the trans-Rhenian Church which it proceeded to organize was given the same character. It is easy to understand what additional strength and glory the prestige and authority of the Papacy won thereby. While in Rome itself the Popes were still regarded by the Emperor of Byzantium and the Exarchs of Ravenna as Patriarchs of the Empire, and were still obliged to apply to them for the ratification of their election, the new Christians of the North revered in the Popes the Vicars of Christ, the representatives of God on earth. Thus the Papacy had made a position for itself which was henceforth incompatible with the state of subordination to the Emperor in which it had hitherto existed. Sooner or later it would break the traditional tie between itself and the Emperor, which, now that there was no longer an Empire in the West, was merely a burden, a humiliation and an embarrassment. If only the Emperor had still been an effective protector, or if he had at least given evidence of his good will! But he not only dissociated himself from Rome, leaving her defenceless against the advance of the Lombards: he even became her adversary.[3]

[3] In 653 Constans II sent Martin I into exile. In 692 Justinian II would have done the same to Sergius I if Rome had not rebelled.

In the Byzantine *milieu*, torn by theological passions, a new heresy had just emerged: Iconoclasm. The Emperor Leo III not only proposed it (726), but attempted to force it on Rome. This was too much: the Pope refused to submit himself to the will of a master who expected to find him as complaisant as the Patriarchs of Constantinople or Antioch. Gregory II (715–731) confined himself to threats: if the rupture was not effected then and there, it was only because the Imperial tradition was still so potent that he hesitated to take a decisive step. Moreover, to abandon the Emperor was to launch oneself into the unknown, and to risk reprisals which might expose the Church to the gravest perils. Before the Pope could do anything so decisive—before he could assume, in respect of the Emperor, the attitude not of an equal merely, but of a superior—before he could break with the heretic East and establish in the West the bases of a universal Christianity—before he could cease to be Roman in the old sense of the word, and become Catholic—before he could free the spiritual power from the fetters imposed upon it by Caesarism, he must find a powerful and loyal protector. And who, in the Europe of that day, could play such a part? There was only one such man, and he himself was seeking an ally capable of legitimately conveying the crown to him: the Mayor of the Palace of the Merovingian kings.

CHAPTER II

The Frankish Kingdom

1. *The Dislocation of the State*

Of all the kingdoms founded by the Barbarians on the soil of the Roman Empire, that of the Franks was the only one whose frontiers enclosed a compact block of Germanic population. Even before the conquests of Clovis in Gaul the Salic Franks, the Ripuarian Franks, and the Alamans had colonized, *en masse*, the whole of the left bank of the Rhine, and had pushed forward some considerable distance into the valleys of the Moselle, the Meuse and the Scheldt. Clovis himself, in the beginning, was merely one of the numerous petty kings among whom the government of the Salic Franks was divided. His kingdom, which must have corresponded very nearly with the area of the ancient Roman "city" of Tournai, did not provide him with sufficient force to ensure the success of the attack which he was meditating upon Syagrius, the Roman officer to whom the region between the Loire and the Seine, in the heart of invaded Gaul, still owed obedience. He therefore obtained the collaboration of his kinsmen, the kings of Térouanne and Cambrai. But he alone profited by the victory. Syagrius defeated, he appropriated his territory, and took advantage of his now crushing superiority over his former equals to get rid of them. By violence or by cunning he overthrew or destroyed them, and was acknowledged by their peoples, and in a few years he had extended his power to the

whole of the region encircled by the Rhine, from Cologne
to the sea. The Alamans, established in Alsace and Eifel,
who threatened the new kingdom with a flank attack, were
defeated and annexed. Having thus assured himself of the
possession of the whole of Northern Gaul, from the Rhine
to the Loire, the King of the Franks was able to apply himself to the conquest of wealthy Aquitaine. It was then the
country of the Visigoths. Converted to Catholicism since
the year 496, Clovis found in their heresy a pretext for
making war upon them, defeated them at Vouillé (507)
and advanced the frontier to the Pyrenees. Provence still
divided him from the Mediterranean. But Theodoric did not
intend to allow the Frankish kingdom to extend itself to the
gates of Italy; and Clovis had to renounce Provence (which
Theodoric, for greater safety, annexed to his own States).
His sons, however, completed the task so well begun, seized
upon the kingdom which the Burgundi had set up in the
valley of the Rhone (532), and took possession of Provence
from the Gulf of Lyons to the Rhone. Henceforth the whole
of ancient Gaul was subject to the Merovingian dynasty.

Conformably with the Mediterranean character which
Western Europe retained until the end of the 7th century,
it endeavoured, to begin with, to expand in a southerly
direction. For a time Frankish armies disputed Northern
Italy with the Lombards. But the Musulman invasion, as
we have already seen, was to call a sudden halt to the
traditional southward orientation of the Northern countries.
The last of the Merovingian conquerors, Dagobert I, directed his efforts towards Germany, and even advanced as
far as the Danube. Then the expansion ceased, and decadence set in.

The closing of the Mediterranean by the Musulmans
marked not only a new political orientation of Europe, but
also, one may say, the end of the ancient world.

For until the reign of Dagobert I the Merovingian State
had not broken away from the Roman tradition. The social
state of the country, after the profound disorder inflicted
upon it by the invasions, reassumed its old Roman character. The lands of the Imperial fisc, it is true, passed to the
king, but the great Gallo-Roman landowners, with rare ex-

ceptions, had retained their domains, organized as they had been under the Empire. In this connection it is impressive to note that Pope Gregory the Great, in order to restore the administration of the enormous territorial properties of the Church, merely reconstructed the Roman domainal system.

Commerce, once peace was re-established, resumed its activity. Marseilles, the centre for the great maritime trade with the East, became the resort of those Syrian merchants who were also to be found in the more important cities of the south of Gaul, and who, with the Jews, were the principal traders in the country. In the towns of the interior there was still a middle class of traders, some of whom, in the middle of the 6th century, are known to us as wealthy and influential notables.

And thanks to this regular trade, which maintained a considerable circulation of merchandise and money among the population, the king's treasury, fed by the market dues, had always important resources at its disposal: as great as, if not greater than, those which it derived from the revenue of the royal domains and the booty of war.

It is true that the surviving civilization of the Empire had fallen into a state of extreme decadence, but it had retained its essential characteristics.

It is evident that the important officials, who were chosen from among the magnates, were singularly independent in their attitude to the supreme power, and there is no doubt that the impost was often collected by the count for his own benefit; which explains why it was beginning to be described, in the language of the day, as an "exaction."

The enfeeblement of the old Roman administration, which had now lost touch with Rome, and of which the king, with some difficulty, was preserving the last vestiges, allowed the aristocracy of great landowners to assume a position of increasing strength with regard to the king and to society. In the north, especially in Austrasia, where the Roman influence was almost entirely effaced, it assumed, from the 7th century, an almost absolute preponderance.

This aristocracy, whose influence was continually increasing, was not in any real sense a nobility. It was distinguished from the rest of the nation, not by its juridical status, but only by its social position. Its members, in the language of their contemporaries, were grandees (*majores*), magnates (*magnates*) and potentates (*potentes*), and their power was derived from their fortune. All were great landed proprietors; some were descended from rich Gallo-Roman families, who were wealthy before the Frankish conquest; others were favourites, whom the kings had generously endowed with estates, or counts who had profited by their position to create spacious domains for themselves. For that matter, whether they were of Roman or Germanic birth, the members of this aristocracy formed a group which was held together by community of interests, and in which differences of origin soon disappeared and were merged in an identity of manners. In proportion as the State which they provided with its most important agents became more incapable of fulfilling its essential and primordial task—that is, of safeguarding the persons and the property of its subjects—their preponderance grew more marked. Their personal situation profited by the progress of the general anarchy, and the public insecurity augmented their private influence. As officers of the king the counts persecuted and fleeced the poor people whom they should have protected; but from the moment when these same poor people, having no alternative, had surrendered their property and their persons, and had been annexed to the domains of the counts, the latter, in their rôle of great landowners, granted them their powerful protection. Thus the very officers of the State worked against the State, and by continually extending their patronage over the inhabitants, and their private property over the land, they deprived the king, with surprising rapidity, of both his immediate subjects and his taxpayers.

For the relation which was established between the powerful and the weak was not the mere economic relation which exists between a landowner and his tenant. Born of the need of effective protection in a society given over to anarchy, it created between them a peculiar bond, as between superior and subordinate, which extended to the whole person, recalling in its intimacy and its closeness the family tie. The "contract of recommendation" which made

its appearance from the 6th century onwards gave the protected man the name of vassal (*vassus*) or servitor, and the
protector the name of ancient or seigneur (*senior*). The
seigneur was pledged not only to provide for the subsistence of his vassal, but also at all times to grant him his
succour and aid, and to represent him before the law. The
freeman who sought protection might preserve the appearance of liberty, but in actual fact he had become a client,
a *sperans,* of the *senior.*

The protectorate which the seigneur exercised over freemen in virtue of the "contract of recommendation" was
naturally exercised with greater strictness over the individuals belonging to his domain—old Roman colonists, attached to the soil (*adscripti glebae*), or serfs, the descendants of Roman or Germanic slaves, whose very persons, by
virtue of their birth, were the lord's private property. Over
all this dependent population the seigneur exerted an authority which was at once patriarchal and patrimonial, like
that of a magistrate and judge combined. In the beginning
this was merely the factual position. But nothing more
clearly illustrates the impotence of the State than the way
in which it was forced to recognize the situation. From the
6th century onwards the king granted privileges of immunity in ever-increasing numbers. There were privileges
granting a great landowner exemption from the right of the
public functionaries to intervene in his domain. Thus the
privileged landowner took the place of the officers of the
State on his own territory. His competence, purely private
in origin, received its legal consecration. In short, the State
capitulated to him. And as this immunity became more
widely diffused, the kingdom was covered with an increasing number of domains in which the king could not intervene, so that in the end there was nothing under his immediate control save the few inconsiderable regions which
the great landowners had not yet absorbed.

The situation was the more serious in that of the properties of the king himself, which had originally comprised
all the territorial possessions of the Roman State, there was
nothing left, at the close of the Merovingian period, but insignificant fragments. Morsel by morsel, they had been

ceded to the aristocracy with a view to purchasing its loyalty. The continual divisions of the monarchy among the descendants of Clovis, the alternate division and reunion of the kingdoms of Austrasia and Burgundy, the constant re-tracing of frontiers, and the civil wars that resulted therefrom, offered the magnates an excellent opportunity of bargaining for the price of their devotion to the princes whom the chances of inheritance had called to reign over them, and who, to assure themselves of the crown, were quite ready to sacrifice the patrimony of the dynasty.

For the first time there was a growing opposition which was to manifest itself between the Romanized aristocracy of Neustria and the magnates of Austrasia, who had remained more faithful to Germanic manners and institutions. The advent of the aristocracy very naturally provoked a manifestation of local influence; and so diversity took the place of monarchical unity.

The conquest of the Mediterranean by the Musulmans was fated to precipitate the political and social evolution which was already commencing. Hitherto, in the midst of a society that was tending to become a régime of seigneurial landowners, the towns, and with them a free bourgeoisie, had been kept alive by commerce.

In the second half of the 7th century all trade ceased on the shores of the Western Mediterranean. Marseilles, deprived of her ships, was dying of asphyxia, and in less than half a century all the cities in the south of France had lapsed into a state of utter decadence. Trade, no longer fed by sea-borne traffic, came to a standstill throughout the country: the middle class disappeared: there were no longer merchants by profession; there was no circulation of goods, and as a natural result the market dues no longer fed the royal treasury, which was henceforth unable to defray the expenses of government.

Henceforth the landed aristocracy represented the only social force. The king was ruined, but the aristocracy, with its land, possessed wealth and authority. It only remained for it to seize political power.

2. The Mayors of the Palace

The last of the Merovingians have been described by tradition as "idle kings," *rois fainéants:* but they could more truly be described as impotent kings, for their inaction was explained, not by their idleness or their apathy, but by their weakness and lack of power. After the middle of the 7th century, although they still reigned, it was the magnates who governed, established on the ruins of the monarchy which they had defeated, whose subjects they had divided among themselves, and whose functions they performed. In each of the three portions into which the monarchy was divided—Neustria, Austrasia and Burgundy—as king succeeded to king, the mayor of the palace became metamorphosed into the minister of the king, the representative, at his court, of the aristocracy. In actual fact it was henceforth the mayor of the palace, supported by the aristocracy, who governed the country. Of the mayors of the palace one—the Burgundian—disappeared before long, and the other two came into conflict. The landed aristocracy of Austrasia, more powerful than the great landowners of Neustria, being farther removed from the king and the old Roman administration, inevitably won the upper hand in a State exclusively based on territorial wealth.

The struggle was just as unequal between the mayor of Austrasia, Pippin, who represented the magnates, and the mayor of Neustria, Ebroin, who had remained loyal to the old conception of royalty: Pippin was victorious. Thereafter there was only one mayor of the palace for the whole of the monarchy, and it was the Carolingian family that provided him.

For a long while this family had held in the north of the kingdom a position which it owed to its territorial possessions. Its domains were many, above all in that semi-Roman, semi-Germanic region of which Liége, then a mere village, was the centre, and were distributed on either side of the linguistic frontier, in Hesbaye, Condroz and Ardenne; Andenne and Herstal were its favourite residences. Wealthy marriages increased its ascendancy. Of the union between the daughter of Pippin of Landen and the son of Ansegisel of Metz was born Pippin of Herstal, the first of the race to play a part of whom history has any record. We know that he fought with success against the pagan Frisians, who were troubling the northern parts of the kingdom by their incursions, and that he thereby won a popularity for himself and his family which lifted them out of obscurity. Sending his natural son Charles Martel to continue the struggle against the Barbarians, he himself led his vassals and his loyal supporters, inured to the hardships of frontier fighting, against Ebroin, whom he conquered, and thenceforth he governed the whole kingdom as regent. It was well for the kingdom that the government was in the hands of this robust warrior at the moment when the Arabs of Abderrahman crossed the Pyrenees and invaded Aquitaine. Charles Martel offered them battle on the plains of Poitiers, and the charge of the Musulman cavalry was broken against the ranks of his heavy footsoldiers. The literary decadence of this period was so complete that we have no account of this decisive battle. That, however, is of little importance; its result was enough to immortalize it. The invasion was checked: the invaders retreated, and the Musulmans retained no possessions in Gaul apart from the environs of Narbonne, from which Pippin expelled them in 759.

The victory of Poitiers made Charles Martel the master of the kingdom; and he took advantage of this to give it a strong military organization. Hitherto the army had consisted only of freemen, levied in the counties in time of war. It was a mere militia of footsoldiers, equipped at their own cost; difficult to mobilize and slow in its movements. After Poitiers Charles decided to create a cavalry—following the example of the Arabs—which could rapidly confront the enemy and replace the advantage of numbers by that of mobility. Such a novelty called for a radical transformation of traditional usages. It was out of the question to expect freemen to maintain a war horse and acquire the costly equipment of the horse-soldier, or to undergo the long and difficult apprenticeship that would qualify them to fight on horseback.

To attain his object, Martel had to create a class of warriors with resources to correspond with the part they were expected to play.[1] A generous distribution of land was made to the strongest vassals of the mayor of the palace, who did not hesitate, for this purpose, to secularize a good number of ecclesiastical holdings. Each man-at-arms thus provided with a tenure—or, to employ the technical term, a benefice—was required to rear a war horse and to do military service whenever required. An oath of fidelity confirmed his obligations. The vassal, who originally was only a servant, thus became a soldier whose livelihood was assured by the possession of landed property. This institution was soon introduced throughout the kingdom. The immense domains of the aristocracy enabled each of its members to form a troop of horse, and they did not fail to do so. The original name of the benefice was presently replaced by that of fief. But the feudal organization itself, in all its essential features, was comprised in the measures taken by Charles Martel. This was the greatest military reform that Europe was to experience before the appearance of permanent armies; but, as we shall presently see, its repercussions on society and the State were even more profound than those of permanent armies. Fundamentally it was merely an adaptation of the army to a period when the whole economic life of the country was dominated by the great domain, and it resulted in giving the landed aristocracy both military and political power. The old army of freemen did not disappear, but it was now merely a reserve to which less and less recourse was made.

The monarchy allowed this transformation to be effected, which placed the army beyond its control, leaving it only the vain appearance of power. Henceforth the kings were so completely effaced in the shadow of their powerful mayor of the palace that we can hardly distinguish one from another, so that the historical experts disagree as to their names. Einhard is doubtless only echoing the opinion current in the entourage of the Carolingians when he

---

[1] It is interesting to note that in Russia, in the 15th century, Ivan III created a cavalry arm in the same fashion. He even gave land to serfs. (Milioukov, *Histoire de Russie*, vol. i, p. 117.)

amuses himself by caricaturing the monarchs as stupid and
rustic persons, with unkempt beards and worn garments,
like those of the peasants of their lost domains, and trav-
elling, like the peasants, in an ordinary ox-cart. He has
neither pity nor respect for them; there is nothing about
them that he does not make fun of, down to their long
hair, an old Germanic symbol of the royal power.

3. *The New Royalty*

Despite the service which Charles Martel rendered to
Christianity under the walls of Poitiers, the Church preserved no sympathetic memory of him. It resented his policy of secularization; and it did not forget his refusal to
come to the help of the Papacy, hard pressed by the
Lombards, even when Gregory III paid him the honour of
sending him a special embassy in order to make the solemn
presentation of the keys of the tomb of the Apostles. Less
absorbed in warfare, his son Pippin the Short, on the contrary, who succeeded him in 741 as mayor of the palace
and ruler of the kingdom, was almost from the first in constant touch with Rome.

At the moment of his accession to power the Anglo-
Saxon missions to the pagan Germans beyond the Rhine
had recently begun their task under the direction of St.
Boniface (719, † 755 in Friesland). Pippin's treatment of
St. Boniface was marked by a degree of zeal and benevo-
lence to which the apostles of Christianity were little accustomed. His conduct, however, was inspired by political
interest. He understood that the most effectual means of
mitigating the barbarism of the Frisians, the Thuringians,
the Bavarians and the Saxons, thus making them less dangerous neighbours and paving the way for future annexation, was to begin by converting them. Hence his interest in
the plans of Boniface, and the support which he gave him,
and the favours which he bestowed upon the see of Ma-
yence, which, being created the metropolis of the new
Germanic Church, allied the latter, from its birth, to the
Frankish Church.

Boniface, however, being as an Anglo-Saxon the obedient son of the Papacy, did not set to work until he had asked and obtained the consent and the instructions of Rome. He thus became, thanks to his intimate relations with the mayor of the palace, the natural intermediary between him and the Pope. And by the very force of circumstances, each of them, having need of the other, asked nothing better than to be brought into closer touch with him. Pippin, already king *de facto,* aspired to the status of king *de jure.* But he hesitated to wrest the crown from its lawful possessor, the incarnation of a long dynastic tradition. In order to accomplish without scruple the *coup d'état* which had become inevitable, he must be able to shelter himself behind the highest possible moral authority, by obtaining the public approval of the Roman pontiff. As for the Pope, his position was equally untenable, and clamouring for a solution. The moment had arrived for him to break with the Emperor, whose heretical Caesarism was becoming more and more arrogant, and who, either through impotence, or in a spirit of malevolence, was allowing the Lombards to advance to the very walls of Rome. (Some time after 744 the Lombard king Aistulf had seized the Exarchate.) Here too a *coup d'état* was imminent, and in order to accomplish it the help which Charles Martel had refused some years earlier was required of his son.

With the ground prepared, the alliance established itself automatically. In 751 Pippin's deputies sent to the Pope and solemnly asked him whether it was not fitting that the royal title should appertain rather to him who exercised the supreme authority than to him who enjoyed only the appearance of authority. No less solemnly, the Pope corroborated their opinion on this point of political morality. A few weeks later Pippin had himself proclaimed king by an assembly of magnates. The last descendant of Clovis—Childeric—was sent to end his days in a monastery. We do not know the date of his death. Never was the disappearance of a dynasty attended by such indifference; never was a *coup d'état* so easy and so necessary.

Mounted upon the throne by the help of the Pope, the first of the Carolingian kings was not slow to repay the debt thus contracted. Stephanus II came in person, in the following year, to claim his assistance against the Lombards. This was the first time in the history of the Church that a Pope had been seen to the north of the Alps. With this the die was cast; Rome broke with Constantinople and associated her destiny with that of the dynasty she had lately consecrated.

Pippin solemnly promised to march against the Lombards, and, having conquered them, to give to the Roman Church the territory surrounding the Eternal City. Neither Pippin nor Stephanus was deterred for a moment by the notion that they were thus disposing of a region whose legitimate possessor was the Emperor. The campaign which was fought in 754 gave the victory to the Franks.[2] The Pope[3] received the promised territory: the State of the Church was founded. The capital of the ancient world, now the capital of the Christian world, was amenable henceforth only to the successor of St. Peter. At the same time, this question of the temporal sovereignty of the Pope gave rise to serious complications and conflicts. The Papal State was small and feeble; it was bound before long to succumb to the assaults of the Lombards unless it could count on the protection of the conqueror who had just bestowed it upon the Church. How could the independency of the Papacy be reconciled with the urgent need of military tutelage? While waiting for a more satisfactory solution, Stephanus adopted the emergency measure of bestowing upon Pippin a title which could be interpreted in any sense, according to circumstances, but which established a permanent bond between the Frankish king and Rome: the title of *patricius Romanorum*, Roman patrician.

The first war of the new dynasty was thus undertaken in the interest of the Church; and this was quite consistent with the character which had been impressed upon the dynasty at the outset. The royal power of the Merovingians had been purely secular: but that of the Carolingians reveals a profoundly religious imprint. The ceremony of consecration, which appeared for the first time at the corona-

---

[2] Aistulf presently renewed the campaign, and Pippin returned in 756.

[3] Stephanus III; Stephanus II having died in 752. (*Tr.*)

tion of Pippin, made the sovereign in some sort a sacerdotal figure. The king affirmed his submission to the commands of God and his desire to serve Him, not merely by including the Cross among his emblems, but by entitling himself, in Christian humility, "King by the grace of God." From this time forward—and here the Carolingian monarchy was inaugurating the tradition which was to outlive it by many centuries—the ideal of the king was not to be Caesar, a potentate deriving his power and authority only from earthly sources; but to ensure that the divine precepts prevailed on earth, and to govern in accordance with Christian morality: that is, in accordance with the Church. This, of course, was the ideal which St. Boniface and Stephanus II were bound to set before Pippin, and this ideal he bequeathed to Charlemagne.[4] We find it expressed in all the treatises of the 9th century on the sovereign power; in the *Via Regia* of Smaragdus as in the *De rectoribus christianus* of Sedulius. Actually, it made religion an affair of State. Only those who belonged to the Christian society could belong to the public society, and excommunication was equivalent to outlawry.

[4] The ancient or Roman ideal of monarchical power was replaced by the Christian ideal until its reappearance in the 12th century.

CHAPTER III

The Restoration of the Empire

in the West

1. *Charlemagne* (768–814)

Charlemagne conferred the title of Great upon himself, and
posterity has ratified this title so completely that it has, by
a unique phenomenon, combined it with his name (Charlemagne, *Carolus magnus*). Caesar and Napoleon alone
enjoy a fame universal as his. Just as in the Germanic languages "Caesar" (Kaiser) became the synonym for "Emperor," so in the Slav tongues, and in Hungarian, Charles
(*Carol, Kiral, Kral*) has acquired the significance of "king."
In the Middle Ages the Carolingian legend was one of the
most prolific sources of literature in the vulgar tongue.
From this legend proceeded the oldest French epic poem:
the *Chanson de Roland*. And again, during the Renaissance, it inspired Tasso and Ariosto.

If we examine it more closely, however, we soon perceive that the reign of Charlemagne, from whatever point
of view we regard it, was only the continuation, and, as it
were, the prolongation of his father's reign. It exhibits no
originality: the alliance with the Church, the struggle
against the pagans—the Lombards and Musulmans—the
transformations in the methods of government, the endeavour to rouse scholarship from its torpor—the germ of all
these things is visible under Pippin. Like all those who have
changed history, Charles did no more than accelerate the

evolution which social and political needs had imposed upon his time. The part he played was so completely adapted to the new tendencies of his epoch that it is very difficult to distinguish how much of his work was personal to himself and how much it owed to the force of circumstances.

At the moment when he succeeded to his father (768) the religious question, or, if you will, the ecclesiastical question (which at this period was one and the same thing) was predominant above all others, and its solution was imperative. The conversion of Germany was still incomplete, and no definite *modus vivendi* had been found between the King of the Franks and the Papacy, which was still threatened by the Lombards. We may say that Charles's utmost efforts during the first part of his reign were directed to the accomplishment of this twofold task.

Beyond the Rhine was a powerful nation which still retained its independence and was loyal to its ancient national cult: the Saxons, established between the Ems and the Elbe, from the shores of the North Sea to the Hartz Mountains. Of all the Germans, they alone, in the great upheaval of the invasions, had put to sea in search of new territories. During the whole of the 5th century their ships had harried the coasts of Gaul and Britain. There were Saxon settlements—which have left their traces to this day in the formation of place-names—at the mouths of the Canche and the Loire. But it was only in Britain that the Saxons and the Angles—a people from the south of Jutland, closely akin to them—had established themselves permanently. They drove the Celtic population of the island into the hilly or mountainous regions of the west—into Wales and Cornwall—whence, finding themselves too closely packed, they migrated, in the 6th century, to Armorica, which thenceforth took the name of Brittany, just as Britain[1] itself was called Angle-land, England, after its invaders. Seven small Anglo-Saxon kingdoms, whose names survive to this day in those of as many English counties, were established on the territory abandoned by its old in-

[1] Bretagne = Britanny *or* Britain. (*Tr.*)

habitants. But these insular Saxons did not remain in touch
with their fellows on the Continent. They had so far forgotten them that when, after their conversion by the missionaries of Gregory the Great, they themselves undertook
to convert the Germans, their missionaries went not to the
Saxons, but to Upper Germany.

Even as late as the middle of the 8th century the continental Saxons, by a singular chance, had never been subjected to Roman or Christian influence. While their neighbours were becoming Romanized or were converted to
Christianity, they remained purely German, and during the
long centuries of their isolation their primitive institutions,
like their national cult, had developed and become firmly
established. The Frankish kingdom, their immediate neighbour, was incapable of influencing them by its prestige and
its power of attraction, as the Roman Empire had formerly
influenced the Barbarians. They had preserved their independence, and they clung to this all the more tenaciously
in that it permitted them, under the pretext of war, to
pillage the frontier provinces. They held fast to their religion as the token and guarantee of their independence.

Charles's Saxon campaigns of 780 and 804 may be regarded as the first of the European wars of religion. Hitherto Christianity had been peacefully diffused among the
Germans. On the Saxons it was imposed by force. They
were compelled to accept baptism, and the death penalty
was decreed against those who should continue to sacrifice
to "idols." This new policy was the consequence of the ecclesiastical character which the monarchy had recently
assumed. Holding his power from God, the king could not
permit dissent in the matter of faith or worship among his
subjects. To refuse baptism, or, having received it, to violate
the baptismal promises, was to leave the community of the
Church, and thereby to outlaw oneself: it was to commit
a twofold act of infidelity towards the Church and the
State. Hence the violence and the massacres in the wars
against the Saxons, and hence too the obstinacy with which
they defended their gods, the guardians of their liberty.
For the first time Christianity encountered, among the
pagans, a national resistance; because for the first time it

was forced upon them by conquest. The Anglo-Saxons were converted by the words of a few monks. The Saxons of the Continent fought desperately to preserve their cult, and this struggle was the first of the series of bloody conflicts which the doctrine of the State religion was to provoke in the course of the ages.

It must be recognized, however, that the security of the Frankish kingdom necessitated the conquest of this people, who represented a continual menace on the northern frontier. The annexation and conversion of Saxony brought the whole of the ancient Germany into the community of European civilization. When they were completed the eastern frontier of the Carolingian Empire extended to the Elbe and the Saale. Thence it ran to the head of the Adriatic, across the mountains of Bohemia and the Danube, including the land of the Bavarians, whose duke, Tassilo, was deposed in 787. Beyond this was the region of barbarism: Slavs on the east, Avars in the south.

And the Avars had to be fought immediately. This nation of horsemen, of Finnish origin, who in the 6th century had annihilated the Gepidae in conjunction with the Lombards, had since then established themselves in the valley of the Danube, whence they harried both the Byzantine Empire and Bavaria. Several expeditions were needed to effect their purpose. These were campaigns of extermination. The Avars were massacred to the point of disappearing as a people, and even in our days the Russian proverb: "He has vanished like the Avars," recalls the impression that must have been produced in Eastern Europe by the annihilation of these cruel and savage raiders, who for a century had subjected the Slavs of the Carpathians to an insupportable tyranny. The operation completed, Charles, to guard against further aggression, threw a *march* or *mark* across the valley of the Danube: that is, a defensive territory under military administration. This was the Eastern March (*marca orientalis*), the point of departure of modern Austria, which has retained the name.

Before the end of the 7th century the Slavs had advanced into Central Europe. They had taken possession of the country abandoned by the Germans between the

Vistula and the Elbe, and by the Lombards and the Gepidae in Bohemia and Moravia. Thence they had crossed the Danube, and had penetrated into Thrace, where they scattered through the country until they reached the shores of the Adriatic.

On this side also it was necessary to assure the security of the Empire. From 807 onwards other marches or marks were established along the Elbe and the Saale, barring the further progress of the Slav tribes of the Wends, Sorabi (Sorbs) and Obodrites.

This frontier was at the same time—as the Rhine had been in the 4th and 5th centuries—the frontier between Christian Europe and the pagan world. It is interesting, as illustrating the religious ideas of the time, to note that on the frontier there was a temporary revival of slavery. The Slavs, as pagans, were beyond the pale of humanity, and those who were taken prisoner were sold like cattle; and the word for slave in all Western languages (*esclave, sklave, slaaf*), is merely the name of the Slav people. For the people of the 9th and 10th century the "slave" was what the "black" was for the people of the 17th, 18th and 19th centuries. The economic constitution of the epoch, as we shall presently see, had no need of slave labour, and this, no doubt, explains the fact that there was no great development of the slave trade or of slavery.

At the other side of Europe, along the Pyrenees, the kingdom was in contact not with the pagan Barbarians, but with the Musulmans. Since their defeat at Poitiers they had not again threatened Gaul. The rearguard which they had left in Narbonne had been driven back by Pippin the Short. Spain, where the Caliphate of Cordova had lately been established, no longer looked toward the north, and the activities of the brilliant civilization which unfolded itself under the first Omayyads were directed towards the Islamic settlements on the shores of the Mediterranean. The rapidity of the progress made by Islam in the sciences, arts, industry, and commerce, and all the refinements of civilized life, is almost as amazing as the rapidity of its conquests. But the natural consequence of this progress was to divert its energies from the great enterprises of proselytism and to concentrate them upon itself. While science progressed and art flourished, religious and political quarrels broke out. Spain had her share of these, like the rest of the Musulman world. It was one of these quarrels that gave rise to Charlemagne's expedition beyond the Pyrenees. Three Arab emirs, at war with the Caliph of Cordova, had applied to him for assistance. He came in person, in 778, at the head of an army, and drove the Musulmans back across the Ebro, but he was unsuccessful at the siege of Saragossa,[2] and recrossed the Pyrenees after a somewhat inglorious campaign, the only result of which was the erection of the Spanish March between the Ebro and the Pyrenees. This afterwards served the petty Christian kingdoms which had established themselves in the mountains of Asturias as an advance-post against the Arabs in the long struggle which was to terminate, in the 15th century, in the liberation of the Peninsula.[3] Charlemagne's contemporaries were hardly aware of this expedition. The memory of Count Roland, killed in a skirmish with the Basques, who fell upon the baggage-train of the army in the pass of Roncesvalles, was perpetuated, at first, only among the people of his province in the neighbourhood of Coutances. It took the religious and warlike enthusiasm that seized upon Europe at the time of the first Crusade to make Roland the most heroic of the paladins of the French and Christian epic, and to transform the campaign in which he fell into a gigantic attack upon Islam by "Carles li reis nostre emperere magne."

Of all the wars of Charlemagne the campaigns against the Lombards were the most important in respect of their political results, and they also very plainly reveal the intimate connection between Charles's policy and that of his father. The alliance with the Papacy compelled them to fight the Lombards, not only in the interests of the country, but also in the interest of the King of the Franks. Pippin, towards the end of his reign, had hoped to conclude a

[2] This city, however, had declared itself independent of the Omayyad Caliphate.

[3] Barcelona was taken in 801 by Louis, ruling in Aquitaine, and the March was then established.

pacific agreement with the Lombards. Charles, accordingly, married the daughter of their king, Didier. But this marriage was like all royal matches in which there is no compatibility of thought and interest; it served no purpose. The Lombards continued to threaten Rome, and their king entered into dangerous intrigues against his son-in-law with the Duke of the Bavarians and Charles's own sister-in-law. Charles repudiated his wife and crossed the Alps in 773. The dynasty was dethroned, and Charles proclaimed himself King of the Lombards. Didier, after prolonged resistance in Pavia, was sent to a monastery.

Thus the Lombard State, whose birth had destroyed the political unity of Italy, brought upon the country, as it perished, a foreign conqueror. Henceforth it was merely an appendage of the Frankish monarchy, and it broke away from the Franks at the end of the 9th century only to fall, before long, into the hands of the Germans. By a complete reversal of the course of history, the Lombard power, which had formerly annexed the north of Europe, was now annexed by it; and in a certain sense this destiny was merely a consequence of the political upheavals which had shifted the centre of gravity of the Western world from the Mediterranean to the north of Gaul. And yet its fate was decided by Rome—but by the Rome of the Popes. One does not see what interest could have induced the Carolingians to attack and conquer the Lombard kingdom if their alliance with the Papacy had not constrained them to do so. Here for the first time the influence is plainly manifested which the Church, once rid of the Byzantine tutelage, was henceforth to exercise over European politics. Henceforth the State could not dispense with the Church; between the two an association of mutual service was established, which, by constantly bringing the two powers into co-operation, led also to the continual amalgamation of spiritual and political questions, making religion an essential factor of the political order. The reconstitution of the Roman Empire in the year 800 was the definitive manifestation of this new situation, and the pledge of its future duration.

2. *The Empire*

Enlarged by conquest until it extended to the Elbe and the Danube in the east, and to Benevento and the Ebro in the south, the Frankish monarchy, at the close of the 8th century, comprised nearly the whole of the Christian Occident. The small Anglo-Saxon and Spanish kingdoms, which it had not absorbed, were a negligible quantity; moreover, they paid the monarchy a deference which practically amounted to the recognition of its protectorate. And in actual fact, the power of Charlemagne extended to all countries and all peoples that recognized in the Pope of Rome the Vicar of Christ and the head of the Church. Outside this area was the barbaric world of paganism, the hostile world of Islam, and the old Byzantine Empire: Christian, indeed, but marked by a highly capricious orthodoxy, which was centring itself more and more upon the Patriarch of Constantinople, and ignoring the Pope. Further, the sovereign of this immense monarchy was at once the debtor and protector of the Church. Its faith was as firmly founded as its zeal for religion was ardent. Is it surprising that under these circumstances the idea presented itself to the Papacy of profiting by so favourable a conjunction to reconstitute the Roman Empire?—but a Roman Empire whose head, crowned by the Pope in the name of God, would owe his power only to the Church, and would exist only to aid the Church in its mission: an Empire which, not being of secular origin, would owe nothing to men, and would not, properly speaking, be a State, but would be conterminous with the community of the faithful, whose temporal organization it would be, directed and inspired by the spiritual authority of the successor of St. Peter. In this way Christian society would be given its definitive form. The authority of the Pope and that of the Emperor, while remaining distinct one from the other, would nevertheless be as closely associated as the soul with the flesh in the human body. What St. Augustine had desired would be accomplished. The terrestrial State would be but the preparation for the journey to the Celestial City. A grandiose but purely ecclesiastical conception; Charlemagne seems never to have realized exactly its whole scope and all its consequences. His simple and positive genius could not have understood that the part which was assigned to him went far beyond that of a mere protector of the Pope and of religion. It may be, however, that he had some suspicion of the fact, and that before crossing the Rubicon in support of the Church he may have shown some hesitation and asked for further light on the matter. To make short work of the affair, the Pope, sure of his man, ventured on a sudden *coup*.

In the year 800, in the basilica of the Lateran at the termination of the Christmas mass, Leo III went up to the King of the Franks, and amidst the acclamation of the people placed the crown upon his head, and having saluted him with the name of Emperor, prostrated himself before him and "adored" him in accordance with the Byzantine ritual. The decisive step was taken; the Roman Empire was reconstituted, and by the hands of the successor of St. Peter.

Charles manifested some displeasure. He must have thought it strange that he, who had come to Rome merely to quell a revolt, and who a few days earlier had sat as judge between the Pope and the magnates of the city, should now receive the Imperial crown from one whom he regarded as his protégé. In 813 he had the offending ceremonial altered for the benefit of his son Louis, whom he appointed his successor; the crown was laid upon the altar, and Louis set it on his head with his own hands, without the intervention of the Pope. This innovation, which was subsequently abandoned, did not in any way affect the character of the Empire. Willy-nilly, it remained a creation of the Church; something external to and above the monarch and the dynasty. Its origin was in Rome, and the Pope alone could dispose of the Imperial crown.

This he did, of course, not as prince of Rome, but as the successor and representative of St. Peter. Just as he received his authority from the Apostle, it was in the name of the Apostle that he conferred the Imperial power. That power, and his own authority, proceeded directly from the same divine source, and the mosaic of St. John Lateran, which represents Leo III and Charlemagne kneeling at the feet of St. Peter, and receiving from him, one the keys, and the other the banner, symbolizes very exactly the nature of their powers, combined in their origin but distinct in their exercise.[4]

But in order that practice should correspond with theory, in order that the spiritual and the temporal power should not encroach upon each other, or rather, in order that their inevitable mutual encroachments should not lead to conflicts, and shake the majestic edifice that rested upon them, it was necessary that they should be associated, and that they should, as it were, keep step in a spirit of intimate and absolute confidence. But charged, as they were, the one with the government of men's souls, and the other with the government of their bodies, who was to indicate the exact limits of their competence? It is all the more impossible to trace them, inasmuch as the Pope's authority over the Catholic hierarchy was still undefined. The Emperor appointed bishops, convoked synods, and legislated in respect of matters of ecclesiastical discipline and religious instruction. In the case of a Charlemagne, this presented no inconvenience. But after him? How safeguard the Pope against the intentions of his successors? And how, on the other hand, were his successors to be safeguarded against the intentions of the Pope? For if the Imperial idea brought the State into the Church, it also brought the Church into the State. And what would happen when the successor of St. Peter felt it incumbent upon him to intervene in the civil government, to correct or guide it?

Until such time as the future should propose and debate these formidable problems, the restoration of the Empire was evidently to the common advantage of religious and civil society. Thanks to the zeal and vigilance of the Emperor, the Church enjoyed a tranquillity, an authority, an influence and a prestige which it had not known since the days of Constantine. Charles extended his solicitude to the material needs of the clergy, their moral condition, and

---

[4] In his official title Charles styles himself *Deo coronatus*, which perfectly corresponds with the conception which we are endeavouring to explain.

their apostolate. He showered donations upon sees and monasteries, and placed them under the protection of "advocates," appointed by himself; and he made the tithe compulsory throughout the Empire. He was careful to appoint as bishops only men as noted for the purity of their morals as for their piety; he encouraged the conversion of the Slavs on the frontier; above all, he urged the bishops to improve the education of the clergy, and, faithfully seconded by Alcuin, he required the cathedral and monastery schools to observe the exact rules of the chant, and imposed upon them the graphological reform which gave rise to the Caroline "minuscule," so clearly formed that the Italian printers of the Renaissance borrowed from it the characters of modern typography. The study of the Holy Scriptures was revived, and also of classic literature, and in the schools a generation of clerks was trained who professed the same disdain for the barbarity of Merovingian Latin as the humanists were to nourish, seven hundred years later, for the scholastic jargon of *magistri nostri*. There were even those who studied the most varied rhythms of prosody, so that modern scholars have been able to compile an anthology of 9th century poems, some of which are not lacking in charm. But this poetry was merely the recreation of workers whose inspirations and tendencies were essentially religious. The so-called Carolingian Renaissance was as the poles removed from the Renaissance properly so-called. There was nothing in common between the two, apart from a renewal of intellectual activity. The true Renaissance, purely secular, steeped itself in the ideas of the classic authors. The Carolingian Renaissance, exclusively ecclesiastical and Christian, regarded the classic authors merely as models of style. For them, study was justified only by its religious aims. The three fingers that held the pen were, so they told themselves, the symbol of the three Persons of the Holy Trinity. Like the Jesuits of the 16th century, the Carolingian clerks wrote only to the glory of God, and while we must not carry the comparison too far, their attitude toward antiquity was not dissimilar to that adopted by the Company of Jesus.

It was not only for the sake of the Church that Charlemagne founded and endowed schools. Since lay education had disappeared the State had perforce to recruit the élite of its officials from among the clergy, or else relapse into barbarism. Under Pippin the Short the chancellery was staffed exclusively with ecclesiastics, and we may conclude that Charlemagne, when he required that the teaching of grammar should be perfected, and that handwriting should be improved, was as much concerned with the linguistic and calligraphic accuracy of the diplomas issued in his name, and the capitularies which he promulgated, as with that of the missals and antiphonaries of the Church. But he had more than this in mind. He had evidently conceived the notion of educating lay officials by sending them to school with the Church, or rather, by having them reared in the Church schools. Just as the Merovingians had sought to graft their administration on to the Roman administration, so, in creating a body of State functionaries, he sought to imitate, as far as possible, the methods employed by the Church for the training of the clergy. His ideal, without a doubt, was to organize the Empire on the pattern of the Church: that is, to provide it with a personnel taught and trained in the same fashion, speaking among themselves and addressing the sovereign in the Latin tongue, which, from the Elbe to the Pyrenees, was to serve as the administrative language, as it was already the language of religion. His practical mind must inevitably have realized the impossibility of maintaining the administrative unity of his vast Empire, in which so many dialects were spoken, by means of illiterate functionaries, each of whom would know only the tongue of his own province. This difficulty would not have existed in a national State, where the vernacular might have become the State language, as it had in the little Anglo-Saxon kingdoms. But in this medley of peoples that was the Empire the political organization had to assume the same universal character as the religious organization, and to superpose itself on all the subjects of the Empire, just as the religious organization embraced all believers. The intimate alliance of Church and State was yet another reason why Latin should become the language of the lay administration. From whatever standpoint we consider the question, it is evident that without the use of Latin administration by the written word would have been impossible. The requirements of the State necessitated the use of Latin; it became, and it was destined to remain for centuries, the language of politics and of business, and also the language of science.

Charlemagne, however, fell very far short of success in creating the educated and Latinized officialdom which he had hoped to bequeath to his successors. The task was too difficult and too enormous. But he gave proof of a touching sincerity and good will. He himself learned to write in his old age, and nothing, perhaps, could give us a better idea of the energy and perseverance of this great man than the passage in which Einhard describes him as employing the hours of his wakeful nights in tracing letters on a slate. At his Court a sort of little academy, directed by Alcuin, provided a literary education for sons of some of the greatest families of the Empire, who were destined for a career in the Church, as bishops, or in the administration, as counts, advocates or *missi*. All his children received the training in grammar and rhetoric which constituted the literary education, and there is no doubt that the Imperial example found many imitators among the aristocracy.[5] The few laymen and laywomen who produced Latin works during the reign of Louis the Pious and his sons—for example, Nithard and Duodha—or who, like Count Eberhard of Friuli and Count Robert of Namur, took some interest in men of letters, show that all these efforts were not wasted. However, this attempt to extend the ecclesiastical education to the upper classes, born of the desire to perfect the organization of the Empire, was not destined to outlive the latter.

The institutions of the Church furnished Charlemagne with the inspiration of many other reforms. His capitularies, drawn up after the model of the decisions promulgated by the synods and councils of the Church, reveal innumerable attempts at reform, or improvement, or innovation, in every

[5] The daughters of Charles the Bald were educated by Hugbald, of the Abbey of Saint-Amand.

department of civil life and administration. He introduced, in the palace tribunal, in place of the barbarous and formalistic process of Germanic law, the procedure by inquest which he borrowed from the ecclesiastical courts. The ideal of administrative control which was realized by the creation of the *missi dominici*—itinerant commissaries whose duty it was to supervise the conduct of the functionaries—was very probably borrowed from the Church and adapted to the needs of the State.

The passion for amelioration and reform that marked the whole of Charlemagne's legislative achievements was only the continuation, or, to be more exact, the efflorescence of the attempts at improvement to be noted in Pippin the Short. Pippin had tried to remedy the chaos into which the monetary system had lapsed. Charles accomplished the task which Pippin had begun. He finally abandoned the coining of gold, which had become too rare in the West to keep the mints at work. Henceforth only silver monies were minted; and the ratio which he fixed between them continued in use all over Europe until the adoption of the metric system, and is still current in the British Empire. The unit was the livre or pound, divided into 20 sous, each consisting of 12 deniers. Only the deniers were real money; the sou and the livre were nominal values; and so they continued until the great monetary reforms of the 13th century.

It is, of course, impossible to give in these pages even an approximate idea of the content of the capitularies. The majority of them indicate a programme rather than effective reforms, and it would be a great mistake to suppose that their innumerable decisions can ever have been carried into effect. Those that were actually realized—as, for example, the institution of the courts of aldermen—were far from penetrating to every portion of the Empire. Such as they are, the capitularies remain the finest surviving monument of the Carolingian Empire. But it is obvious that the power of the monarchy was not commensurate with its intentions. The personnel at its disposal was insufficient, and, above all, the power of the aristocracy constituted a limit which it could neither surmount nor suppress. The realization of the politico-religious ideal of Charlemagne would have necessitated resources and a degree of power and authority which the social and economic constitution of the period were unable to place at his disposal.

CHAPTER IV

Economic and Social Organization

1. *The Disappearance of the Cities and of Commerce*

The most important fact, from the social point of view, of the period extending from the Musulman invasions to the Carolingian epoch, was the rapid reduction, and, in the end, the all but complete disappearance, of the urban population.

In the Roman Empire the cities constituted, from the first, the very basis of the State. The political organization was essentially municipal. The country was merely the territory attaching to the city; it had no independent existence; it produced only for the city and was ruled by the city. Wherever the Roman State was established it founded cities and set them up as administrative centres. In the Roman Empire the provinces were so intimately related to the cities on which they were dependent that the same word, *civitas*, was employed to denote the city and the province. And this state of affairs continued until the end of the Byzantine Empire.

The constitution of States whose administrative and social organization no longer corresponded with the urban type of the Roman State was therefore a most surprising novelty, and one hitherto quite unknown in the Western world. It was explained—at all events, as far as the administrative function of the towns was concerned—by the fact that the conquerors of the Empire found it impossible to preserve unaltered all the institutions of the Empire. And it was these institutions of the Empire which had assured the existence of the cities in the provinces occupied by the invaders—Gaul, Spain, Italy, Africa and Britain. Some of them, of course, beside the shores of the Mediterranean—Marseilles, Narbonne, Naples, Carthagena—carried on a more or less important maritime trade, and almost all the towns in the interior of the country depended on their regular commercial activities; so that the majority of their population consisted of a middle class of shopkeepers and artisans. But none of these cities were comparable with the great ports or industrial centres of the East: Alexandria, Constantinople or Antioch. They existed less by virtue of their own energies than by the general operation of the political and economic activity of the Roman world. Their importance was due to the place which they occupied in the State, to their function as administrative centres, to the presence in them of a numerous staff of officials, and to the relations which the population of the provinces necessarily maintained with them. In short, their situation was fairly analogous to that of those modern cities whose only distinction is that they are royal residences, or have the advantage of possessing some important State institution. Rome herself differed from the provincial cities in this respect only by reason of the glory and importance which she derived from the presence of the Emperor and the central government. The history of her decadence, from the moment when Constantine deprived her of the rank and the advantages of the capital of the world, was repeated, on a smaller scale, in all the cities of the West, as the officials abandoned them amidst the turmoil of invasion, and later, under the rule of the Germanic kings; so that the offices, law-courts and schools were closed, the postal service no longer operated, the inertia and incapacity of the administration allowed the bridges and aqueducts to fall into ruin, and the police and the revictualling services disappeared.

The sea-borne trade, until the period of the Musulman conquests, had maintained, in the coastal towns, a commercial activity by which the adjacent regions of the interior profited. It is true that this trade had lost its principal export market now that an impoverished and depopulated Rome no longer required the grain of the provinces for her subsistence. Nevertheless, until the middle of the 7th century the Western ports of the Mediterranean were still assiduously frequented by Syrian and Jewish merchants. In the time of Gregory of Tours a Jewish colony of some importance existed at Clermont-Ferrand. The papyrus employed in the Merovingian chancellery was imported from Sicily, which shows that navigation was still providing articles of current consumption. But these relations with the Byzantine world came to an end once the preponderance of Islam made it impracticable for Christian traders to risk themselves beyond the waters of Greece and Southern Italy. From this time forward the sea no longer excited the spirit of enterprise in the Western countries. Now, when men looked out seawards, there was dread in their hearts, lest enemy sails should appear on the horizon. And just as the Mediterranean was in the power of the Musulmans, so the North Sea was traversed only by the ships of the Scandinavians. Washed by the waves on the south, north and west, the Carolingian Empire no longer showed the slightest trace of maritime activity. Its only ports—Quentovic, at the mouth of the Canche, and Duurstede—still maintained a certain degree of commercial activity until the 9th century, when they were devastated by the Normans, after which they lapsed into complete decadence. From the 8th century onwards Europe existed for three hundred years without any intercourse with the countries overseas.

The inevitable consequence was an almost complete cessation of trade, and apart from a few local industries, such as the weaving of cloth, which still survived in Flanders, there was an almost total failure of industrial activity, and money no longer circulated.

Henceforth, in the depopulated cities, the deserted quarters fell into ruin, serving as quarries to the few inhabitants who, gathered together in some corner of the old city area, found means to defend and shelter themselves by utilizing the materials furnished by the deserted buildings. At Nîmes the walls of the Roman circus served as the ramparts of the little town that nestled amidst the ruins. At Treves a window of the ancient palace, adapted as well as might be for purposes of defence, became one of the gates of the city, and the *porta nigra*, whose blocks of stone were too heavy to be carried away, was deprived, for the benefit of the local smithy, of the iron cramps which bound them together. Even in Italy, where the decadence was less profound, it was none the less lamentable. Rome seemed lost within the vast circuit which the wall of Aurelian described about what was left of the city. In 848 Pope Leo, to guard against a sudden attack, caused the inhabited portions on the left bank of the Tiber to be enclosed (the "Leonine city"), and turned the tomb of the Emperor Hadrian into a fortress.

In Gaul, urban life was so completely extinct that the kings no longer dwelt in the towns, where they were unable, owing to the complete lack of transport, to obtain the necessary victuals for their retinue. Henceforth they lived all the year round on their domains, passing from one to the other as they emptied the barns and granaries. And like the kings, the provincial officers lived in the country, on their own estates, or on those of the persons under their jurisdiction, on whom they imposed the *droit de gîte*. By a curious phenomenon of regression, the administration, on losing its urban character, became nomadic instead of sedentary.

Ruined and depopulated though they were, the cities had not lost all their significance. Abandoned by the civil administration, they remained the centres of the religious organization. The episcopal see established under the Empire in the capital of each "city" was still extant, and the strong Roman scaffolding of the Church still rose from the ruins of the State. And so, in the heart of a purely agricultural society, something of the municipal character of the ancient State was preserved by the Church. It was owing to the Church that the cities did not disappear altogether, but waited for the still distant day when they would become the cradles of the new middle class.

Just as the Pope, after the Emperors had deserted Rome, took it upon himself to protect the Eternal City, so in each "city" the bishop extended his authority over the few inhabitants who grouped themselves about the Cathedral and provided for the needs of the clergy. Thus the religious life and the religious organization maintained, amidst the ruins of the ancient cities, a small assemblage of laymen who continued as best they could to carry on the Roman trades and practise the Roman technique, but who had no longer anything in common, whether in the spirit that inspired them or in the administration that governed them, with the municipal populations of old.

2. The Great Domains

The disappearance of the towns led to a profound transformation of rural economy. The products of the soil, which had flowed into the urban markets, gradually lost their purchasers. Once the division of social labour came to an end, which in all advanced societies places the town and the countryside in the mutual relation of consumer and producer, the agricultural population began to produce only for its own needs; or in other words, as it now constituted the nation, it was henceforth both the producer and the consumer of the products of the soil. There was now only one kind of wealth—landed property—and only one kind of worker—the tiller of the soil—and the only economic relations which existed between man and man were conditioned by their quality of landowner or tenant.

Since no dates are available, we cannot form a very exact idea of the agricultural crisis which must have been provoked by the restriction, and then the complete disappearance, of the urban markets. Very probably it finally ruined such small landowners as still survived. As for the great domains, it would certainly have increased their area and modified their organization. It increased their area by forcing the small farmers, deprived of their outlet, and therefore of their resources, to attach themselves to the neighbouring domain, adding their land to it in return for tenant rights. It modified their organization by forcing them to adapt themselves to a system in which there was no such thing as production for sale. The transformation must have begun some time in the 5th century; by the end of the 8th century it was complete. Its final stage was the great domain of the Carolingian epoch, an exact description of which may be found in the polyptych of Abbot Irminon and the *Capitulare de villis.*

The pattern followed was that of the great ecclesiastical domain, better organized than others because the Church had not abandoned the use of writing; and we may be confident that beyond the Rhine the domains of the Church were the earliest types of domainal organization.

The domain, as an economic phenomenon, was entirely original; there was nothing of the kind at any period of Graeco-Roman antiquity. It was doubtless related, by direct filiation, to the great estate of the late Roman Empire; it preserved, in its essential features, the organization of the Roman *villa*, whose name is retained, and the institution of the *colonatus* appears to have been the preponderating influence in the condition of its tenants. But its actual operation, both in principle and in effect, was something quite new. One may define it by saying that the idea of profit was completely unknown to it. This will be readily understood if we consider that since it could not regulate production with a view to export and sale outside the domain, it was forced to regulate it with a view to its distribution and consumption within the domain. Its aim was to ensure that the domain should be self-sufficing, living on its own resources, without selling and without purchasing. This system is commonly described as "closed economy"; it would be more exactly described as "economy without outlets." For it was the absence of outlets that produced this self-sufficiency of the domainal constitution. And from this many very important consequences followed, which dominated the entire economic life of the Middle Ages down to the 12th century. With them, indeed, the economic life of the Middle Ages originated. To begin with, the regression of agricultural methods is obvious. It was useless to make the soil yield more than was required to satisfy the needs of the cultivator, for since the surplus could not be exported it would neither improve the condition of the tiller of the soil nor increase the rental value of the land. The farmer was therefore satisfied with a minimum of care and effort, and agronomic science was allowed to fall into oblivion, until the possibility of selling the crops should once more encourage the owners of the soil to adopt improved and therefore more lucrative methods. But then the land would begin to be regarded as a value, and not as a mere means of subsistence.

Another characteristic of domainal exploitation was the almost complete substitution of payments in kind for payments in money. It goes without saying that this was a natural and necessary consequence of the absence of sale outside the domain. The landowner, whose livelihood depended on his domain, fixed in natural products, and sometimes even in raw material worked up by the peasant, the quota of each tenure in what might be called its alimentary revenue. At stated periods, in conformity with a permanent assessment, the various tenures would have to deliver to him grain, eggs, cheese, smoked meats and ells of cloth.

It would be a great mistake to suppose that we are confronted here with a return to an age preceding the invention of money, and the rather unfortunate description of "natural economy" so often applied to this system is a very imperfect definition of its character. As a matter of fact, money did not cease to exist as an instrument of exchange and a measure of values. We do not find that natural products of any kind took the place of money from the 9th to the 12th century, or fulfilled its function. All that we can truthfully say is that inside the domain it was very naturally replaced by the practice, imposed by necessity, of supplying consumer's goods. Outside the domain it was in normal use, and the few commodities—eggs, poultry, and the like—which the peasants took each week to the little local markets with which no society can dispense entirely, were paid for in deniers and oboli.

We must consider, too, that the prestation[1] of each tenure was invariable, and that for so long as he furnished it the tenant enjoyed a hereditary right to the land which he occupied. And this too was the inevitable consequence of the economic system from which the idea of profit was ab-

---

[1] Payment in kind. (*Tr.*)

sent. What mattered to the landowner was the annual regularity of his income in kind, and the best way of guaranteeing this was to give it the character of a permanent tax. Between the lord of the domain and his peasants there was no relation comparable to that which subordinates the workers to a capitalist. The domain was not in any sense an exploitation, whether of the soil or of human beings. It was a social institution, not an economic enterprise. The obligations of its inhabitants were not based on personal contracts, but depended on right and custom. Each domain had its own law, established by traditional usage. The seigneur was at once more and less than a landed proprietor in the Roman or modern meaning of the term; less, because his property right was limited by the hereditary rights of his tenants to their tenures; more, because his power over these tenants was far in excess of that of a mere landowner.

In fact, he was their lord and they were his men. Many of them, the descendants of enfranchised slaves or body-serfs, constituted part of his patrimony. Others, the heirs of colonists of the Roman epoch, were *adscripti glebae*. Others, again, bound to the seigneur by "recommendation," lived under his protection. Over all of them, in various degrees, he exercised a patriarchal authority, and all were subject to his private jurisdiction. It was by virtue of this family group, which he protected, and ruled, that he was powerful. For at this period of sparse population men were far more important than land; there was more than enough land, but men were rare, and the great thing was to keep carefully as many as the seigneur possessed. There were consequently many provisions for preventing a man from leaving the domain. Over his serfs the seigneur possessed the right of pursuit; they could not, without his consent, marry wives outside the domainal community. Adscription to the soil, originally confined to the descendants of slaves and colonists, was gradually extended to freemen living under the seigneur's jurisdiction. This gradual extension of servitude to the whole agricultural population was the most notable phenomenon of the 9th century and the two following centuries. As a general rule, the peasant of this epoch was not free; he was so far from being free that in contemporary documents the words denoting the peasant (*villanus, rusticus*) became synonymous with serf (*servus*).

It must not be supposed that those who were subject to this servitude felt it as a burden. On the contrary, it was so completely adapted to their condition of hereditary tenants under the protection of a powerful lord that they regarded it as their natural state and submitted to it of their own free will. It was a necessary result of the domainal organization: the inevitable juridical consequence. How could liberty be valued by men whose very existence was guaranteed only by the place they occupied on the land, and under the jurisdiction of their seigneur, and whose security was therefore all the greater in proportion as they were more intimately incorporated in the domain?

Whether lay or ecclesiastical, the great domain of the first few centuries of the Middle Ages (before the 13th century) had nothing in common with the great exploitation. By the end of the Roman Empire the *latifundia* with their slaves had already disappeared, and it seems that the landed proprietors were progressively abandoning agriculture on the grand scale and dividing their estates into tenures. The complete cessation of the trade in agricultural products naturally favoured this tendency, and in the great domain of the Carolingian epoch and the following centuries we see its almost complete triumph. The domain was divided into two very unequal parts: the seigneurial land (*terra indominicata*) and the mansionary land (*mansionaria*). The first, by far the less extensive, was exploited directly and wholly to the profit of the seigneur. The work on this land was performed by domestic serfs who did not possess tenures, much like our agricultural labourers, or by tenants who were subject to *corvées*. The mansionary land was reserved for such tenants. It was divided into units, of variable extent according to the quality of the soil and the region; but each was large enough to support a family. These were the manses (*mansus*), and their possession was hereditary, subject, as we have seen, to prestations in kind and in labour. The whole constituted a rural *villa*. The common centre was the seigneurial court (*hof, curtis*), in which lived the seigneur's intendant or bailiff, the mayor (*meyer, major, villicus*) entrusted with the supervision of and jurisdiction over the villeins (*villani*). The court, surrounded by a moat and a palisade, served as the master's residence when he resided on his estate, and included the barns and granaries where the crops and other revenues were stored. It was here too that the domainal tribunal assembled, composed of tenants and presided over by the mayor or the seigneur. Here and there, even in the 9th century, and more and more frequently as time went on, a chapel, built by the seigneur, and served by a priest whom he chose and appointed, provided for the needs of religion. Many rural parishes owe their origin to these domainal chapels; and these, too, explain the right of presentation which many local seigneurs retained until the end of the *ancien régime*, and of which traces still linger in certain countries.

Surrounding the cultivable land, the woods, meadows and marshes were apportioned to the use of the seigneur and the villeins, in proportion to the share of the soil which they exploited. Often, if a stream crossed the domain, the seigneur built a mill upon it, for his own use and that of the inhabitants. A portion of flour was deducted from each sack by the miller, to provide for his maintenance: and this was the origin of the customary dues which survived until the French Revolution.

Despite local differences, the general features of the organization just described were to be found everywhere; but this organization was more perfect on the ecclesiastical properties than on those of the lay aristocracy. It exercised such a profound influence on society that in all Western European languages it has left its traces on the geographical and onomatological vocabulary. One has only to consider the number of French place-names ending in *ville* or *court*, or in the Germanic languages in *hof*, and the frequency of such family names as Lemaire, Mayer, De Meyer, Le Mayeur, etc.

Ordinarily a large domain consisted of several *villae*. That of Saint-Germain des Prés, in Charlemagne's day, comprised a whole series, scattered about from Brittany to the banks of the Moselle. The monasteries of the northern regions almost always endeavoured to acquire, in the wine country on the banks of the Rhine, the Moselle or the Seine, a *villa* which would furnish them with the wine that could no longer be obtained through the channel of trade.[2]

This last feature adds the final touch to the rural economy without outlets, of which the domain of the early years of the Middle Ages was the organ, just as the trade guild would subsequently be the organ of the urban industrial economy. Despite their profoundly different character, both were alike in one respect. Both economies were based on petty exploitation, with the result that they preserved intact, through the centuries, in the one case the bourgeois artisan, in the other the small farmer. Paradoxical though it may seem, it may truthfully be said that the great domains of the Middle Ages safeguarded the class of peasants. For them servitude was a benefit. At a time when the State was powerless, and when the earth alone supplied men's wants, it assured them of a protector and guaranteed them the possession of a share of the soil. Since it was not organized with a view to profit, the domainal constitution imposed only small prestations in return for considerable advantages. As the peasants were part of the seigneur's property, he was interested in their preservation: he defended them in the event of war and fed them from his stores in time of famine. War and famine were the two plagues that afflicted them in turn; war being a consequence of the increasing weakness of the State, and famine the inevitable result of commercial stagnation. A bad harvest was an irremediable disaster at a time when a country could not make good the deficit from the surplus of a neighbouring country. The period extending from the 9th to the 12th century is *par excellence*, in the economic history of Europe, the age of alimentary crises. They recurred every few years with the regularity of a natural phenomenon.

But while they were much more numerous than those of the following centuries, these famines were also less cruel.

---

[2] The Abbey of Saint-Trond, for example, had vineyards at Briedel and Pommeren on the Moselle.

This is explained by the absence of an urban population and the very low numerical strength of the rural population. The domainal organization which we have described, with its small productive power and its peasant class consisting almost entirely of tenants, evidently presupposed an extremely restricted number of inhabitants. There were, of course, landless folk, "poor men," as the contemporary texts describe them; men of a wandering habit, begging their way from monastery to monastery, hiring themselves to the villeins at harvest-time. But these disinherited children of a social order which was based on the possession of the soil were neither a responsibility nor a danger, which is proof of their small number.

It is impossible to estimate, with any approach to accuracy, the density of the population, as no reliable data are available. All that we can say is that in the Carolingian epoch the population was very small; undoubtedly smaller than at any previous epoch, owing to the extinction of the urban population. And it seems to have remained almost stationary until the beginning of the 11th century, for the natural excess of births did no more than fill the gaps constantly made by famine, war, and the disturbances and catastrophes of every kind that descended upon the West from the middle of the 9th century.

BOOK THREE

Feudal Europe

CHAPTER I

The Dissolution of the Empire

1. *Internal Causes*

Despite the fame of Charlemagne, we must be under no illusion as to the solidity of his political achievement. As a matter of fact, nothing could exceed the fragility of the Empire. The weakness of Louis the Pious, the quarrels of his sons, and the incursions of the Normans, Slavs and Saracens, merely hastened a dissolution whose causes were internal, and so obvious that they force themselves upon our attention.

The immense territory of the Empire, stretching from the marches of the Elbe and the Danube to the march of the Ebro in Spain and the Papal possessions in Italy, had none of the essential characteristics of a State. The Merovingian kingdom did at least endeavour to establish itself on the basis of the Roman institutions. However crude its organization, its administrative absolutism was, after all, a political system. We shall seek in vain for anything of the kind in the Carolingian monarchy. Here all seems incoherent. The power of the sovereign, which should have set the whole mechanism in motion, was not able to impose itself sufficiently. Obliged to reckon with the aristocracy to whom they owed their crown, Pippin the Short and Charlemagne could not refuse it a place in the government. The magnates of the kingdom deliberated with them, assembling at court in a *conventus* at the feasts of Christmas and Easter. But what were the competences and what the attributes of these councillors? They were as vague and unsettled as the very composition of their assemblies; aggregations of ecclesiastics and laymen who, without title or mandate, were considered as representing the people. *Lex fit consensu populi et constitutione regis,* says a capitulary; the law is made by the assent of the people and the king's constitution. A fine formula, but actually devoid of meaning. As a matter of fact, many of the capitularies were never submitted to the assemblies, and in the case of those that were submitted to them we do not know what part the assemblies played in the matter. Nothing could be less deserving of the name of laws than these capitularies, a heterogeneous mass of administrative decisions, regulations, statements of principles, emergency measures, or perpetual edicts; and in most cases we do not know whether they were ever put into force, nor whether they related to the whole Empire or merely to one of its regions. Moreover, they are full of contradictions, and we never know whether the later texts abrogate the earlier ones, or whether we should seek as far as possible to reconcile them. The general impression emerging from this confusion is that of a royal will, ardently desirous of good, eager for progress, order and justice, and endeavouring, without success, to realize them. As manifested and expressed in these documents, the royal power seems that of an absolute sovereign, but of one whose absolutism is doubly limited. It is limited, in the first place, by Christian morality, and it accepts this limitation. It is limited further by the necessity of avoiding anything that will displease the aristocracy, and to this limitation it submits. It is evident that in his heart the Carolingian Emperor felt responsible only to God, and that if he tolerated the intervention of the magnates it was because he could not do otherwise. Between him and the magnates with whom he took counsel there had been from the beginning a lack of confidence, and before long their relations were vitiated by a lack of good faith. In short, we may say that the Carolingian constitution was based on a disagreement. The two forces that seemed to be in alliance were in reality two adversaries.

The more powerful of the two, under Charlemagne, tricked out in the glamour of his victories, and in the novel dignity of the Emperor, was the sovereign. But the aristocracy was the more vigorous; circumstances and the organization of society were on its side. This aristocracy declared that it was the people, and to a certain extent it was right; for the people had disappeared into the aristocracy. It had absorbed the people into its domains, and for all those who were dependent upon it—that is, for the greater part of the population—it replaced the public power of the State by a private power of protection and jurisdiction. The direct subjects of the sovereign, outside the jurisdiction of the aristocracy, were very few in number, and becoming fewer year by year. Charles saw the danger, and he tried to guard against it. He attempted, by reducing the burdens that military service and the judicial service imposed on freemen, to safeguard those who had preserved their liberty, which was becoming increasingly rare. His measures met with the common fate of all attempts to deter social evolution from gravitating in the direction of interests and necessities; they could not prevent the inevitable. The peasants continued to cede their lands to the magnates and attach themselves to their domains.

And here again we recognize the disagreement at the base of the Carolingian organization. In this matter of the maintenance of freemen the interests of the Emperor and those of the aristocracy were in direct conflict. But it was to this very aristocracy that the Emperor had to entrust the realization of his plans, for it was from their ranks that he recruited his officials. The rest of the aristocracy had to choose between their own advantage and that of the sovereign. They could serve the sovereign only to their own detriment. How could he hope that they would decide in his favour?

And against this inertia or this ill-will there was no remedy whatever. In law, no doubt, the Emperor could dismiss the counts, since he appointed them. In actual fact he could do nothing against them. For they were not the mere instruments of his power, mere agents, independently selected, strangers to the men under their administration, and passing, at their master's orders, from one district to another. On the contrary, each one of them belonged to the region which he governed; there he was the largest landowner, as his family might have been for generations, and the man of the greatest influence; his family estates were scattered all over his county; the inhabitants, from father to son, were his serfs or his tenants; he was born in their midst, and there he would die, unless he fell far from home on the battlefield; and it was the same with his father, to whom he almost always succeeded in the dignity of count. Thus, in the region over which he presided he was regarded as a seigneur rather than a representative of the Emperor. Consequently, if he were sent elsewhere or divested of his charge, his successor would seem, in the eyes of the people, a usurper and an intruder.

This impotence of the State with regard to its agents is explained by the financial situation. What was left of the Roman impost had disappeared at the close of the Merovingian epoch, when it was commuted into fines which were usurped by the magnates. The Imperial treasury was still fed from two sources: one of them—war booty—intermittent and capricious; the other—the revenue of the domains belonging to the dynasty—permanent and regular. Only this latter source was capable of furnishing the necessary resources for current requirements. Charles gave it his careful attention, and the well-known *Capitulare de villis* proves, by the minuteness of its details, the importance which he attached to the good administration of his estates. But their yield consisted of prestations in kind, just enough to revictual the court. Properly speaking, the Carolingian Empire had no public finances, and when this has been said we can appreciate how rudimentary was its organization compared with that of the Byzantine Empire or the Empire of the Caliphs, with their taxes levied in money, their financial control, and their fiscal centralization, which provided for the salaries of officials, public works, and the upkeep of the army and the fleet.

Reduced to the resources of his private domains, the Emperor could not meet the expenses of an administration worthy of the name. Now if the official is to be dependent on the State, the State must not only appoint him, but must also pay him. Here, having no money, the State was obliged to have recourse to the gratuitous services of the aristocracy, which placed it in the paradoxical situation of taking as its collaborators the members of a social class whose power was bound to increase as that of the State diminished. The danger of this arrangement was so evident that attempts were made to guard against it. From the end of the 8th century a special oath of fidelity, like that sworn by the vassal, was required of the counts when they entered upon their duties. But the remedy was worse than the disease. For the bond of vassalage, by attaching the functionary to the person of the sovereign, weakened or even annulled his character as public officer. It made him, moreover, regard his function as a fief; that is, as a possession to be enjoyed, and not as a power delegated by the crown and exercised in its name. Further, this system, at each succession to the throne, gave rise to a crisis of the most dangerous character. The new sovereign found himself confronted with the alternative of retaining in office the confidants of his predecessor, or replacing them by confidants of his own. In the first case he was reduced to governing with a staff whose members were unknown to him; in the second he was bound to provoke, from the very first, a formidable sense of resentment.

However we look at it, the administrative organization of the Empire was lacking in the features which are essential to any State administration: subordination and discipline. Compared with that of the Church, where the hierarchy allotted to every man his rôle and his responsibility, it seemed to be plunged into the crudest anarchy. The institution of the *missi dominici* was evidently designed to improve the system by the exercise of control. Here Charlemagne's personal initiative is clearly manifested, and his tendency to ameliorate lay institutions by following the example of the Church. Just as the Church was divided into archiepiscopal sees, each of which comprised a certain number of dioceses, so he divided the Empire into vast circumscriptions (*missatica*), each of which included several counties. In each of these circumscriptions two Imperial envoys (*missi dominici*), an ecclesiastic and a layman, were entrusted with the supervision of the officials, the noting of abuses, the interrogation of the people, and the annual production of a report on their mission. Nothing could have been better, nothing more useful and salutary than such an institution—so long as there was any sanction behind it. But in actual fact there was no such sanction, since the so-called functionaries, as we have seen, were practically irremovable. We cannot find that the *missi dominici* were anywhere successful in curing the defects of which they must have noted many in all directions: the reality was more powerful than the good intentions of the Emperor.

The creation of the *missi* is enough to prove that Charlemagne—doubtless under the influence of his ecclesiastical counsellors—had acquired a very clear notion of the imperfection of his means of government. His ideal—but he had not the power to realize it—was to reform them in accordance with the example furnished by the administration of the Church. The spirit by which he was actuated was, we may say, entirely Roman. It is a complete illusion to see in him, as so many have done, the adept of some sort of indefinable Germanism, of which we shall vainly seek for any traces in his achievements. Here legend has seen more clearly than many of the historians. In the popular memory of the Germans Charles has remained the legislator *par excellence*, the conqueror of barbarism, the founder of the social order. For the pagan or semi-pagan peoples he was actually all these things, but it was by virtue of his ecclesiastical government. The definitive establishment of the Church in Germany and the subordination of the people to its dogmas and its moral laws was so far his personal achievement that he appears in tradition as a quasi-sacred personality. It was doubtless this tradition that inspired the imagination of Albrecht Dürer, when he gave him the strange and majestic appearance that makes us think of a lay Pope rather than an Emperor. The close alliance of State and Church, the identification of political unity with Christian unity, and its necessary consequence of a State religion—this is the essential Carolingian achievement; it was this that survived the dynasty, and determined, for centuries to come, the development of European society.

2. *The Pope and the Emperor*

The death of Charlemagne (January 28th, 814) did not provoke the slightest crisis. In 813 he had caused five provincial synods to frame a series of dispositions regarding the organization of the Empire. They were ratified the same year by a General Assembly convoked at Aix-la-Chapelle, in the course of which he took the precaution of setting the crown, with his own hands, on the head of Louis, his only surviving son.

Louis succeeded to the throne in an atmosphere of general approval. The Empire was rejoicing in the profoundest peace; nothing in the outer world gave warning of the imminent outbreak of the disorders which would presently overwhelm it. The essentially ecclesiastical ideal of the Imperial power which Charles had cherished was revealed in the education to which his son had been subjected. It was wholly Latin and clerical, and it was for good reason that the second Carolingian Emperor was known to tradition as "the Pious." But his piety, if we may say so, was pre-eminently a political piety. It was blended with a conception of the secular power which regarded the maintenance and protection of the Church as its *raison d'être*. Charles, who had become Emperor late in life, had retained something of his independence as a sovereign, something of his original character as King of the Franks; but with his son this independence disappeared. Louis, on his accession, abandoned the title of King of the Franks and Lombards; the only title which he bore was that of Emperor: signifying that his authority was as universal as that of the Pope, extending, like the latter, to all Christians. And this, of course, had been the tendency of the Carolingian policy since the coronation of the year 800. There was no opposition of tendencies between Charles and Louis, despite the enormous difference of personal genius and power. The Imperial power, as Louis understood it, was only the com-

plete and logical development of the idea that had dominated Charlemagne throughout the latter part of his career,
and the great Emperor himself had willed and prepared the
spirit in which his weak successor was to reign.

Louis found himself at once confronted by a question
which his father had been spared, and which would presently enable him to test the solidity of the Empire. He had
three sons: Lothair, Louis, (the German) and Pippin. How
should he order his succession? The idea of equal partition
among the sons of the sovereign had always been applied
from the beginning of the Frankish monarchy. On the other
hand, the Imperial power was by its very nature as indivisi-
ble as the power of the Pope. Should he then regard the
Empire as so indissolubly merged in the State that the succession to the State must be ruled by the same principle as
succession to the Empire? Or, distinguishing the one from
the other, should he proceed to partition the State, while
reserving the Imperial authority to one of the heirs? Louis
decided on a measure which, without breaking altogether
with the custom of partition, nevertheless sacrificed it to
the principle of unity. In 817 he associated with himself,
as co-regent of the Empire, his eldest son, Lothair, and appointed him his heir. At the same time the two younger
sons received each a sort of appanage with the title of king:
Pippin being King of Aquitaine and Louis of Bavaria. In
so doing Louis decided against the old conception of the
secular monarchy as it had been held and put into practice
by the Merovingians, and in favour of the new ecclesiastical conception of the Empire; and we can hardly doubt
that he made these arrangements by agreement with the
Pope. But the younger sons considered that they had been
unjustly treated, and only waited for the opportunity of
taking their revenge. The opportunity came to them: they
had no need to provoke it. A widower, in 819 Louis had
married, for her beauty, Judith, the daughter of the Duke
of the Alamans. Amorous and sensual by temperament, as
were nearly all the early Carolingians, he soon fell under
the domination of his wife, and when in 823 she made him
the father of a fourth son, Charles (the Bald), he had not
the energy to check the intrigues into which she entered

in order to assure this child of the largest possible share of the paternal heritage. Judith had no difficulty in persuading Louis and Pippin to see things as she did, and to incite them against Lothair, and it was an easier matter still, by means of promises, to assure herself of the help of the aristocracy. Two parties, or rather two factions, were thus formed within the Empire: one adopting as its programme the sharing of the succession among all the sons of the Emperor, and the other remaining faithful to the idea of unity.[1] The first of these parties had the best of it at the outset: Lothair, deprived of his title of regent, went to Italy to submit his quarrel to the Pope, while Louis, in obedience to Judith, proceeded to a fresh partition of the monarchy between his four sons. The advantages which he lavished upon Charles resulted in a quarrel with Louis the German and Pippin, who made it up with Lothair. In 833 the latter crossed the Alps at the head of an army, accompanied by Pope Gregory IV, joined his brothers, and marched with them against his father. They met in the Rhenish plain, near Colmar. The victory was apparently Lothair's, but actually the Pope's. In the name of the peace of the Church, of which the Empire was only the temporal power, he claimed the right to intervene, restored Lothair to his original dignity, and imposed on the old Emperor, as guilty of troubling the peace of Christendom, a humiliating penance. The first consequence of the intimate conjunction of Pope and Emperor followed with pitiless logic: the Emperor gave way, the Pope increased his influence, and the original alliance of the two powers was replaced by the subordination of the Emperor to the Pope.

But this was not what Louis the German and Pippin had wanted. They took up arms again, and the struggle continued, with a sort of muddled obstinacy, between rival ambitions and personal interests. Neither the death of Pippin (838) nor that of the Emperor interrupted it. Not un-

---

[1] These are, as it were, party labels. Actually only the ecclesiastics can have had a programme; the laymen grouped themselves according to their sympathies and interests.

til 843 did it finally terminate—thanks to the exhaustion of
all parties—in the Treaty of Verdun.

This was a compromise, but one that strangely diminished the scope of the Imperial idea. The entire monarchy was divided into three equal parts. The middle portion, cutting across Europe, and extending, without regard
for natural frontiers or the character of the peoples, from
Friesland to the Papal States, was allotted to Lothair. He
retained also the title of Emperor, exercising an ill-defined
primacy over his brothers Louis and Charles, who reigned
respectively over the regions to the east and west of him.
Thus the identity between the Empire and the Frankish
State which had existed under Charlemagne and Louis the
Pious disappeared. The Imperial unity now existed only in
theory; its universality no longer corresponded with the
reality of things, as the Emperor actually ruled over merely
a third of Western Christendom.

After the death of Lothair (855) matters were even
worse. He too had three sons, and they, in their turn, divided his territories between them. The eldest, Louis II,
took for his share Italy and the Imperial title. Under
Lothair the Emperor had still been at least as powerful
as the two kings, his brothers. Under Louis II he was no
more than a secondary sovereign, infinitely less influential
than his uncles Louis the German and Charles the Bald.
The contrast between the Emperor as he was and the Emperor as he ought to have been was steadily increasing.
One may say, indeed, that even though there was still an
Emperor, he had no longer an Empire.

This continual decline of the Imperial power was accompanied by the correlative and simultaneous increase of
the power of the Pope. Once the equilibrium between the
two forces set over Christendom was broken, one of them
was bound to profit by the losses of the other. Already circumstances had led Gregory IV to judge between Louis
the Pious and his sons. Under Louis II, Nicholas I (858–
867) claimed and enforced the superiority of the pontifical
over the Imperial power. With him the political alliance
which had been concluded under Charlemagne came to an
end. The head of the Church, in virtue of the divine origin

of his power, regarded himself henceforth as the judge and the director of the depositories of the temporal powers, whether kings or emperors. Amenable to him as Christians, liable to his moral jurisdiction as sinners, it was essential that they should be subject to a sanction which would guarantee their obedience. Henceforth the Pope could and must, if he judged it necessary to the service of God and the Church, intervene in the affairs of the princes, and Nicholas unhesitatingly entered upon the path which was afterwards to be followed by Gregory VII and Alexander II, and which led Innocent III and Innocent IV to the theocratic hegemony which was ended by the catastrophe of Boniface VIII. He had no occasion, however, to intervene in matters of high policy. The excommunication which he thundered against the King of Lotharingia, Lothair II, on the occasion of his divorce, and which ended in the humiliation of the culprit, was no more than a moral manifestation, but its repercussions were felt throughout Europe.

The "false decretals" which were published in the middle of the 9th century in Northern France, and whose apocryphal texts, cleverly forged, gave the Pope a power over the whole body of the episcopate which he had never yet actually exercised, helped to confirm the primacy of Rome. Nicholas even sought to compel the Eastern Church to recognize this primacy, and launched his excommunication against the patriarch Photius: the only result being still further to aggravate the conflict which was poisoning the relations between the Greek and Latin halves of Christendom.

The death of Louis II (875) furnished the Papacy with a fresh opportunity of affirming its superiority over the Empire, and of showing that the Empire was dependent on the Papacy and not on the dynasty. Louis had no children, and his nearest male relation was Carloman, the son of Louis the German, whom he had appointed his heir. John VIII (872–882) decided otherwise, summoned Charles the Bald to Rome, and crowned him.

Since the middle of the 9th century the ascendancy of the Pope over the Emperor had continued to increase. But if it was possible to exercise this ascendancy, it was only

because the Emperors consented. By himself the Pope, reduced to the possession of his little Roman State, would
have been absolutely incapable of resisting the least aggression. Further, in the last resort he owed the authority
which he enjoyed, and of which he had given such striking
proof, to the Carolingians whom he had crowned, and who,
in return, granted him their protection. A paradoxical situation, which permitted the Pope to dominate the Emperor
for so long as the Emperor guaranteed his liberty; which
allowed the spiritual power precedence over the secular
only by virtue of the support which it received from the
latter! And now the political anarchy into which Europe
was falling, with increasing rapidity, at the close of the 9th
century, suddenly deprived the Pope of this indispensable
protector. Charles the Bald was the last Emperor to enjoy
any real prestige, to exercise any real power. After him,
under the irresistible pressure of feudality, under the blows
of the Normans, the Saracens, the Slavs and the Hungarians, under the influence of regional particularism, and of
personal ambitions and intrigues and rivalries, what was
left of the Carolingian order foundered, and the princes,
whether they called themselves kings or emperors, were
equally powerless. Henceforth Rome was abandoned to her
fate, and the Papacy suddenly found itself confronted with
dangers far greater than those which had menaced it of
old, in the days of the Lombards. For while the Lombards
persisted in their attempt to conquer Rome, they wished
no harm to the Pope. Now, on the contrary, the very liberty
of the Papacy was threatened. Since the Pope had the
disposal of the Imperial crown, it would be possible henceforth to obtain it by subjecting him to violence and compelling him by threats to exercise his power. Already, after
the death of Charles the Bald, Charles the Fat, marching
upon Rome at the head of an army, had forced John VIII
to crown him (881). Then, not long afterwards, the world
witnessed the sorry spectacle of the simultaneous debasement of Pope and Emperor. After the deposition of Charles
the Fat and the final rupture of the Carolingian unity two
Italian magnates, the Marquis of Friuli, Berenger, and the
Duke of Spoleto, Gui, disputed for the ancient Lombard

crown, and each had himself crowned king in Pavia. The Imperial dignity was vacant: Gui resolved to seize it. He had only to enter Rome with his soldiers in order to obtain it from the Pope, Stephanus VI (891), and some time later he compelled Stephanus' successor, Formosus, to confer it also on his son, Lambert.

To what a depth had the Empire and the Papacy fallen in the course of a few years! Formosus felt that the only means of restoring them was to appeal to force. Arnold, Duke of Carinthia, had just won a brilliant victory over the Normans, and seemed to hold forth the promise of a glorious reign. The Pope solicited his assistance against the odious tyranny to which he was subjected. Arnold crossed the Alps, took Rome—defended by the Spoletans—by assault, received the Imperial crown (896), and returned to Germany. Lambert could take his revenge. It was tragic and repulsive, as were the political and religious customs of the time. Formosus being dead, Lambert proceeded, in the presence of the corpse, to a simulacrum of judgement, after which the Pope's body was delivered to the populace, who proceeded to fling it into the Tiber. Arnold did not cross the Alps again, and the Papacy was more than ever the plaything of ambitious intriguers, who disputed for the Empire as others quarrelled elsewhere for a fief or a province, and the world took little more heed of them. Lambert dead, Berenger of Friuli was once more supreme in Italy. Louis, King of Burgundy, made war upon him, defeated him, and took the opportunity of having himself crowned Emperor by Benedict IV (900). Five years later Berenger took him prisoner at Verona, had him blinded, and drove him out of the peninsula. Then, in 919, he in turn had himself consecrated Emperor by John X. It was difficult to do anything further to degrade the title inaugurated by Charlemagne; and as a matter of fact it was not further disgraced. After the assassination of Berenger of Friuli (924) there was not another Emperor until the coronation of Otto I (962).

3. *The Enemies Without*

The enemies from which the Empire suffered so cruelly
in the course of the 9th century—the Normans and the
Arabs—did not attack it merely because of its weakness:
nor were their attacks deliberately directed against the
Empire. The Normans' sphere of action was the northern
seas; the Arabs', the shores of the Mediterranean; in each
case the regions affected went far beyond the coasts of
the Carolingian State. The aggressions of which the latter
was the victim were no more than an episode in the history
of the maritime incursions which it could not hope to
escape, but of which it was never the only, nor even—at
any rate, in the beginning—the principal object.

The advance of the Arabs in the Western Mediterranean
at the beginning of the 9th century was no longer related
to the great movement of religious expansion which had
followed the death of Mohammed. The political unity of
Islam was broken, since the Caliph of Baghdad was not
recognized by all believers. In Spain, at the close of the 8th
century, a new Caliphate was erected under the Omayyads. In Africa the Berbers of Morocco, Algeria and Tunis
were really independent. Finally established in their new
conquests, these Musulmans of Spain and Africa turned to
the sea. Tunis, founded beside the ruins of Carthage,
looked, as Carthage had done, towards Sicily; and before
long the Tunisians, like the Carthaginians of old, sought to
conquer the beautiful island, always, throughout history,
a bone of contention between Europe and Africa. The
Byzantines were unable effectually to defend this remote
province. Between 827 and 878 they were gradually driven
toward the Straits of Messina, and at last they were obliged
to fall back on the Italian coast. Already in possession of
the Balearics, Corsica, and Sardinia, the Musulmans now
held all the islands of the Mediterranean, which served as
naval stations, and as bases of attack upon the continental
coasts. From Sicily expeditions were despatched against
Calabria, which ended in the conquest of Bari and Tarento.
Other fleets harried the coasts of Central Italy. Pope Leo

IV was obliged to put what was left of Rome in a state of defence against the pirates, who landed, having nothing to fear, at the mouth of the Tiber. The mouths of the Rhone, which were equally unprotected, were even more exposed. The Arabs established military posts along the Corniche, the ruins of which may still be seen. However, they made no attempt to establish themselves in the interior. The possession of the coasts was all that mattered to the new masters of the Mediterranean, and as there was no Christian trade no serious efforts were made to dislodge the Arabs, and the littoral was left in their hands. The Christian population withdrew farther inland, and the derelict towns in the region of Nîmes fortified themselves as best they could.[2]

The Norman invasions were more devastating, and their results were much more important. These were the sudden incursions of a people of whom so little was known that they had not even been given a name, and for want of a better description the inhabitants of the northern coasts, who were the first to come into contact with them, gave them the name of the region from which they came: they were Noord-mannen, Northmen, Normans.

The maritime raids of the Scandinavians can be explained only by hypotheses—though these are plausible enough. The first condition of such raids was obviously the need experienced by part of the population to seek abroad the means of subsistence which the poor and thankless soil of their native country did not provide in sufficient abundance to satisfy a hardy and vigorous people. If to this economic distress we add intestine quarrels between local chiefs, and allow for the pride of the vanquished, who would refuse to submit to the conqueror, but would rather put to sea with their comrades in arms, hoping to return in triumph after profitable adventures, we shall have some idea of the motives which from the close of the 8th century impelled the Danes, Norwegians and Swedes to set sail

[2] In 916 Pope John X, with King Berenger and Byzantine reinforcements, captured the fortified camp of the Musulmans in the Garigliano. Henceforth Central Italy was free of the enemy.

across the North Sea, the Baltic, the blue wastes of the
North Atlantic, and even the sunny waters of the Mediterranean. The Swedes, moreover, were actuated by a motive
unknown to the Scandinavians of the West. The influence
of the two great Empires of the South—the Byzantine Empire and the Empire of the Caliphs—was felt, like a gleam
of golden light, even in the frozen ends of the earth. From
the latter part of the 7th century trade routes had been
coming into existence, on the one hand between the Baltic
and the Caspian, from the Gulf of Finland, the Neva, Lake
Ladoga, Lake Onega, to the course of the Volga, and on
the other hand between the Baltic and the Black Sea.

More than 200,000 Arabic and Byzantine coins have
been exhumed from the soil of Sweden, the oldest dating
from 698. The Swedes began at an early date to adventure
on the paths that led to the lands of the sun and fortune.
The Slavs called these strangers by the name of *Rus,* which
their mutual neighbours the Finns had given them. These
Scandinavian Russians soon established themselves in large
numbers in the *pogostes* (markets) which the Arab or
Khazar merchants visited at fixed intervals in order to buy
their honey and their furs. There they quickly replaced the
other foreigners; to such an extent that along the course of
the Dnieper the rapids have retained throughout the years
the names which the Swedes bestowed upon them. Towards the middle of the 9th century they imposed themselves as masters on the population in the neighbourhood
of the *pogostes.* According to tradition, Rurik founded
Novgorod, and two of his companions, Askod and Dir, took
possession of Kiev, the most important commercial centre
of the whole of the southern plain. In 892 Olaf, Rurik's
successor, established himself in Kiev, which was then beginning to extend its political domination over all the surrounding regions. From this moment may be dated the
birth of a Russian—that is, a Swedish—State in the basin of
the Dnieper. The princes, and their comrades in arms and
in trade, who continued, until the beginning of the 11th
century, to receive reinforcements from their country of
origin, preserved almost until this period their Scandinavian

tongue and customs.[3] But in the end they were absorbed
by the population whom they governed and exploited, and
thus the name of these hardy adventurers of the 9th century, by an extraordinary trick of fortune, has been borne,
through the vicissitudes of history, by the greatest of the
Slav peoples and the most far-flung Empire in the world.

Owing to the situation of their country, the Danes and
the Norwegians looked to the West. The lands which
tempted them to adventure were not, like the Byzantine
Empire or the Arab Empire, flourishing States, full of cities,
and promising great commercial profits, but purely agricultural regions, having nothing to buy or sell. Thus, while
the Swedes, on finding themselves in touch with societies
which were, economically speaking, highly developed, were
anxious above all to trade with them, the Danes and Norwegians made their appearance as pirates and pillagers or
sea-rovers.[4]

And while they assailed the coasts to the south and the
west, their vessels explored the northern waters. Norwegians installed themselves in the Faroes at an early date;
and in 874 they discovered Iceland, which they colonized,
and a century later they sailed westward to the shores of
Greenland. But the European countries naturally offered
them the greatest hopes of booty. England was the first to
suffer their attacks. As early as 793 a landing was effected
in Northumberland, where the monasteries of Lindisfarne
and Jarrow were pillaged and burned. After this raid followed on raid, the incursions becoming more frequent and
more devastating. The Anglo-Saxon kings were unable to
repulse the invaders. By the middle of the 9th century the
greater part of Eastern England belonged to them, and in
878 Alfred the Great was obliged by treaty to abandon
to them all the country lying to the east of a line drawn

[3] These newcomers were known, in Russian, by an old Swedish word meaning "foreigners" (vaering). Hence the Varangians,
βαραγγοι, of the Constantinople guard, which was at first composed mainly of Scandinavians.

[4] The Russians, however, attacked Constantinople in 865,
907, 941, 944 and 1043.

from London to Chester, which for long afterwards was known by the name of the Danelaw.

Nor did Ireland escape the Scandinavian invasion. Dublin, from the middle of the 9th century to the beginning of the 11th, was a sort of Norman colony. From the insular outposts the hardy adventurers boldly set sail for the south. They infested the coasts of Portugal and Spain, where they attacked Lisbon and Seville (884), passed the Straits of Gibraltar, pillaging Algeciras and the Balearics, reached the mouths of the Rhone, and at times—as far-travelled rivals of the Moslem pirates—they landed on Italian soil.

The Frankish Empire, owing to its nearness, the extent of its littoral, and the great number of deep rivers debouching into the sea, was bound to be—and was in fact—the greatest sufferer at the hands of the Northmen. From the reign of Louis the Pious to the beginning of the 10th century their incursions were incessant. At the outset they appeared now at one point, now at another, baffling the defenders by the sudden and unexpected nature of their attacks. They ascended, in succession, as far as their waters were navigable, the Rhine, the Scheldt, the Meuse, the Seine and the Loire, completely devastating their banks. Then, as they became familiar with the country, they set to work in a more methodical fashion, concentrating on the region extending from the north of the Seine to Friesland. The port of Duurstede, pillaged four times in rapid succession (834–837), was left a heap of ruins: Utrecht was destroyed in 857. It seems that a pagan, Scandinavian State was on the point of being founded in Friesland, for in 850 the Emperor Lothair, unable to repulse the viking Rurik, granted him in fief the banks of the Waal, and in 882 Charles the Fat renewed this concession in favour of Godefroid, another Barbarian. The year 879 marked the apogee of the crisis. A veritable army landed on the banks of the Rhine and the Scheldt, and basing its operations on a series of fortified camps—at Gand and Courtrai, then at Elsloo, near Maestricht, and finally at Louvain—for several years it systematically exploited the country. In 884 Charles the Fat succeeded in turning it aside from Rhenish Germany only at the price of a humiliating treaty. It then marched upon the Seine, and for a year it besieged Paris, but did not succeed in taking the city (885). Having wasted all the north of France, it returned to Louvain in 891. There it was attacked and at last annihilated by Arnold of Carinthia. After this the Northmen risked only a few raids on the Low Countries. But the Seine was long their objective. At last, in 911, Charles the Simple, unable to repulse them, ceded in fief to their chieftain Rollo the regions lying between the Seine and the Epte, which thereafter constituted the Duchy of Normandy. This was the end of the invasions. Scandinavia, exhausted by its effort, and sated with conquest, ceased to discharge its surplus population upon the Continent.

The success of these aggressions is to be explained only by the weakness of the Carolingian State and its increasing decomposition. To resist the Barbarians a fleet would have been necessary. But how could a fleet be built without financial resources? And how could fortresses be built to defend the coasts? While the kings were fighting among themselves, and the monarchy was decaying, how could the State concentrate its efforts and send its armies against the enemy? As a matter of fact, the kings abandoned the attempt, leaving it to the aristocracy to check the invaders as best they could, by local and uncoördinated efforts. The chroniclers of the period have recorded the heroism of many of the feudal seigneurs, who, like the Counts of Paris, Robert the Strong and Eudes (the future king), made their reputations in these conflicts. But others beheld in them only an opportunity of blackmail—of obtaining still greater wealth, inasmuch as they alarmed the feeble kings by threatening to ally themselves with the Barbarians. Even without the Norman invasions the great Carolingian scaffolding must have collapsed. The shocks to which it was subjected only hastened its fall.

The cession of Normandy to Rollo took place only a few years later than the conquest of Kiev by Oleg.[5] The com-

[5] It was only in the course of the 11th century that the Scandinavians became assimilated to the Slavs. In 1018 Kiev was still wholly Scandinavian.

parison between the two States is interesting. In Russia the Northmen were and remained the masters of the country, and they instituted a government in accordance with their national customs, treating the Slavs as their subjects. In France, where they were in contact with a superior civilization, their attitude was very different. Rollo and his followers went over to Christianity, and the process of assimilation began immediately. It proceeded with astonishing rapidity. Twenty-five years after their arrival the Scandinavian tongue was no longer spoken save at Bayeux, and doubtless along the coast, where the place-names ending in *beuf* remind us of the presence of a people speaking a Germanic tongue. The process of Gallicization was so complete that there is not a single Scandinavian word in the Norman dialect. Nor was there anything Scandinavian in the institutions of the Duchy. These were immediately adapted to the environment, and did not in any essential feature differ from those of the other great fiefs. Fifty years after Rollo's time Normandy was as French a province as Burgundy or Champagne. It must not be forgotten that it was here that the *Chanson de Roland* was born, and that it was on Norman soil that some of the finest specimens of Romanic architecture were erected, such as the great churches of Caen and Bayeux. But of Germanism not a trace remained. So little had survived that when the Normans invaded Sicily, and then England (1066), they appeared as French conquerors. What did survive was the spirit of adventure, which, from the beginning of the 11th century, drove masses of them southwards into Italy. There forty Normans, returning from a pilgrimage, had taken service as mercenaries, and spread the news of what was to be gained in that country. But we must doubtless regard this movement, like the Flemish and Brabantine migrations of the period, as to some extent the consequence of over-population.

CHAPTER II

The Division of Europe

1. *The Treaty of Verdun*

The Roman unity was replaced, in the epoch of the Invasions, by States which were independent of one another,
conquered by different peoples, and governed by dynasties
belonging to these peoples. The Europe of that age, in
respect of its political division, was much nearer to the
Europe of the modern epoch than it would be again for a
long time to come. All these States—excepting the Anglo-
Saxon kingdoms and the Visigoth kingdoms of Spain—were
fused together in the Carolingian conquest, and absorbed
into the great politico-religious unity of the Empire. It was
upon its ruins that the States of continental Europe established themselves. But the process of their formation was
very different from what it had been at the end of the
Roman Empire. There was nothing national in the partition
of the monarchy under the sons of Louis the Pious. The
question of different peoples did not enter into the case.
But how should it have done so? Since the government to
which they were subjected was of a universal and ecclesiastical character, the political divisions of the monarchy did
not have the effect of subordinating them to one of their
number. The Carolingians were, so to speak, transferable;
they could govern anywhere; their nationality mattered no
more than the nationality of the Pope mattered to the
Church. The difference between Romans and non-Romans

—a very real difference, but one of which the peoples were not conscious—was of no practical consequence. The quarrel between Lothair and his brothers—the one wishing to preserve the unity of the Empire to his own advantage, the others wishing to divide it—ended in the compromise of Verdun (843).

This was the first of the great treaties of European history, and none was to have more lasting consequences. Even to this day we see its traces in Western Europe, where—between France and Germany—Holland, Belgium, Switzerland and Italy represent the share of Lothair.

But we must hasten to observe that it was history that gave the treaty this significance: not those who negotiated it. All they wanted to do was to divide the Empire into three equal parts. The standpoint from which they regarded the matter was imposed upon them by the economic constitution of the period. Society was purely agricultural; there was no commerce; there were no longer any towns. All they could do, therefore, was to give each party to the treaty, as far as possible, a region whose revenue would be approximately equal to the revenue of each of the other shares; and they had not to take into consideration such matters as trade routes and highways and the extent of the coasts, and all the other considerations which would have rendered the partition of Europe on the lines then followed quite impossible at a later period. The whole destiny of Europe depended on the share to be awarded to Lothair, the elder and the holder of the Imperial title, which gave him at least a moral supremacy over his brothers. Evidently he must be given the central portion. It consisted of Italy, plus a region bordered on the east by the course of the Rhine, and on the west by the Rhone, the Saône and the Meuse, a line running from Mézières to Valenciennes, and finally, the course of the Scheldt.

This central portion being thus delimited, the rest went to his brothers: Charles the Bald taking all that lay between the western frontier and the sea, and Louis all that lay to the east, as far as the confines of the marches established against the Slavs. It was due to chance that Louis' share consisted entirely of Germanic peoples, and that of Charles

of peoples almost entirely Romanic. But we have only to
consider Lothair's share to realize how little attention was
paid to national differences. Nothing could have been more
contrary to all geographical and ethnographical considerations. Intersected by the Alps and the Jura, it included,
counting from north to south, Frisians, Flemings, Walloons,
Germans, Provençaux and Italians. Evidently no more regard was paid to the populations than modern States have
paid to the negro tribes on partitioning Africa. And this
method answered very well: no one had cause for com-
plaint, since the peoples were conscious only of the rule of
the aristocracy, and the aristocracy was everywhere local.

There were no nations in the 9th century. There was only
Christendom. All Europe could be cut up into States, as
into dioceses, and no one would be injured thereby. The
division concerned the dynasty; it was made over the heads
of the peoples, and no one was inconvenienced. The Treaty
of Verdun was therefore perfectly adapted to a Europe in
which the only policy was universal, and the domainal
economy had no outlets. Without these two essential conditions it would have been impossible in the form which it
actually assumed.

Thus, the first step on the path which was to lead Europe, at the cost of so much bloodshed, to its division into
national States, was taken without any regard for the various nationalities, and was even—as a matter of fact—directly
opposed to national considerations. The same spirit was
manifested throughout the Carolingian decadence.

On the death of Lothair (855) his three sons divided his
Empire. The eldest, Louis, took Italy, with the Imperial dignity; the second, Charles, the territory extending from the
Jura to the Mediterranean; the third, Lothair, the territory
to the north of the Jura. This time the partition seems to
have been determined by geographical considerations, but
the nationalities were once more completely disregarded.
The kingdom of Lothair II was heterogeneous in character;
it was impossible to give it a national name, so it was called
by the name of its king—Lotharingia. When Charles died
childless (863) his two brothers naturally divided his share
between them, Louis taking the South and Lothair the

North. But the procedure was less regular when Lothair II
died in his turn—also without lawful heirs (869). If the previous rule had been followed, Louis II should have inherited
his kingdom. But as the unfortunate man was too feeble,
his uncles, Louis and Charles, each hoped to secure the
succession. They met at Meersen, and instead of fighting
they negotiated. Lotharingia was divided into two parts,
and on this occasion more or less along the linguistic
frontier; not on principle, but because it was thus divided
into two approximately equal shares. Charles the Bald, on
the death of his brother Louis (876), attempted to seize
his States. He was defeated by his nephew Louis III, then
King of Germany, at Andernach. This was the first battle
in which a French and a German army fought for the prize
of Lotharingia, although there was as yet no talk of France
or Germany. Contemporaries, indeed, gave the same name
of France to the kingdom of the East and to that of the
West, merely adding the adjective, Eastern or Western.
Charles died (October 6th, 877) before he could repeat
his attempt. His son, Louis the Stammerer, who succeeded
him, died not long afterwards (August 10th, 879) and
Louis III adroitly took advantage of the disturbances which
broke out at this moment among his vassals in order to obtain the cession of all the territory which Charles the Bald
had acquired. This time the whole of Lotharingia was annexed to the Eastern kingdom.

While this northern portion of the territory of Lothair I
was thus disputed, another fragment, in this same year of
879, set itself up as a kingdom. Count Boson of Vienne,
son-in-law of the Emperor Louis II (875), had himself
elected, by a few bishops and magnates, king of Lower
Burgundy or Provence. The power of the aristocracy was
growing greater and greater. However, this was still no
more than a local manifestation. In 885, the Carolingian
family being almost extinct,[1] the whole Empire, with the
exception of Burgundy, adopted Charles the Fat as the sovereign. And this again shows how little influence national

[1] There were left only Charles, son of Louis the German, and
a younger son of Louis the Stammerer.

questions exercised over all these events. For Charles was the youngest son of Louis the German: yet the whole of France recognized him.

But his incapacity, and the shameful treaties which he concluded with the Normans, exhausted the patience of the aristocracy. Arnold, who was governing Carinthia, rebelled against him. He was deposed by the Easterners in 887, and went to end his days in a monastery, while the magnates bestowed the crown upon Arnold of Carinthia. Arnold himself was a scion of the Carolingian stock, but he was only the bastard son of Carloman, the son of Louis the German. The legitimate heir of the Carolingians was the little Charles the Simple, but he was still a child, and no one recognized him as king. The magnates of the Western kingdom followed the example of the Burgundians: they gave themselves a king, and they chose Eudes, Count of Paris, who had defended the city against the Normans in 886, and whose father, Robert of Paris, had been slain while fighting them. At last, in 888, a new kingdom, once more the creation of the aristocracy, made its appearance in Upper Burgundy (from the Jura to the Pennine Alps), Count Raoul being chosen king. As for Lotharingia, which had acknowledged Arnold, he now (in 895) constituted it a kingdom for the benefit of his son Zwentibold. Probably the magnates of the country had insisted on this step.

However, when Eudes died in 898, Charles the Simple, who had come of age, was proclaimed King of France: so the dynastic idea was not yet extinct. Arnold died in the following year (899), and Zwentibold was killed by the magnates in 900. As Charles the Fat had done formerly, Charles the Simple might have restored the Carolingian unity. But he did nothing of the kind. The magnates of Francia Orientalis recognized as their king the son of Arnold, Louis the Child, who was barely seven years of age, and who, once more, was related to the Carolingians.

Was there in these happenings the beginning of national division? The French did not recognize Arnold in 887; the Germans refused to acknowledge Charles the Simple in 899. But it is impossible to regard these facts as due to a national division. The French, in 883, recognized Charles

the Fat because he had been Emperor since 881. Charles
the Simple was not Emperor, and Louis the Child was a
Carolingian. Here the partition of the monarchy was continued within the dynasty. But the dynasty was badly
shaken, and the Italian princelings were contending for the
Empire. It was plain that the European unity was breaking
down. The aristocracy were disposing of its crowns as they
chose. On the other hand, those who dwelt on the periphery of the Empire had lost all interest in what was happen-
ing in the centre, in the old historic region between the
Seine and the Rhine, as is proved by the separation of Burgundy and Italy. Now, the princes who acknowledged
Louis the Child were mainly Trans-Rhenian. The national
ideal found so little support among the aristocracy that after
the death of Louis the Child in 911 the magnates of Franconia, Swabia, Bavaria and Saxony, the four German duchies, appointed Duke Conrad of Franconia king, while the
magnates of Lotharingia, both German and Roman, breaking away from Francia Orientalis, to which they had been
attached since the reign of Arnold of Carinthia, acknowledged as their sovereign, after the death of their king
Zwentibold, the King of Francia Orientalis, Charles the
Simple, who left them their autonomy under Regnier Long-
neck. The Trans-Rhenians, by appointing Conrad, had definitely broken with the Carolingian dynasty; henceforth this
was merely a local dynasty; it had lost its universal character. We may date the final dissolution of the Carolingian
unity from the election of Conrad; it was inevitable from
the moment when the dynasty ceased to wear the Imperial
crown. The greater Francia no longer existed. Henceforth,
it is interesting to note, its name was restricted to the territory over which a Carolingian was still reigning. But it was
now merely a special name. Henceforth one has to speak
of the kingdom of France and the kingdom of Germany.
They were separate kingdoms, and they would follow their
own destinies, although the distinct nationalities did nothing to cause the separation, and were not even conscious of
it. Of the vanished Carolingian unity they both, however,
preserved the common heritage, which survived everything, even the Empire: namely, the indissoluble union of

the royal power with the Church; as much on account of the intellectual superiority of the Church as by virtue of the still subsisting conception of the duties of royalty.

2. *The New States*

Between the two distinct States which had now emerged from the Carolingian unity—France and Germany—there was no necessary and inherent motive of hostility. The nationalities of the two States were different, but not more different, each from the other, than were the peoples within each State: for example, the Bavarians and the Saxons, or the Flemings and the Provençaux. There was no tradition of antagonism. On the contrary: the two countries had lived together side by side and under the same institutions. Their economic constitution did not urge them to encroach upon each other. And yet there arose between them, immediately, that "Belgian question" which one might really call *the* Western question, and which ever since, under various forms, has made periodic reappearances in the course of European history. On this occasion it appeared as a Lotharingian question.

The Lotharingian aristocracy remembered that Lotharingia had been a kingdom. It did not matter that this kingdom had contained nationalities whose languages were different; it nevertheless formed a single social group. On this frontier, when the Carolingians were born, in this extreme north of the Roman world, where Roman and Germanic influences mingled, a sense of autonomy had sprung up among the magnates. They had had kings of their own—Lothair II and Zwentibold—and they wished to continue the tradition. They had not acknowledged Conrad of Franconia, elected by the German duchies; they had placed themselves under the sceptre of Charles the Simple, who left them under the authority of their Duke Regnier; and he assumed an attitude of such independence that his son Gislebert had already hopes of obtaining the royal title. Conrad could do nothing to prevent him. But as soon as Germany possessed a strong monarch, in the person of Henry the Fowler, the king intervened.

For the Carolingians, Lotharingia had been part of France since the reign of Charles the Simple. For the kings of Germany, it was necessarily part of the German kingdom. It was bound to belong to the stronger country, and the stronger country was Germany. Henceforth there was no intermediate State, in the north, between the two great Western kingdoms. The Franco-German frontier was the Lotharingian frontier (the Scheldt-Meuse frontier). So it was to remain for centuries. The new situation, which came about against the will of the country, was a ferment of discord for the future. The discontented aristocracy had a power at their back to support them. Their manners and customs drew them toward the West rather than the East. Here was the seed of future danger. The oscillations of political preponderance in this Lotharingian territory were to have their repercussions in European history.

Lotharingia became a German duchy against her will, because Germany was stronger than France.

Why was she stronger? Not because she was wealthier or more populous. She was stronger because her king was stronger. And why was he stronger? For two reasons: firstly, because the social evolution of the country was less advanced; secondly, because the Eastern frontier was attacked by the Barbarians.

The social evolution of the country was less advanced in the sense that the local aristocracy comprised fewer powerful families; the further one went from the Rhine, the less developed was the domainal organization. The inhabitants, who were still very much nearer to their old tribal system, lived under the provincial protectorate of a local dynasty. In Saxony and Bavaria especially, far from the administrative centres, the old tribal feeling persisted. The hereditary dukes were recognized as true national chieftains. Nearer the Rhine, in Swabia and Franconia, the social organization was more complex and more advanced, so that there the power of the dukes was less national in character. And across the Rhine, in Lotharingia, matters were very different. There the duke was merely the head of the aristocracy; the dukedom had no national roots, for there was not, properly speaking, a Lotharingian nation.

In Germany, then, the situation was simple. In the place of a multitude of magnates, four dukes, or five at most, held the power in their hands. If they recognized the necessity of allying themselves with the prince whom they accepted as king, they could group the whole country about him.

And this they very soon realized. For the situation of Germany was extremely perilous: not in the West, where the Lotharingian question was mainly dynastic, but in the East, where it was national. It was in the East that Germany was in contact with barbarism, and the Carolingian decadence had given the Barbarians their chance. The Wends, along the Elbe and the Saale, and the Czechs further to the south, had begun to assail the frontiers; and presently a more terrible enemy appeared, the last comer among the European peoples: the Magyars or Hungarians.

They were the last wave of that Finnish inundation which since the days of Attila had never ceased to beat upon the frontiers of Europe: bringing first the Avars, and finally these Magyars, who, like the rest, having traversed the Russian Steppe, made their way into the Danube corridor, driven onward by the Petchenegs. Their earliest raids occurred at the close of the 9th century, when Arnold of Carinthia fought against them. Their arrival in Europe was of the greatest importance to the Western Slavs, whom they cut in two. They destroyed the kingdom of Moravia, founded by the Czechs of Bohemia. The latter were henceforth separated from the Croats and the Serbs, and also from the Poles; so that they were isolated from the Byzantine influence which had recently manifested itself in Bohemia by the despatch of the evangelists Methodius and Cyril, for whom Ratislav, the Prince of Moravia, had sent in order to escape the Frankish influence. From the Danube the Hungarians flung themselves upon Germany and Italy: as terrible as the Normans, and equally adventurous. One of their raids penetrated as far as the Rhine, and as they retired they ravaged Burgundy.

Against these perils Conrad could do nothing. But the case was altered after the election of the Saxon Henry the Fowler (Henry I) in 919. It might have seemed that the royal power was still declining, since after a Carolingian, and after Conrad, a Saxon king was elected.[2] But this Saxon was the most powerful of the German dukes, and his purely military rule did much to enhance the importance of royalty. With his Saxons, Henry repulsed the Slavs, enforced an oath upon the Duke of the Bohemians, and defeated the Hungarians, who had penetrated as far as Merseburg (933). He consolidated the royal power to such effect that the princes acknowledged his son Otto as his successor during Henry's lifetime.

Henry had based his power mainly on his duchy of Saxony. Otto entered upon the stage as King of Germany. At his inauguration the dukes served him at table. Despite their revolt, he succeeded in associating them with his military achievements. These continued those of his father. Like his father, he consolidated the German rule in Lotharingia. But his most important work was done in the East. The Hungarians were finally defeated at Augsburg (955). Henceforth they settled down and became Christians, and in so doing, despite their Finnish origin, they entered once and for all into the European community; which proves that racial differences are of no significance that the historical environment is everything. In the Slav country bishoprics were founded at Meissen, Merseburg, Zeitz, Brandenburg, Havelberg and Oldenburg, which were attached to the archbishopric of Magdeburg, founded in 968. An expedition was despatched to Poland, where Duke Mesko I took the oath, paid tribute, and became a Christian (966), a fact of considerable importance, in so far as it attached Poland to Rome. In the same way, Harold Bluetooth, King of Denmark, was compelled to found bishoprics and to become a convert.

Germany was thus able to turn her attention to the East. She began by reconquering from the Slavs the territory on the right bank of the Elbe, which the Germans had abandoned at the time of the great invasions. So far, however,

[2] Conrad was a Franconian, and therefore a native of a comparatively advanced and highly developed country. Henry, a Saxon, was more backward, and a stronger ruler. Here we see the same contrast that was to appear again, later, when Prussia took precedence of the three German States.

there was no German colonization of the country, for Germany had no surplus population. What Otto wanted was to settle the Barbarians on the land, and convert them to Christianity. He himself effected a rapprochement with the Church, as the Carolingians had done, but in a somewhat different manner. With the Carolingians the head of the State was closely related to the head of the Church. For Otto such a state of affairs was impossible, both because in his day the Papacy was completely degraded, and because he was not Emperor. It was to the bishops—and not to the Pope—that he looked for support. Through them he was able to oppose a personal policy to that of the secular magnates, and it was from among the prelates that he recruited his counsellors. His brother Bruno was Archbishop of Cologne, and Otto created him Duke of Lotharingia. This is a characteristic example: the bishops were about to become rulers. Otto considered them rather in their secular aspect than from the spiritual standpoint. One might say that what distinguished his policy from that of the Carolingians was that the latter clericalized the State, while he secularized the Church. But if the Church was to furnish him with reliable support it must be powerful. Hence the wholesale gifts to the bishops, the donations of estates and counties. The King of Germany could make such gifts, though the King of France could not, because many of the counties were still dependencies of his own, and because he confiscated the estates of those magnates who ventured to resist him. It was because the evolution of Germany was less advanced, in a feudal sense, that his royal policy was practicable, and it was for this reason that he was able to make his bishops princes of the Empire. The whole of Germany and Lotharingia became covered with episcopal principalities: a feudal system of a special type, which the monarch could extend at will. The prince-bishops were trained in his chapel, like a species of ecclesiastical page. They owed him everything, and wherever they were found, under Otto and his successors, they were distinguished from laymen by their conception of the king's sovereign rights. Their skilful training, and their spiritual education, nurtured in them the idea of discipline. In their eyes the king, not the State, was

the stronger, since they themselves were given a portion of
the State. Bishop Gerard of Cambrai (1012–1031) refused
to introduce the "peace of God" in his diocese because it
was the sole prerogative of the sovereign to maintain the
public peace. From the bishops, from the 10th century onwards, the Lotharingians learned to admire the discipline
of the Germans. The more scholarly they were, the better
they served the king. Many of them maintained very notable schools: the schools of Liége were especially celebrated. Here again the Carolingian tradition was revived.
For the rest, neither Otto nor his successors meddled in
questions of dogma. It was enough for them that they had
the Church well in hand. Their *Reichskirche* had something
in common with the *Landeskirchen* of a later day.

The Pope, absolutely powerless, did nothing to obstruct
the great episcopal policy of the King of Germany. Far from
attempting to assert his primacy over the king, he found
in him a protector; John XII called on him for assistance,
and on February 2nd, 962 restored the Imperial dignity for
his benefit. This merely placed the Church more than ever
in Otto's hands, until the day when it brought upon Germany the War of Investitures.

The acquisition of the Empire by Otto was simply a consequence of his personal power. Already the Marquis of
Ivrea, Berenger, fleeing before King Ugo of Italy, had declared himself Otto's vassal, and in 951 Otto crossed the
Alps and assumed the title of King of Italy. The peninsula
having been left to its devices for a moment, had taken the
opportunity of rending itself to pieces, with the result that
for centuries it was tied to Germany.

Otto's intervention was not to be explained, like that of
the Carolingians, by his interest in the Papacy. For him,
intervention was a dynastic affair, which was quite unre-
lated to the interests of Germany. There was nothing to
draw Germany to the south of the Alps. Her intervention
in Italy was actually inconsistent with her movement of expansion towards the East. Was Otto already thinking of the
Empire when he undertook this first expedition? In any
event, having undertaken it, he was bound to go to Rome
and there become Emperor. Whatever strong power ap-

peared in Europe, it must needs gravitate toward Rome.

The Empire having been restored for Otto's benefit, Rome and Italy filled an increasingly important place in the policy of the German sovereigns. Would they be able to support the burden? Already, when Otto was dead (973), Otto II had to march against the Saracens of the South, was defeated by them in Calabria, and died shortly afterwards in Rome (983). Otto III, his son, lost in Imperial dreams, had to establish himself in Italy, forgetting Germany, and there he died in 1002. In Poland, meanwhile, Boleslas Chrobry had asserted his independence, while the Polish and Hungarian Churches, under the Archbishops of Gnesen and Gratz, had detached themselves from the German Church; the Wends, under Otto II, had revolted and shaken off the yoke, and under Svend Forkbeard paganism had reappeared in Denmark. Henry II, the last of the Saxons, neglected the task of re-establishing his authority on the confines of his kingdom, occupying himself only with Italy, where the Marquis Ardoin of Ivrea (1014) was proclaimed king. It was evident that the Imperial ideal was getting the better of the ideal of kingship. As a matter of fact, there was no King of Germany; the king was presently known as *Rex Romanorum*, and the Emperor as *Imperator Romanorum*. There were no words to describe Germany; she was merged in the Empire. Her kings exhausted their strength in maintaining the Empire. They were all Germans, but they had no German policy. All their strength lay to the north of the Alps, yet they were continually drawn to Italy. They were destined to wear themselves out in pursuit of their policy. Germany has been the victim of the Empire, but her history is confounded with that of the Empire.

The Kings of Germany had evidently undertaken a task beyond their strength. One may ask what would have been the destiny of Europe if instead of squandering their strength to the south of the Alps they had persistently pushed eastwards.

As for the German people, we cannot say that their kings had abandoned them. The people wanted nothing. No necessity, save that of defence, drew them eastwards. The

Italian expeditions, thanks to the economic system of the period, did not exhaust their resources. The sovereigns of the 11th century could not conceive of their mission as other than a religious, or shall we say, an ecclesiastical mission. The Carolingian tradition was all-powerful. We can very well understand that Otto could not escape from its influence. So far no such thing as a national policy was possible. The only conception that a powerful monarch could entertain of his power was the conception of Christian universality. In the absence of a national consciousness, the more primitive the economic constitution of the State, the more permissible was it for governments to indulge in universalist idealism; or, in other words, since policy could not be inspired by interests it had its being in the sphere of ideas.

Having died out in Germany with Louis the Child in 911, the Carolingian dynasty survived in France until 987. On the death of Eudes of Paris (898) the magnates of the kingdom had returned to the royal family of tradition, and had acknowledged Charles the Simple as their king, and they turned away from him on the death of Charles the Fat only because he was a minor. However, Charles the Simple and his successors had little of the Carolingian but their names: Charles, Lothair, Louis. None of them bore the Imperial title, none even thought of claiming it. The grandson of Charles the Simple, Lothair, uttered no protest when Otto was crowned in Rome. The only ideal in respect of which they were still faithful to their family traditions was the tenacity with which they endeavoured to recover Lotharingia. Lothair had the satisfaction of advancing as far as Aix-la-Chapelle, where he came near to taking Otto II unawares, and of turning the eagle that surmounted the palace roof to face the east. But his forces were not in proportion to his enterprise. In that same year, 975, Otto II, by way of reprisals, led an army up to the very walls of Paris. Lotharingia, conquered for a moment, was lost to France; only the bishopric of Verdun still remained a French possession.

Lothair's son, Louis V, reigned but a year. At his death only one Carolingian was left—his uncle, Charles, the brother of Lothair, whom Otto II had made Duke of Lotharingia. He tried in vain to conquer the crown, supported by some of the magnates of his duchy, but he was taken prisoner by Hugh Capet in 991. His son Otto, whose name proves that he had become an alien to his race, succeeded him as Duke of Lotharingia. With him the glorious Carolingian dynasty ended in obscurity. We do not even know the exact date of his death (1005 to 1012).

The impotence of its last representatives, which contrasts so strongly with the success and enterprise of the German kings, is not by any means to be explained by their incapacity. Louis, the son of Charles the Simple, and Lothair were both energetic and enterprising princes. But the ground crumbled away from under their feet. The aristocracy had finally acquired an irresistible ascendancy in the countries over which they reigned. The king had only as much power as the aristocracy chose to allow him; and it chose to allow him as little as possible, the better to absorb the counties, and to constitute, by their agglomeration, its feudal principalities. If there had been a question of resisting an invasion it would perhaps have grouped itself about the crown. But since the Normans had established themselves on the coast in 911, France had no external enemies. The magnates were wholly indifferent to the fate of Lotharingia; its possession was merely a dynastic question. The king wanted Lotharingia mainly because it would give him increased power; for he really had no power save in his last domains, and over his last vassals in the Laon country. He could do nothing independently in the interior. If he wanted to take action against one of his vassals he had, for that purpose, to ally himself with another.[3] Lothair endeavoured in vain to prevent the Count of Flanders, Arnold, from advancing to the south of the Lys. The loyalty of his vassals was becoming more and more doubtful. In 922 a party was formed among them which abandoned Charles the Simple and declared Robert of Paris king. Robert was killed in the following year. He was replaced by Duke Raoul of Burgundy, and Charles the Simple died in captivity. Under Louis IV, Hugh the Great, son of Robert, was all-

[3] For example: with Flanders against the Normans.

powerful. It was to him that the king owed his election, and he attempted to exercise tutelage over the monarch. Before long he openly rebelled against his authority, and Otto I of Germany had to come to the assistance of the lawful king and save his crown for him (946). Naturally enough, the King of France had to do what he could to restore his power by directing his efforts toward the outer world. If he contrived to maintain himself within his frontiers, this was not because he was strong like the King of Germany, but because he was weak. His vassals were loyal to him because he was not dangerous, and the most powerful among them found it in his interest to seek his support in order to prevent others from attempting to dispute his authority.

On the death of Louis V, and in the absence of a possible Carolingian heir—for Charles, Duke of Lotharingia, the last representative of the dynasty, was not accepted by the aristocracy of France—the election of Hugh Capet (June 1st, 987) followed, in accordance with the traditions of his family: two of his ancestors had been kings, and the Archbishop of Reims, Adalbéron, supported him. With his accession to the throne a new dynasty began, which was to endure for eight centuries, and achieve hegemony in Europe.

There was nothing to suggest this. The date of the election of Hugh Capet is a date of great significance: but the fact of his election was not important. Nothing was changed; or hardly anything. There had already been Capetian kings: so his election was not a novelty. The conception of royalty was not in any way modified by it.

To suppose that Hugh and his successors had a different conception of royalty from the last of the Carolingians would be completely erroneous. Nothing was changed: neither the title, nor the emblems of royalty, nor the organization of the court. The king was still anointed by the Church; he still considered himself the temporal guardian of order and the protector of the Church. The Carolingian ideal was the royal ideal: there was no other. What is more, the royal power had only *de facto* limits. No one, save the Church, could say where this power should stop. All depended on the strength of the king and of the aristocracy. It was a delicate matter to say just how far the royal power should extend.

The Capetians accepted the situation. They were not by any means feudal kings in the sense of considering that their power was legally restricted by that of the aristocracy. They were simply opportunists, who knew how far they could go. They knew this better than the Carolingians, and for two reasons. Firstly, with their accession the kingship had become purely elective. True, it had become elective in the case of the Carolingians; but they, none the less, constituted a dynasty. The Capetians, on the contrary, had to create a dynasty. It was this necessity that dictated their policy: they were careful to give the magnates no cause of discontent which might excite their mistrust. They kept out of difficulties at home and abroad. This explains why the Capetians allowed the question of Lotharingia to drop. They were content to live, and to leave behind them—as it was their good fortune to leave—an heir whom they had elected in their own lifetime. For them, as for the first Ottos, the hereditary principle was thus established as a fact; but while in Germany it was imposed by the prestige of strength, in France it insinuated itself by virtue of weakness.

The first Capetians dug themselves in, without any undue *amour-propre*. Philip I, defeated by the Count of Flanders, Robert the Frisian (1071), was reconciled with him and married his stepdaughter. The kings were sustained only by their own domains of Paris, Amiens, Orléans and Bourges. They could not create prince-bishops, like the Ottos: the great lay nobles had absorbed all the territory. The kings let them go their way; and it was the Church, not the king, that organized the "peace of God." They contented themselves with taking part in the feasts and assemblies of the magnates, and giving diplomas to the abbeys. They were so modest that they have no history. They married mere princesses. They did not leave their own territories, or show themselves abroad: they neither despatched embassies nor received them. Robert the Pious, the son of Hugh (946–1031), refused the crown of Italy, which he was offered by the *grandi* of Lombardy. Henri I (1031–1060) allowed the Emperor Conrad to take possession of the kingdom of Burgundy. Philip I (1060–1108) did nothing to make his reign remarkable. But the Capets endured, and they struck roots in the soil. At the same time their residence, Paris, which they rarely left, was gradually becoming a capital. It was the first capital that Europe had known. Hitherto the kings had moved about: the Capets, territorial princes, settled down and provided the country with a centre. There was no reason why Paris should become the capital of France. It became the capital because it was the residence of the Capets.

So, while the German kings, fortified by the vigour of a primitive society, spent and exhausted their strength in grandiose enterprises, filling Christendom with the sound of their names, but without attaching themselves to the soil, the kings of France, living humbly and modestly amidst a more advanced society, which restricted their power, were quietly and obscurely building up the future. Compared with their immoderate and poetical German contemporaries, they were prosaic and practical. They were sensible folk, who knew their strength, and imperceptibly increased it. And when, under Louis VI, the son of Philip I, an age of peril began with the conquest of England by William the Conqueror (1066), the monarchy showed that it was already sufficiently established to enter upon the conflict which was henceforth to shape the history of France.

CHAPTER III

The Feudality

1. *The Disintegration of the State*

We are accustomed to give the name of "feudal" to the political system which prevailed in Europe after the disappearance of the Carolingian dynasty. This habit of ours goes back to the French Revolution, which indiscriminately attributed to the feudal system all the rights, privileges, usages and traditions which were inconsistent with the constitution of the modern State and modern society. Yet if we accept the words in their exact sense, we ought to understand, by the terms "feudal" and "feudal system," only the juridical relations arising from the fief or the bond of vassalage,[1] and it is an abuse of language to stretch the sense of these terms to include a whole political order, in which the feudal element was, after all, only of secondary importance, and, if we may say so, formal rather than substantial. We shall follow the common usage, but we shall also call attention to the fact that the most significant feature of the so-called feudal system was the disintegration of the State.

Everything tended to accomplish this disintegration, once it had proved to be materially impossible, after the kingdoms founded by the Germanic invasions were estab-

---

[1] The old feudal seigneurs, down to the close of the 18th century, were under no illusion in this respect. It was generally admitted by all that "fief and justice have nothing in common." In reality, feudal law was a special kind of law, like commercial law.

lished, to continue the Roman State. Disintegration was already on the way at the close of the Merovingian period, when the monarchy, on which everything depended, recovered its influence for the time being, through its great conquests and its alliance with the Papacy. But these conquests, and this influence, retarded only for a moment the process of disintegration, for the causes of the latter were inherent in the social order itself. The king alone could maintain the political organization of the State. Theoretically the State was monarchical and administrative; but we have seen how weak it was, even under Charlemagne. It was weak because its political constitution did not match its economic nature. Since commerce and the towns had disappeared the State had entered upon a period when the great domains absorbed both the land and the inhabitants, placing the revenue of the former and the arms of the latter at the disposal of a class of magnates. These were rendered the more independent by the fact that their economic life was subject to no perturbations; the whole produce of the domain was applied to the maintenance of the domain itself. There was therefore nothing to be feared or expected from the State. This decided the fate of the monarchy. Sooner or later, accordingly as the evolution of society was more or less advanced, it was doomed to allow its rights and prerogatives to pass to the magnates who were now almost its only subjects, since they had interposed themselves between it and the people, and it was obliged to govern through them. To an ever-increasing extent, its only effective power was that which it derived from its own domains. Where it was reduced to the exercise of a purely political sovereignty its rule soon became purely formal. Deprived of taxes, deprived of the possibility of paying its functionaries, how was it to maintain itself? By throwing itself upon the Church, as it had done in Germany? But this had been possible only because in the time of the Ottos the lay aristocracy was still in an undeveloped condition. And again, the episcopal principalities were themselves destroying the State. Thanks to them the monarch alone was strong from the military point of view. But his governmental efficacy was not enhanced by them, and the State was destroyed notwithstanding his military power. Thus, in the economic circumstances of the age the power of the king was inevitably bound to decline, until it depended entirely on his military activity and his personal prestige. And in fact, since the days of Charlemagne the decadence of the monarchy had progressed very rapidly. The king's position, in respect of the magnates, was growing steadily weaker. Matters had gone so far by the close of the 9th century that the monarchy had become purely elective.

It might have disappeared. It did not disappear, and this was characteristic of the age.[2] It did not occur to the magnates that they could dispense with the king. They still had a lingering sense of the unity of the State. Here, above all, the Church had to intervene, for it did not acknowledge the magnates; for the Church the king was the guardian of the providential order of the world. And he, for his part, protected the Church and guaranteed its property. And the magnates themselves needed a king as judge and arbiter: just as in the law-courts there must be a judge or magistrate who presides over the proceedings and pronounces sentence. The king was indispensable to the social order, to the "public peace." But it was clearly understood that the king reigned and did not govern.

And yet, in law, there was no limit to his power. He took no oath of capitulation. He renounced no prerogative. Theoretically he was absolute. But he was paralysed. The members no longer obeyed the head. As far as appearance went, nothing was changed. The kings continued to employ all the old formulae, to receive, in the official language, all the marks of respect. But they had allowed the reality of power to pass into the hands of the aristocracy. The modern jurists have constructed the prettiest theories of the State of the early Middle Ages, and of the rights of the monarch: but they are only theories. The reality was very different. The State was disintegrating, falling to pieces, and from its ruins it reconstructed itself in another form. After Charles the Bald there were no more capitularies, and not

[2] The election of the king was a mark of progress in the sense that it assured the unity of the monarchy: there would be no more partitions of kingdoms.

until the 12th century do we find the king acting again in a legislative capacity.

What had happened was simply this: the power had spontaneously declined from the hands of the king into those of the aristocracy, which included his officials. We may therefore say, with perfect truth, that the official usurped the functions which he performed. The thing happened quite naturally, without deliberate intention, without any violent disturbances, because the official was the seigneur of many of the persons under his administration, and the proprietor of a good portion of his circumscription.

It should be noted, however, that there was a very clear distinction between his private powers over his estates and his men, and the public power, the crown rights which he exercised in the king's name, but henceforth for his own benefit. He possessed the first in his own name as a part of his patrimony. The second he held only by delegation from the crown. If the count, in his county, was supreme justiciary, military commander, collector of what remained of the old Roman *census,* beneficiary of the *droit de gîte* and collector of market tolls, this was because he was a functionary. But all these powers, which he exercised in the king's name, he exercised for his own benefit, and the king could not prevent him from doing so.

Further, the power of the aristocracy broke up and reconstituted for its own benefit the circumscriptions of the State. The State, since the Merovingian epoch, had been divided into counties. These counties were very small, so small that the count-officials were able easily to cover their counties in the course of a day. But from the 8th century onwards the more powerful of these counts had begun to usurp the power in a number of counties adjacent to their own. Fortunate marriages, friendly arrangements, violence, the king's favour, or the fear which they inspired in him, soon enabled them to amalgamate, in a single territory, a greater or smaller number of the old circumscriptions. The new county established by these encroachments became a principality, just as the count became a prince. The name borrowed from the Roman bureaucracy still adhered to him, but this sometime agent of the central power, having absorbed the power which was delegated to him, and enlarged the circumscription in which he exercised that power, was now, and would remain for centuries, a petty local sovereign.

All this was accomplished in the midst of unspeakable violence and treachery. The 10th century, like the 15th, was an epoch of political assassination. The territorial power of the feudal princes was no more scrupulous in the choice of means than that of the absolutist monarchs or the tyrants of the Renaissance; it was merely more brutal. Each sought to increase his power to the detriment of his neighbour, and any weapon was permissible. The passion for land ruled the actions of all these feudal magnates, and as there was no one to stop them, they struck at each other with all the brutality of their instincts. The king was powerless, and when on occasion he attempted to intervene his functionary made war upon him. It was thus that Charles the Simple died in the prison of the Count of Vermandois.

Nevertheless—and here the feudal element appears—the princes were bound to the king by the oath of fealty. The old subordination of the functionary had been transformed into the oath. The feudal seigneurs were the king's men, his faithful servants. In theory, the king was still the supreme possessor of the powers which had been usurped from him, and this the feudal oath acknowledged. We must not say, therefore, that the feudal system broke down the State, for the truth is the reverse of this. It still maintained a bond—or at least a formal bond—between the king and those parcels of the kingdom of which the great functionaries who had become princes had possessed themselves, and whose feudal oath made them vassals. Here was a principle which the jurists would exploit at a later period, when the king was strong once more. For the time being the king gave way to the seigneurs, and recognized the usurpations which he could not prevent. The hereditary principle was in force among the feudal magnates. The son succeeded to the father, and from the 11th century onwards the hereditary principle was extended to women.

The king, who still regarded himself as the possessor of all the power of the State, was now envisaged by the princes, his great vassals, only from the feudal standpoint. For them he was no more than a magnate to whom they were allied by a contractual bond. They owed him aid and counsel, and the king owed them protection: if he attacked them, taking his king's point of view, they considered themselves justified in marching against him. The princes envisaged the monarchy otherwise than the king himself. But the consequences of this difference of conception were not felt until a later date; and until the 12th century the kings, with rare exceptions, allowed matters to go their way.

Thus, from the end of the 9th and the beginning of the 10th century the State was reduced to an empty form. The provinces had become principalities, and the functionaries princes. The king, except on his own territory, was merely the "enfeoffed sovereign" of his kingdom. A multiplicity of local sovereignties had replaced the old administrative unity derived from the Roman Empire. But it must be recognized that this was the normal and sensible situation, which was in correspondence with the social condition, and therefore with the needs, of the community. The agrarian and domainal constitution of the epoch made it impossible to maintain the administrative unity that even a Charlemagne could not transform into a living reality. How could the political power have remained centralized in the hands of the king at a time when the people were entering *en masse* into the cadres of the great estates, into dependency on the seigneurs? Political power was bound to follow effective power, and to crystallize itself, so to speak, around those who really possessed that power. The protection of human beings is not merely the primordial function of the State: it is also the origin of the State. Now, the king no longer protected his subjects; the magnates protected them. It was therefore necessary and beneficial that they should dismember the State to their own advantage. They certainly had public opinion—or shall we say, the sentiment of the peoples—on their side. Nowhere do we see that the "little man" attempted to save the monarchy. He no longer knew what monarchy was.

It was in the restricted centres of the territorial principalities that a system of government and administration was

first organized that actively influenced those who were subject to it. The kingdom was too extensive. It had inevitably
to restrict itself to an administration which could not be
adequately supervised, and which did not reach the masses.
It was otherwise with the new system. The territorial
princes were in touch with reality; their private function
enabled them to govern effectively a territory of moderate
extent: the number of their dependents and vassals was in
proportion to its area, and provided them with a staff. Each
of these princes set to work in his own way; their methods
varied in detail, but were broadly the same. It was this obscure task that was the most important feature of the period, as regards the formation of society, and where it was
first undertaken—in the Low Countries and in France—
society was more advanced than elsewhere. The kings were
in the front of the stage; the emperors occupied themselves
with high policy. But it was the princes who created the
first original type of political organization that Europe had
known since the Roman Empire.

They had, of course, no theory, no conscious conception.
Practice automatically fitted itself to the reality.

The foundation of the territorial organization was the
landed property of the prince, since it was from this that
he derived his power. The principal "counts" of his domain,
or the most favourably situated, were provided with defensive works, and became castles (*bourgs*), the centres of the
military, financial and judicial organization. They were
usually great walled enclosures, with dwelling-houses,
store-houses, and lodgings for the garrison of knights. A
châtelain, whom the prince chose from among his men acted
as his substitute in the circumscription, which bore the
name of *châtellenie*. It was the châtelain who commanded
the fortress, watched over the countryside, and presided in
the local court of justice. In order to support the châtelain
and the knights of the castle prestations in kind were levied
on the population: and here the principle of the salary
made its appearance, a principle unknown to the kings: of
payment in the form of fixed dues to be made to the public
authority. Moreover, as early as the 11th century we find
traces of a county impost (*petitio bede*), and this was a

fresh sign of progress, despite the still primitive form of assessment and collection. Thus, at a time when the king had no financial resources outside his domains, the prince was organizing them. Moreover, the prince minted money, for he usurped the right of coining money with the other crown rights, and he made a handsome profit by debasing the coinage. He had also the market tolls, and, of course, he continued to take his share of the fines.

From every point of view, then, his power was greater than that of the king. For while the king was now elective, the principality was hereditary, and at an early period—as early as the 10th century—the right of sole succession was established, so that the principalities were not divided. It is interesting to note how unchanged they continued until the end of the *ancien régime*, which preserved them as provinces. The prince, from the 10th century, had a historiography. He had a court, modelled on that of the king: chancellor, marshal, seneschal, cup-bearer. He had his vassals, who were more loyal to him than he was to the king, by reason of their proximity, and the greater disproportion of their powers. He was the advowee of all the monasteries within his territory, and he exacted dues or services from them. The documents call him *princeps, monarcha, advocatus patriae, post Deum princeps.*

He was in actual sense the territorial chieftain, the head of the *patria*, and we should note that in the Latin of the Middle Ages people were beginning to apply this beautiful word to these little local "counties." In them was formed, for the first time, the patriotism which in modern society has replaced the civic sentiment of antiquity. There was something in it of the sense of family, and it was embodied in the man who from father to son was the chief and protector of the group. His armorial bearings became those of the people, and their common loyalty to him was a bond of service. Nothing like this had existed under the Merovingians or Carolingians, and in later periods men had this feeling only for their kings. Modern patriotism, born of the dynastic sentiment, was in the first place nurtured in the principalities.

The prince was really the protector of his men. He discharged his duty in person: his life, and his social function, were active in the extreme. Not only did he lead his men to the wars, and with them fling himself upon the enemy: he also presided in his courts of justice, supervised the work of his tax-collectors, and gave his personal decision in all important questions; and above all, he watched over the "public peace." He assured the safety of the roads, and extended his protection to the poor, and to orphans, widows, and pilgrims; and he fell upon highway robbers and hanged them. He was the supreme justiciary on his own territory, the guardian and guarantor of public order, and in this respect his function was essentially social in character. When one speaks of the "bloodthirsty" feudal magnates one should make reservations. The feudal seigneur was bloodthirsty when abroad, in his enemy's country, but not in his own; and one thing is certain—that society began to receive its political education within the *cadre* of the feudal principalities. The great State of which the principalities were the dismembered parts did not really influence people; its activities were carried on over their heads. The monarchy had designed the framework of political life, introduced Christianity, allied itself with the Church, and created an ideal of royalty which still survived, and would be a force in the future. But it had no actual hold upon men and women. To reach them, to govern them, the immediate, firm and active power of the local princes was needed. And these princely men-at-arms with the fantastic names, these rough soldiers, despite their pillaging of their neighbours' territories, must be given their place among the civilizers of Europe. In the political and social life of the continent, they were the first instructors.

2. Nobility and Chivalry

In the 10th century a new juridical class had sprung up in the European States: the nobility. Its importance is sufficiently shown by the fact that in lay society the nobles alone had political rights. Later on the bourgeoisie would take its place beside the nobility. This place would become

more and more considerable, but down to the end of the
ancien régime it would still be regarded as a secondary
place. In the history of Europe the nobles have played—
though under very different conditions—almost the same
part as the patricians in Roman history, while the bourgeoisie may be compared with the plebeians. It is only in
the modern State that they have become merged in the
mass of the citizens, much as in the Empire the general
bestowal of civic rights effaced the old difference between
the patriciate and the plebs.

The noblesse exercised so great and so general an influence over the history of Europe that it is not easy to
realize that it constituted an original phenomenon, and one
peculiar to the Christian society of Western Europe.
Neither the Roman nor the Byzantine Empire, nor the
Musulman world, had ever known a similar institution.
Doubtless all primitive societies have comprised a nobility
of mythological origin. But these nobilities disappeared on
the advent of civilization: like the old Germanic nobility,
which did not outlive the invasions. The nobility of the
Middle Ages, five centuries later, was quite a novel creation, and very different in character.

It was preceded by the powerful aristocracy, partly
Roman, and in part consisting of the parvenus and functionaries who had been making their appearance, and playing a more and more important part, since the formation of
the new kingdoms. But this aristocracy was not a nobility,
in the sense of being a juridical class to which a man belonged by birth. It was merely a social class, which consisted of a group of powerful individuals. Moreover, whatever its actual power, it possessed no privilege in law. The
greatest landowner of Charlemagne's day was in the same
position, in a court of justice, as the simple freeman.

Two causes contributed to the formation of the nobility:
the constant diminution of the number of freemen, and the
feudal form of military service: and of these two causes the
second was far more important than the first, and could
even have dispensed with its action.

The domainal system, as it expanded, resulted in the
juridical degradation of the rural population, reducing it

to a more or less complete servitude. Those who had retained their liberty were in a privileged situation, and from the 10th century the word *liber* took on the meaning of *nobilis*. The old juridical usages relating to the family and inheritance now applied only to these privileged persons. The common law of freemen was modified into a special law. The *connubium* was enlarged in Roman law: at the beginning of the Middle Ages it was reduced. Family right was finally the apanage only of the few; and the same was true of free hereditary property (*allodium*).

These freemen, whose numbers it is impossible to estimate, naturally retained the right to bear arms. Their estate enabled them to maintain a war horse. They were above all warriors.

But beside them, and far more numerous—at any rate, in France—was another class of freemen: the vassals. Their means of livelihood was provided not by their personal property, their *allodium*, but by the fief which, in this agricultural age, served as their salary. Like the others, and even more than the others, they were warriors. But unlike the first class, they were not hereditary warriors; for the fief did not pass from father to son unless the son was a good soldier. If the father left only daughters, or sons incapable of bearing arms, the fief lapsed to the seigneur. But such a case was rare. In France, from the time of Charles the Bald, the fiefs were hereditary, and while in Germany their hereditary character was not formally recognized until the reign of Conrad, they were certainly handed down from father to son before that date.

In addition to these free soldiers—some the proprietors of *allodia*, others the holders of fiefs—there were also soldiers who were not free. These were loyal and sturdy serfs whom the seigneurs took with them as bodyguards when they went to the wars, and employed, in times of peace, in confidential posts, as *ministeriales* or *Dienstmannen;* in Germany, more especially, they were numerous, and they constituted the aristocracy of servitude.

All, whether free or not, were united by the sense of professional community, and were regarded with special consideration by the rest of the population; for since all the intellectual functions were allotted to the clergy, only the trade of arms could give the laymen a privileged position in society.

The warrior entered the military class only on coming of age. A special ceremony was necessary before he could be admitted; at this his arms were conferred upon him by the seigneur or by one of his companions. By this ceremony he was consecrated knight, *chevalier*, which meant simply horse-soldier. It gave the recipient of the honour the advantages and the prestige of his position. At first, unless the son of a knight was himself dubbed knight, he was a villein merely, and his daughters, since they could not be knighted, enjoyed no special consideration. But this was evidently a transitory phase; and fact was followed by law. As a general rule, the son of a knight would himself become a knight. He was therefore counted, from birth, as belonging to the military caste; and the daughters of a knight would be regarded as belonging to the same social class. And as soon as this state of affairs was reached—which in France, at all events, was by the close of the 10th century—the nobility was born: that is, a hereditary class, conferring a particular rank in the State, independently of social position. All those who belonged to the *milicia*, or whose ancestors had belonged to it, were *nobiles*. It was not absolutely essential that the "noble" should be free; for in the end the *ministeriales* came to be regarded as nobles.[3]

Thus the class of vassals was practically merged in the nobility. However, nobility did not depend upon the possession of a fief. After all, a man could be knighted who did not possess a fief; and it was not for some time—not until the 13th century—that the plebeian was debarred from the possession of a fief. It was therefore the social function that made the noble; but it was a social function that presupposed economic independence, based upon the noble's personal property (his *allodium*) or his feudal property (his fief). The nobility was really the army. Hence its privileges. They were explained by the nature of the service rendered, and conferred as consideration for that

[3] But this was not definitely the case until the 14th century.

service. The noble did not pay the count an impost on account of his land, because he furnished him with military service. This was the sole privilege, so-called, of the nobility: it had no others. His special juridical situation, his special status in respect of his family, and the special procedure by which he benefited in the law-courts, were merely the survival of the common law of freemen, which had been modified for villeins.

The importance of the nobility resided in its social rôle. Uplifted by its military functions above the rest of the population, in constant touch with the princes, it was the nobility and the nobility alone that furnished the administrative personnel, just as it was the nobility alone that constituted the army. It was from the nobility that the châtelains were chosen, the mayors, and all the other agents of the territorial administration. It was therefore regarded not only as a military but also as a political caste. Beside the nobility was the clergy. Below the nobility and the clergy was the mass of plebeians, by whose labour they lived; in return for which service the clergy directed their souls while the nobility protected their bodies. This is not a theoretical *a posteriori* view. The writers of the period were perfectly well aware of this mutual relation, and recorded it in plain language.

This nobility was extremely numerous; especially when the domainal system was well developed, so that the number of fiefs could be readily increased. One may say that the evolution of society was in proportion to the numbers, or rather to the density of the chivalry, which decreased as one proceeded from the French frontier in the direction of the Elbe. In France and the Low Countries one could count on finding a number of knights in every country town, and we certainly shall not be far out if we estimate that in these countries they represented at least one tenth of the population.

We must not imagine that their mode of life was especially refined. Their fiefs and their little domains just enabled them to live. Their military equipment consisted of a lance, an iron casque, a buckler, and a suit of buckram. Only the wealthiest knights possessed a coat of mail. They were formidable soldiers, however, and when war left them any leisure they kept themselves in training by means of tourneys that were like veritable battles. They attended them in their hundreds, grouped according to regions, and charged one another heavily until more than one was left on the ground. Further, they were the most turbulent of men, furiously destroying one another in the private wars and family vendettas in which they were continually involved. In vain did the Church, from the close of the 10th century—first of all in France, and later in Germany—restrict the days of battle by the "peace of God"; custom proved to be too strong for it. At the end of the 11th century the chronicler Lambert of Waterloo related that ten of his father's brothers were slain by their enemies on the same day, in an encounter near Tournai; and about the same time the Count of Flanders, Robert the Frisian, drawing up the list of murders committed in the neighbourhood of Bruges, stated that it would take more than 10,000 marks of silver to pay the "compositions" in respect of these murders.

Naturally, in such an environment there was no intellectual culture. Only in the wealthiest families would a clerk teach the daughters to read. As for the sons, who were in the saddle as soon as they could mount a horse, they had no knowledge of anything but fighting. Their literature consisted of soldiers' songs, such as the song that Taillefer sang at the Battle of Hastings. They were violent, gross, and superstitious, but excellent soldiers. Consider the exploits of the Normans in Sicily, the conquest of England, the Flemish knights who so amazed the Emperor Alexis as they passed through Constantinople, and above all the extraordinary enterprise of the Crusades. The qualities that made the knights of France and the Low Countries the finest warriors of their time had nothing to do with race; they were the fruit of training. This training was better in the West because there the chivalry was more numerous, and it was so because of the greater extension of the domainal system.

At the close of the 11th century chivalry was extremely widespread. But "chivalrous" manners—by which I mean the code of courtesy and loyalty which distinguished the gentlemen after the age of the Crusades—had as yet no existence. To produce them greater refinement was necessary. Still, the two sentiments on which they were based were already widely diffused among the knights: namely, devotion and honour. Nothing could exceed the piety of these soldiers, despite their superstitions and their brutality. They were scrupulous in their respect for the right of sanctuary: they would halt in their pursuit of an enemy as soon as they saw the towers of a monastery upon the horizon. They followed with exemplary piety the relics which the monks carried in procession through the countryside. They went on distant pilgrimages, to Rome and to Jerusalem; and it would even seem that the songs of the feudal epoch were evolved on the pilgrim routes. As for honour, the sentiment which the modern world has inherited from them, this was wholly a military virtue. It was not precisely the honour of our day, which is more refined. It was, before all, the sentiment of fidelity and loyalty. These knights were ready enough for treachery, but they did not break their given word. Homage (*homagium*)—a word which has gradually lost its full meaning in our language—meant for them the complete offering of their person to their seigneur. Felony was in their eyes the worst of crimes.[4] They regarded everything from the personal point of view, as between man and man. The sentiment of obedience and discipline was entirely foreign to them. The moment that they considered they had been injured they rebelled, and their habit of plain speaking was quite extraordinary. Their economic independence naturally generalized among them certain mental and moral attitudes, which persisted under different conditions, though they assumed more refined forms. It was then that the normal foundation on which the nobility was to build in later times was laid. It was easily comprehensible, and entirely dissimilar to the foundation from which the bourgeoisie rose to a position of influence. To the very last the great majority of the nobility would retain the traces of their descent from a class of men to whom all

[4] See Ganelon in the *Chanson de Roland*.

notions of profit and productive labour were alien. To a certain extent the ancient idea that labour is unworthy of the freeman was revived by the chivalry of Europe. But the freeman of antiquity devoted his leisure, which he owed to the labour of his slaves, to public affairs: the knight of the Middle Ages profited by the gift of land which he received to devote himself to the calling of arms and the service of his lord. When centuries had passed, and when the nobility had gradually been ousted from the rank which it held of old, the expression "to live like a nobleman" finally came to mean, "to live without doing anything."

BOOK FOUR

The War of Investitures and the Crusade

CHAPTER I

The Church

1. *The Papacy*

As the Empire declined the Papacy, as we have seen, profited by its rival's loss of vitality and prestige. But it could not of its own strength maintain itself at the height to which it had climbed. It had leant on the Empire: it had, so to speak, climbed upon its back. When the Empire collapsed the Papacy was involved in its fall. To begin with, assailed by the self-made kings who fought one another for the possession of Italy and the Imperial crown, it became the prey—at the beginning of the 10th century—of the Roman feudality. The lords of the Roman Campagna fought among themselves to obtain the Papacy for their own family. True, the Pope was still appointed by the clergy and the people of the city, but it was only too easy to impose him on the electors by force, or to overthrow the pontiff elect who did not suit the book of the more powerful party. The election of the Pope by the community of the clergy and the faithful took place regularly as long as there was a strong power at the side of the Papacy. At first it was supervised by the exarch, then by the *missi*. But since the Empire had fallen into decadence the Pope was appointed under pressure from the feudal signori. The Popes of this period appeared and disappeared at the will of the feudal factions: some were assassinated, others died in prison. In this Roman environment, whose immorality was equalled only by its brutality, the intrigues of the women more than once disposed of the tiara. Marozia and Theodora, working through their successive husbands or lovers, had it conferred upon their sons; the legend of Pope Joan is merely an exaggeration, to the point of caricature, of the only too actual scandals of the period. One of Marozia's sons, Alberic of Tusculum, finally became the lord of Rome and the maker of Popes. He took the precaution of making the Romans acknowledge his son Octavian as his successor, and the future Pope. When he died Octavian succeeded him as the master of the city, and in 955, at the age of 18, he received the sovereign pontificate as he might have received a fief, under the style of John XII. And yet it was this feudal Pope who was the instrument of the restoration of the Empire. We need hardly say that the sole consideration that moved him to restore it was his own interest, and for him this great action was no more than a mere expedient. When in 962 he summoned Otto I to Rome, and set the Imperial crown upon his head, he did so because at this moment he was soliciting Otto's help against the Marquis Berenger of Ivrea, the so-called King of Italy, his mortal enemy. The traditions of the age of Leo I and Charlemagne were so degraded that John can hardly have supposed that Otto's conception of the Empire was more exalted than his own of the Papacy. No Roman of his day had any understanding of the great words that had once dominated history. When he saw that the new Emperor was taking his position seriously, and that his lordship of Rome was threatened, he made haste to betray him and intrigue against him. Otto returned to Rome, convoked a synod, which deposed John XII, and made the Romans swear an oath to the effect that they would not in future appoint a Pope without his consent, or that of his son. Leo VIII was elected in his presence: then he departed. But the Romans had yielded only to force. Otto had hardly left Rome when they drove Leo from the throne, and recalled John: and after his death, heedless of their oath, they replaced him by Benedict V. Otto had to return and besiege the city. Seizing Benedict, he exiled him to Hamburg, and restored Leo. On the death of Leo, John XIII, appointed under German influence, was soon driven from the throne by a revolt, and in 966 the Emperor had to cross the Alps once more in order to restore him.

We see that in all these conflicts the Pope, as compared with the Emperor, was merely the lord of Rome, and almost like a disobedient vassal. The contrast is obvious between the majestic memories evoked by his name and the local rôle to which he was restricted. Thanks to its remoteness from Germany, the Roman feudality always recovered its position after it had yielded. Under Otto II the Crescenzi were as powerful in Rome as Alberic had been before them, and the defeat of Rossano did nothing to diminish their influence.

Otto III had a vague dream of establishing the alliance of Pope and Emperor, in accordance with the Carolingian theory, but not the Carolingian reality. He dreamed of making Rome the centre of the twofold power, the indissoluble union, which from that centre would govern Christendom. At the age of twenty-five he entered the city, caused his cousin Bruno to be elected Pope, under the name of Gregory V (996), and received from him the Imperial crown. At Gregory's death Otto chose, as the occupant of St. Peter's throne, the most learned man of his time: Gerbert, Archbishop of Reims, then of Ravenna, who took the name of Sylvester II, thus recalling that Sylvester I of whom legend relates that he baptized Constantine. The Emperor installed himself beside the Pope on the Aventine, in a palace whose pomp recalled that of Byzantium, and whose etiquette borrowed its austerity from the rules of the monastic orders. Losing himself in the idealistic daydreams that betrayed the influence of his mother Theophano, and of the bishops who had educated him, he seems to have believed in the possibility of making Rome once more the centre of the world—but a Rome in which the Pope would share in the Imperial power. Neither he nor Gerbert, lost in their dreams, could perceive the reality. And this reality avenged itself cruelly: a revolt of the Romans forced him to flee, and on January 23rd, 1002, he died at Paterno, at the foot of Monte Soracte: died of the shattering of his dream.

Once more the factions fought for the mastery of the city: the Crescenzi on the one hand, the Counts of Tusculum on the other. Benedict VIII, the creature of the Counts, maintained himself in power by appealing for aid to Henry II, just as John XII had appealed to Otto. He was succeeded by his brother, John XIX (1024–1033), a layman, who received all the degrees of the ecclesiastical hierarchy on one and the same day. He crowned Conrad II. After him a third member of the Tusculum family was elected: Benedict IX. The Crescenzi drove him from the throne, replacing him by Sylvester III, who a little later was expelled in his turn by his adversary, returning at the head of his party. Sylvester then sold his title to Gregory VI, so that there were three Popes at the same time.

We see, then, that the restoration of the Empire had not the effect of strengthening the Papacy. With the exception of Otto III the new Emperors did not continue the Carolingian tradition. They governed with the Church—that is, with the bishops—but not with the Pope. He was useful only because he crowned them.

For the rest, they did not succeed in restoring order in Rome; but this did not concern them greatly. The Pope, moreover, could do little to embarrass them, for he exercised no authority over the Church. And the clergy of Rome, being in the hands of the factions, uttered no protests, and made no effort to restore the throne of St. Peter to its ancient glory, or even to its ancient dignity. The reformation which was to restore it, and which, as a necessary consequence, was to bring it into conflict with the Emperor, came from the outer world.

2. The Clunisian Reformation

The discipline, the morality, the learning and the wealth of the Church had been restored or increased under the Carolingians. They were dependent upon the support of the Carolingians, and therefore upon their power. The decline of the dynasty subjected them to a crisis which, like the crisis of the political constitution, was the point of departure for a renewal of activity. In Germany, where the

Imperial Church, since the reign of Otto, had stood on solid foundations, the crisis was of brief duration, and under the guidance of the bishops the Carolingian tradition was quickly restored, and the intellectual culture of the clergy once again followed the path traced by Charlemagne and by Alcuin. But it was otherwise in the West. The feudal system, in destroying the State as it spread over Western Europe, as a natural consequence undermined the Church. In France, in Lotharingia, and in Italy the position of the bishops was almost the same as that of the Pope in Rome. They had to defend themselves against the feudal authorities of the neighbourhood, or they were imposed upon the clergy by these authorities; they were driven from their sees if they did not please the most powerful party, and were sometimes assassinated if they defied it too openly. The Pope could do nothing for them: in France the king could protect only the bishops of his own domain, whom he appointed. The situation of the monasteries was still more lamentable. The lay seigneurs who forced themselves upon them as advowees, when they did not simply assume the title of abbot, pillaged their estates, created fiefs for their men at the cost of the monastic domains, compelled them to support their servants and their packs of hounds, and, in short, plundered them, and no one could intervene.

As the secular power grew weaker the Church passed through a temporary crisis, from which it emerged more powerful than before, since it was now alone. It was fully capable of maintaining itself, and of applying to its own benefit the forces which had for a time been diverted to the service of the State. This renovation had naturally to come from those of the clergy who were least involved in secular allegiances—namely, from the monks.

The evil afflicting the Church, unlike the malady of the State, was only on the surface. It was feeling the consequences of the feudal expansion, but its constitution, since it stood outside the political community, was not thereby affected. However great the disorder in the Church, it destroyed nothing essential. The episcopal organization survived, just as the monasteries survived; and so did piety, for while learning and discipline declined, piety increased in the sense that it became more widespread. In the 10th century the parishes extended over the whole country. The rural churches became a feature of the landscape. The monastic domains, better organized than those of the lay proprietors, attracted the people *en masse*. Many of the new inhabitants became *cerocensuales* (that is, serfs of the Church); and these, faithful to the saintly patron of the monastery, provided him with a following which spread his cult and lauded his miracles. This, the period of local government, was also the period of local saints: St. Lambert, St. Hubert, St. Bavon, St. Trond. They were, so to speak, the great vassals of God, under whose protection men were glad to place themselves. Their relics exercised a magic influence. The monks bore them in procession about the countryside. They served to dissuade the knights from private warfare. And their miraculous power was reflected upon the monks who guarded them. For the saints, as a rule, dwelt in the monasteries, not in the bishops' palaces. The influence of the abbeys was increased by the fact that many of the rural churches belonged to them, or were dependent upon them; and the monks officiated in them. The contemporary ideal of sanctity was the monastic ideal; the renunciation of worldly joys in order to save one's soul; the withdrawal from social activities, and even from all other virtues than those of renunciation, humility, and chastity. And it was to this ideal that the Church owed its renaissance: not to the bishops, whether they were semi-feudal as in France, or faithful to the Carolingian tradition, as in Germany. Their learning made no impression on this uncultured public. The people wanted saints and workers of miracles.

The feudal nobles, even more than the people, regarded the bishops as their enemies. They pillaged the monasteries, but they respected them, and on their deathbeds the princes who had pillaged them most mercilessly made large donations to them. They all revered holiness, and they deplored the disorder into which the monasteries had fallen, although they were the cause of this disorder.

We can judge of their feelings by the encouragement which they accorded to asceticism whenever this made itself conspicuous. Gérard de Brogne, a knight who had become a religious, and who soon became famous for the discipline that he enforced in the little monastery which he had founded on his estate, was entrusted by the Counts of Hainault and Flanders with the task of reforming the abbeys in their territories. This local movement is significant, and shows how far the ground was prepared for the decisive reformation that proceeded from Cluny. This monastery, founded in 910 by Duke Guillaume d'Auvergne, under the direction of men like Odo († 943) or Odilon de Mercœur († 1099), played a part whose importance might be compared with that of the Jesuits in the 16th century. Here, of course, there was no question of grappling with heresy. The point at issue was the orientation of religious thought and feeling. I think we may say that by the reform of Cluny monasticism set its stamp upon Western Christianity for centuries to come. Of course, the monks had already played an important part: notably in the conversion of England. But the secular clergy were the more important: it was through them that the alliance of Church and State was manifested. The bishops, in the Carolingian epoch, were almost royal officials; in Germany they were made princes. Now, it was precisely this that the Clunisians condemned. For them, the world was the antechamber to Eternity. Everything had to be sacrificed to supraterrestrial ends. The salvation of the soul was everything, and it could be effected only by the Church: and the Church, in order to fulfil its mission, must be absolutely innocent of temporal interests. Here there was no question of the alliance of Church and State, but only of the complete subordination, in the spiritual domain, of man and society to the Church, the intermediary between man and God. Anyone who lent himself to the meddling of the secular power in religious affairs was therefore regarded as guilty of simony. The priest belonged to the Church and the Church alone. He could have no seigneur, just as he could have no family. The marriage of priests, tolerated in practice, was an abomination which must disappear. The complete spiritualization of the Church, the absolute observation of canonical law: this, if not the programme properly so-

called, was at all events the tendency of Cluny. In the
domain of piety it made for asceticism: in the political
domain, for the complete liberty of the Church, and the
breaking of the ties that bound it to civil society. In this
sense, Cluny might be described as anti-Carolingian. But
it was Papist; for obviously the Church, in order to be
independent, must gather round its head, who was in
Rome.

The political consequences implied in this reform were
not immediately manifested. At first there was nothing to
be seen but a renaissance of the ascetic life at Cluny, while
in all parts of the country princes and bishops called upon
the monks to regenerate the abbeys in their territories.
From the middle of the 10th century the reform spread
through the whole of France, and into Italy, Flanders, and
Lotharingia—whence, at the beginning of the 11th century,
it overflowed into Germany. And wherever it made its way
there was an increase of piety—of the outward piety which
consists, above all, in obedience to religion, in respecting
the feasts of the Church, in resigning oneself wholly and in
all things to the Church, the bride of Christ, His representative on earth, the mystical source of grace and salvation.
More knights adopted the religious life,[1] more princes died
in the monastic habit,[2] and more than ever new monasteries
were founded. There were many new foundations in the
10th and 11th centuries.

The Church was regarded as a purely superhuman institution. Men lived in an atmosphere of wonder; miracles
were matters of everyday experience. Every epidemic gave
rise to miracles. Every plague, every famine provoked extraordinary manifestations, such as the great procession of
Tournai (11th century). At Saint-Trond the annual prod-
uct of the offerings of the faithful surpassed all the other
revenues of the monastery. The building of the new church
at Cologne having been decided upon, the people volun-
tarily carted thither the stones and columns brought down
the Rhine. The "peace of God" which interrupted the

---

[1] Pippin, who became Abbot of Stavelot.
[2] Godefroid le Barbu, Duc d'Ardenne.

private wars on the occasion of the great annual feasts was one of the results of the extraordinary influence which the Church exerted over men's thoughts and feelings. But the riots which broke out in the 11th century to mark the popular disapproval of married priests were also the direct result of this influence.

There were plenty of conservative thinkers who were alarmed by the new dispensation. Egbert of Liége and Sigebert of Gembloux considered that the monks were going too far: they were dismayed by the arrogant and absolute nature of their opinions. And such feelings were at first very general among the Imperialist clergy. Gérard of Cambrai refused to introduce the "peace of God" in his diocese. Yet all the noblest minds, all the purest hearts turned to the new movement as to a great ideal. And no one dared to oppose it, for that would have been to make war on God Himself.

The power of the movement has left its traces to this day. It was then that the first great churches were built; it was then that religious art began to make temples too vast for the people, but still too small for the Divine Majesty.[3] The 11th century was an extraordinary period of church-building, the point of departure of the great schools of Western architecture, which hitherto had always been dominated by Byzantium and Ravenna. It also demonstrated the enormous increase of the Church's fortune. As regards the monasteries especially the 10th and 11th centuries were *par excellence* the age of donations. Their wealth naturally enabled them to augment their social influence, to increase their almsgiving, their protection of the poor, etc.

It must once more be noted that while the Church was a sacerdotal caste, and also, more and more, like the nobility, a military caste, it was none the less open to all. A serf could not enter the nobility, but he could enter the Church. He had only to go to school and learn Latin. As soon as he had the tonsure he was *clericus,* and in the prestige that enveloped his class the recollection of his origin was ef-

[3] The Abbaye aux Hommes and the Abbaye aux Dames at Caen; the cathedrals of Tournai, Spire, etc.

faced. Every man, however poor, might be said to carry a bishop's crozier in his pack. From above the clergy might seem to be a closed corporation; but nothing could have been more democratic than its recruitment from below. We must not forget that Gregory VII was the son of a peasant. Later on there would be a change. But whenever there was a renewal of faith in the Church, manifesting itself by a reform, it was accompanied by the regeneration of the Church by the people. This was very notable among the Cluniacs; which was one of the causes of their success.

In short, it was in the 10th and 11th centuries that the Church finally conquered the privileged situation that it retained until the end of the *ancien régime*. Clerics were then exempted from the civil courts, and the ecclesiastical tribunals extended their competence to all civil matters touching the religious life: whether because, like marriage, they were essentially dominated by the sacrament, or because, like contracts, they were accompanied by an oath which made them religious acts.

We see, then, that as it grew weaker the Carolingian State ceased to go hand in hand with the Church, its ally. The Church suffered for the moment, and the secure position of its upper hierarchy, from the Pope to the bishops, was shaken, except in Germany. But the enfeeblement of the Church which resulted was atoned for by complete liberty, and by an orientation of the religious sentiment which, troubling no more about the things of this world, turned exclusively heavenwards. The monks, and above all the Cluniacs, were the propagators of these new tendencies. They had a twofold result: on the one hand, the Church, being the necessary medium of salvation, on concerning itself exclusively with the eschatological motives, obtained an ascendancy over men's souls which it had never before enjoyed. On the other hand, the new tendencies conferred upon it an extraordinary strength, by causing it to reject all tutelage, all secular meddling in its affairs, as an affront to its purity. Lastly, its prestige brought it enormous wealth, in land, in alms, in privileges.

The whole movement evolved outside Rome and apart from the Papacy. But it was bound to reach Rome, suddenly giving to St. Peter's successor—degraded by feudal intrigues and party conflicts, the impotent protégé of the Emperor—the control over this enormous force, which was working for him and awaiting the moment when it should act in obedience to his command.

CHAPTER II

The War of Investitures

1. *The Empire and the Papacy since Henry III* (1039)

By restoring the fallen Empire in 962—the Empire, debased
by its last rulers, and since the year 915 without any ruler
at all—Otto had undoubtedly intended to revive the Carolingian tradition. On receiving the crown from the hands of
John XII, and assuming the title of Emperor of the Romans
(*Romanorum imperator*), he conferred upon himself the
rôle of the temporal head of Christianity, which was the
very essence of the Imperial dignity. The power which he
assumed was a universal power, universal as obedience to
the Church. But what a contrast between that which was
and that which should have been! Under Charlemagne, under Louis the Pious, even under Charles the Fat, the Empire
included almost the whole of the West; its actual extent,
we may say, coincided with its universality. Otto, on the
other hand, reigned only over Germany and Italy. In reality, the Empire as he founded it, and as it continued to
be after his day, consisted merely of a constellation of
States, to which, from Conrad's reign, was added the kingdom of Burgundy, acquired by cession from its last king,
Rudolph III (1033). While it possessed the title, it had no
longer the reality of Christian universality.

Nor had it preserved that intimate union with the Papacy, that collaboration of the spiritual and the temporal
power in the government of the world, which lay at the

basis of the Carolingian conception of empire, and constituted its majesty. Under the new Emperors the Pope was
either in open rebellion against the monarch who should
have been his ally, or he was his creature, with neither influence nor prestige.

Otto's dream of renewing the mystical marriage of the
Papacy and the Empire was cruelly dispelled. The mosaic
of St. John Lateran had become a lie. The Pope, in the new
order of things, played so subordinate a part that the King
of Germany, even before his coronation in Rome, assumed
the title of King of the Romans, thus indicating his right to
the crown which the Pope, like a sort of master of cere-
monies, set upon his head, and which he could not dream
of refusing.

Henceforth, in fact, the Imperial dignity was merely an
appendage, a consequence of the German monarchy. It was
the King of Germany, the king recognized and accepted by
the German princes alone—for the princes of Italy and Burgundy never took part in his election—who bore the title of
Emperor. But the Empire—and here we find ourselves in
the presence of tradition—although it belonged to the King
of Germany, was by no means a German Empire. Debased
though it was, its universality prevented it from becoming
nationalized. Being Roman, it could not become the property of any nation. Just as Charlemagne and his successors
were not Emperors of the Franks, so Otto and those who
followed him were not Emperors of the Germans. Instead
of Germany having nationalized the Empire to her own advantage, her kings, one may say, by the very fact that they
knew themselves to be Emperors designate, denationalized
themselves to her detriment. Their mission, from the first
day of their reign, was out of proportion to their country:
exceeding it and reducing it to no more than a part of the
whole over which they reigned. In short, the new Emperors
were condemned to occupy the unprecedented situation
of being neither universal sovereigns nor German sovereigns. In the one case, reality was the obstacle; in the other,
tradition.

Down to the end of the 12th century they were incontestably the most powerful of the continental monarchs, and

yet, when we come to consider them closely, we quickly perceive that their strength was more apparent than actual. The Imperial territory has the appearance, at first sight, of a vast, imposing mass, containing in itself all the conditions of a formidable expansion. Washed on the north by the North Sea and the Baltic, in the south it extended to the shores of the Adriatic, and it was seemingly destined, by the possession of Italy and the shores of Provence, which it had acquired with the kingdom of Burgundy, one day to dominate the Mediterranean. Unfortunately, it did not and it could not constitute a State. The power of the Emperors was based, after all, only on the Church, or rather, on the episcopal principalities, whose extent and resources each of the Emperors, after Otto, had taken pains to augment, and whose incumbents they appointed from among their loyal followers. It was from these principalities that they drew the better part of their revenues and their military contingents. As for the lay princes, in proportion as the feudal evolution favoured by the economic causes responsible for propagating the domainal institution made its way into Germany, they became, as in France, more and more independent; but unlike the King of France, the Emperor possessed no dynastic territory, no principality of his own, whose soil and whose inhabitants belonged to him, and where he felt that he was on firm ground. He had no capital; and he wandered about the Empire, an eternal traveller, sometimes beyond the Alps, sometimes in Saxony, Swabia, or Franconia. And naturally, this wandering power had no secular administration. There was and there could be no such thing; for the economic conditions which had ruined the Carolingian administration still existed, and were still producing their inevitable results. Conrad II was obliged formally to recognize the hereditary character of the fief. The parcelling out of the Empire into principalities was more accentuated with each succeeding reign. And the further it was carried, the more truly could it be said that the Emperor could really count on no one but the bishops.

We must not exaggerate the power which he derived from them. Actually it was not very great. It sufficed to make him more powerful than any individual prince; it was not enough to enable him to intervene beyond his frontiers and impose his will upon the foreigner.

Partially subdued by Otto I, under Otto III the Slavs rebelled, and from that time no fresh attempt was made to force Christianity upon them, or subject them to German hegemony. This too, since the end of the 10th century, had been declining in the countries of the north. It was not the Emperors, but the Danish princes of England who introduced Christianity into Denmark (during the reign of Canute the Great, 1018), into Norway (under Olaf the Saint, 1016), and into Sweden (under Olaf the Child, 1006). Bohemia and Hungary had completely shaken off the dependence which Otto I had imposed on them for a time. In the West the situation was equally unpromising. After the death of Otto II there was no longer any question claiming the least pre-eminence over the kings of France. The acquisition of Burgundy by Conrad II was a proof of the weakness rather than the strength of the Empire, for it signified only a nominal enlargement. The German sovereigns never attempted to rule over the country; they left it so completely to its own devices that the inhabitants did not even realize that they had passed under the sovereignty of a German dynasty. On the western frontier of the kingdom of Germany, Lotharingia, which had been forcibly annexed in 925, was still turbulent and discontented, and would evidently break its fetters, despite the loyalty of the bishops of Liége, Utrecht, and Cambrai, if only the feudal princes could induce the prudent Capetians to support their rebellion. The misadventures of Henry III, who, after years of conflict, could neither suppress their rebellion against him —for they had rebelled under the leadership of Duke Godfrey the Bearded—nor even force the Count of Flanders, Baldwin V, who had deliberately defied him, to lay down his arms, leave no room for doubt that the Empire would soon have succumbed if its internal troubles had been complicated by the necessity of waging war beyond the frontiers. Fortunately the old enemies of the Empire in the East—the Slavs, Danes, Bohemians and Hungarians— were neighbours no less friendly than the kings of France. In the 11th century Bohemia and Poland were at war. The

Emperors did not meddle in their conflict, apart from endeavouring, by political intrigues, to profit by them.

It was thanks to the security which he enjoyed as far as his neighbours were concerned, a security which he wisely did nothing to compromise, that the Emperor was able to employ such forces as he possessed in his endless Italian enterprises. Every coronation in Rome necessitated a military expedition, and it was only by fighting his way that the Emperor could reach St. Peter's. Once there, he could rely on the bishops of his own appointment; but the lay feudality and the Roman factions did not accept the German yoke, and took advantage of every least occasion to rebel against it. Italy gave the Emperor nothing but fatigue, anxiety and danger, but being Emperor he could not renounce it, although the burden paralysed and exhausted him. In the beginning the conquest of the entire peninsula had appeared indispensable. The Byzantines and the Arabs were then contending for the South. Otto II attempted to subdue them, but his disastrous defeat at Rossano (982) was at all events a salutary lesson for his successors. They no longer risked such perilous adventures: so that Sicily, Apulia and Calabria, which the Emperors would not attempt to conquer, fell, before their eyes, into the hands of the Normans: a paradoxical spectacle.

The story of the foundation of the Norman State in the south of Italy reads like a *chanson de gestes*. This extraordinary episode gave striking proof of the military strength of the Northern chivalry, and was a prelude to those two even more astonishing episodes: the conquest of England and the first Crusade.

In 1016, when the Saracens were besieging Salerno, forty Norman knights, returning from a pious pilgrimage to the Holy Land, passed that way, following the customary route (for the pilgrims used to cross Italy to Bari, where they embarked for Constantinople), took advantage of this opportunity of breaking a lance in the name of Christ. It was a wonderful country, and the state of anarchy in which they found it—attacked by the infidels and rebelling against the Byzantines—held a promise of profitable adventure. Normandy soon had wind of the matter, and little companies of younger sons, or warriors in search of loot, set out to join their compatriots. They took service indiscriminately with all the disputing parties, which bid against one another for the swords of these formidable warriors. It mattered nothing to them whether they fought against Byzantium or for it; since gain was their only motive. About 1030 one of them, Raoul, had already acquired such a position that Prince Pandolfo of Capua gave him, as fief, the county of Arezzo. The Normans had now won a foothold in the country; they were soon to take complete possession of it. In 1042 one of their leaders, Guillaume, was proclaimed Count of Apulia. It was too late to resist these auxiliaries, who had now become conquerors on their own account. Pope Leo IX, to whom the Prince of Benevento had appealed for assistance, marched against them with a body of German troops, who were defeated, leaving the Pope a prisoner in the hands of the Normans (1053). Meanwhile, Robert Guiscard installed himself in Calabria, and in 1057 inherited the county of Apulia.[1]

Between the pontificates of Leo IX and Nicholas II the attitude of Rome toward the Normans underwent a complete transformation. The schism between the Latin and Greek Churches, which had so long been threatening, became definitive in 1054, after which date the Pope was directly interested in the expulsion from Italy of the few Byzantine troops which still remained there.

On the other hand, the nature of the Pope's relations with the Emperor Henry III foreboded a serious conflict in the near future. It was therefore not surprising that he should conclude a close alliance with his enterprising neighbours in the South, and that he should favour their expansion.

[1] The story of these Normans offers a convincing proof that the south of Italy was economically more advanced than northern Europe. The princes of the country hired the Normans as mercenaries, and in this anarchical region—for it was divided into a score of petty and hostile States—they went to work much as the great military companies attempted to do in the 14th century. They were pure mercenaries, who carved out principalities for themselves. It was because there was money in the country that they were able to obtain immediate reinforcements from Normandy.

In 1059—though he was really disposing of territory which did not belong to him—he gave Capua as fief to Richard of Arezzo, and to Robert Guiscard, Apulia, Calabria and Sicily. Two years later Guiscard seized Messina, and thirty years later still the island was completely liberated from the Musulman invasion. The last of the Byzantine outposts in Italy were similarly conquered. Bari and the Lombard duchies were annexed (1071); and then, not content with having expelled the Greeks from the peninsula, Robert attempted to gain a footing on the Adriatic coast, seizing Durazzo and sending expeditions into Thessaly. His death in 1085 interrupted these plans for the time being. Nevertheless, they proved the warlike vitality of the new State, which, thanks to the astonishing energy of its adventurous conquerors, had succeeded in installing itself at this southernmost point of Europe, where for 500 years, despite the Lombards, the Carolingians, the German Emperors and the Musulmans, Byzantium had succeeded in maintaining an outlet toward the West. What none of the successive masters of Italy had been able to do the Normans had accomplished in less than fifty years. The State which they had founded at this meeting-point of three different civilizations was very soon to assume a political importance of the first order, when it would play an unexpected part in the destinies of the Empire.

Nothing could show more clearly how deceptive was the Empire's appearance of strength than the completely passive attitude of Henry III in respect of the young and enterprising power which was growing up upon his frontiers. For him there could be no Italian question; he was not strong enough. It was enough for him that he had arrived at a provisional solution of the question of the Papacy.

The situation of Rome, at the time of his coronation, was more deplorable than ever. While the Cluniac reformation was taking hold on men's souls, and the Church was aspiring, in all its purest and most ardent elements, to assure its spiritual domination by a more fervent piety and a stricter discipline, the see of St. Peter offered the scandalous spectacle of three Popes quarrelling or bargaining for the tiara. Full of zeal for the religious reformation, Henry wished to prevent once and for all the repetition of those incessant conflicts and feudal intrigues which had for so long prevented the Papacy from fulfilling its mission. A synod which he convoked at Sutri deposed the three rival pontiffs, and the Romans were bidden to appoint a candidate chosen by the monarch—the Bishop of Bamberg, Suidger, who assumed the title of Clement II (1046). The other Popes who succeeded him during Henry's reign—Damasius II (1048–1049), Leo IX (1049–1054) and Victor III (1055–1057) —were, like him, Germans, or at any rate subjects of the Empire, and imposed upon the Romans by the Imperial will. Further, they were all excellent pontiffs, and convinced Clunisians, who restored to the Papacy the prestige and influence which the Church had wished to see it recover. But it recovered them only in violating, by a flagrant contradiction, the very principles by which it was henceforth inspired. True, the tyranny of the counts of Tusculum no longer falsified the pontifical elections for the benefit of unworthy favourites; but was not the intervention of the Emperor, however beneficial its results might be, a direct encroachment upon the domain of canonical law, and, to speak plainly, a flagrant act of simony? Henry had not realized that in restoring the Papacy he would inevitably be provoking a conflict between it and the Empire. It was evident that by choosing his Popes from the ranks of the Clunisian clergy he was hastening the moment when his interference would be regarded, by the very Popes who owed the triple crown to him, as an insupportable and criminal usurpation. Leo IX, having been appointed by Henry, was seized with conscientious scruples, and had himself reelected by the Romans in accordance with the traditional forms. Sooner or later the dormant conflict was bound to become manifest. The unexpected death of the Emperor in 1056 brought about the crisis.

2. The Conflict

His successor, Henry IV, was a child of six, under whose reign Germany was for a long time paralysed, in the first place by a stormy regency, and then by a dangerous revolt of the Saxons. Rome took advantage of the circumstances. On the death of Stephen IX (1058) the aristocracy, reverting to tradition, hastened to proclaim one of its faithful supporters, Benedict X. But times were altered; the series of the feudal Popes—and also that of the Imperial Popes—was brought to an end by the election of Nicholas II, who owed the pontificate to the party of reform. The Church had decided to throw off all tutelage—that of Germany no less than that of the Roman barons. The name chosen by the new pontiff recalled the Nicholas who, in the 9th century, had so vigorously proclaimed the superiority of the spiritual weapon. The Church could not more plainly have indicated its intention of effecting a new orientation.

During the fifteen years which had elapsed since the pontificate of Clement II, the Papacy, thanks to the nominations of Henry III, had not only recovered its position at the head of the Church, but was regarded with a veneration and had acquired an influence such as it had never yet enjoyed. The religious renewal which had been accomplished outside the Papacy was now directing the prayers and the devotions of the whole Church, clergy and faithful, toward the successor of St. Peter. The immense moral force which had been evoked by the asceticism of the monks had at last given Rome the head for whom she was waiting, and who was assured beforehand of her enthusiastic obedience. The loyalty to Christ which had inspired men's souls was now confounded with loyalty to His Vicar. When he spoke his words would be heard and revered to the ends of Catholic Christendom. And the Catholic world had not only increased its fervour: it had also extended its area. Since the beginning of the 11th century Christianity had spread into Denmark, Sicily, and Norway, and even remote Iceland, and although the Papacy had taken no part in these new conquests it was towards the Papacy that they now gravitated. Never had Rome possessed so vast a spiritual domain, so potent an authority. Her definitive rupture with the Greek Church in 1054 had shown what confidence she had in her own strength.

How could she continue to tolerate the simoniacal protection of the Emperor? How continue to allow him to dispose of the tiara on behalf of the German bishops, humbling her universal power to benefit the sovereign of a single nation? The minority of Henry IV enabled her to shake off the yoke. In 1059 Nicholas II, in order henceforth to guard the nomination of the Popes from any alien influence, confided it to the College of Cardinals. Thus, at one stroke, he put an end to the tumultuous elections which had caused the long decline of the Papacy, and to the interference of the Emperor. Henceforth the election of the Vicar of Christ would be a matter for the Church alone, which would choose him in peace and liberty. A special clause in the Bull decreed that the election, contrary to the tradition hitherto followed, need not necessarily take place in Rome: the Cardinals were free to assemble where they chose if they thought themselves unsafe in Rome at the moment of the Consistorium.

The conflict between the Papacy and the Empire may be dated from this reform. It was henceforth inevitable, and Nicholas II had no illusions as to the future. It was not due merely to chance that he concluded a treaty of alliance with the Normans in the very year in which the right of electing the Pope was conferred upon the Cardinals.

At the same time the Pope took measures to prohibit the marriage of priests, and in prevention of simony, which showed that he could henceforth count upon the support of the masses. In the north of Italy the people rebelled against the Imperial bishops who attempted to disobey the orders of Rome. However, the insurgence of the *pataria*— the *canaille*—as the princes of the Church and their supporters disdainfully called their enemies—was not exclusively due to religious motives. Under the influence of reviving commerce a new social class, the bourgeoisie, was growing up in the Lombard cities, and it took advantage of the motive provided by piety in order to rebel against the bishops, whose administration took no account of its new requirements.

It was the Bishop of Lucca, the protector of the *patarias*, who in 1061 succeeded to Nicholas II, taking the name of Alexander II. Thus the first election of a pontiff by the Cardinals called to the throne of St. Peter a declared anti-

Imperialist. Henry IV was as yet in no position to interfere. His governors were reduced to supporting the Antipope Cadaloüs, whom the feudal party in Rome had set up in opposition to Alexander, and who almost immediately disappeared. In 1073 Gregory VII succeeded to Alexander, and at last the war broke out.

The new Pope, since the advent of Nicholas II, had been the inspirer and the private counsellor of his predecessors. When at last he succeeded them, he was firmly resolved to adopt, in respect of the Empire, an attitude which would either lead to war, or would compel the first sovereign of the West to recognize the supremacy of Rome over the temporal power. In 1075 he solemnly condemned, under penalty of excommunication, the investiture of any ecclesiastical function by the secular authority.

Nothing, of course, could be more consistent with the principles of the Church, but nothing could have been more impossible for the Emperor to concede. Since the reign of Otto I, in proportion as the secular princes became more completely feudalized, the Imperial power depended more and more upon the bishops. Reign after reign, the monarchs had accumulated their donations of territory around the episcopal sees, in order to make the bishops more and more powerful. But they had done so, obviously, on condition that they themselves should appoint the bishops and invest them in their office. By giving them the crozier and the ring, the emblems of their function, the Emperor showed the bishops that they were bishops only by the Imperial will—that it was to the Emperor that they owed the government of their diocese and their principality. To give obedience to the Pope, to return to the canonical prescription, and consequently to allow the chapters to appoint the bishops, and therefore to invest them in their secular fiefs, would have been equivalent to placing in unknown and possibly hostile hands the power which the Empire had conferred upon the prelates—in its own interests, not in theirs. Were they to tell the Emperor that he must renounce the power of investiture? But that would have been to tell him that he must henceforth be a nonentity, since he would have been deprived of the very foundation of his power. Gregory

VII was never under any illusion in this respect. But what did the power of the Emperor matter to him? Together with all the most radical partisans of the religious reformation, he regarded the temporal power merely as a source of division. The Church alone was divine, the Church alone could guide man to salvation, and the Church was united in the Pope, "whose name alone could be uttered in the churches and whose feet all kings should kiss."

For these reasons Gregory has been regarded as a sort of mystical revolutionary, an Ultramontane endeavouring to ruin the State. But this is to introduce modern ideas into a conflict where they are entirely out of place. To begin with, in the case of Gregory there was no trace of Ultramontanism. Ecclesiastical discipline was still very far from being dependent on Rome. He made no claim whatever to nominate the bishops. What he wanted was to ensure that the Church should no longer be defiled by secular meddling. As for his conflict with the State, what does the accusation mean? The Empire was not a State. It was actually governed not by the Emperor but by the princes. As we have seen, there was no administration; nothing in the shape of what we must call, for the want of a better term, a central power, giving it a hold over its inhabitants. If the Emperor's power was diminished what injury was inflicted on society? None, since it regarded him with indifference; since it was not he who defended and protected it. No catastrophe could follow from the victory of the Pope, and the Church was bound to benefit by it. If we are to understand the situation we must regard it from this point of view. We must not forget that this was the heart of the feudal period, and that social and political evolution were on the side of these princes, who, as we have seen, were the real organizers of society. And they were on the side of the Pope. The feudality was working for him, just as he, without intending to do so, was working for it. A little while ago it was the rising bourgeoisie that was taking the part of Rome; now it was the feudal magnates. Here what we call the State is not secular society, but the royal power, subjecting the Church and diverting it from its mission in order to support itself.

In the beginning, this exploitation of the Church by the State goes back to the Carolingian tradition. Otto I did no more than somewhat complicate the ecclesiastical policy of Charlemagne. In reality what Gregory was attacking was the political conception that made the Emperor the equal of the Pope. For the alliance of the two powers he substituted, in the affairs of the Church, the subordination of one to the other. Once more, it must not be said that it attacked the State. It would be more correct to say that he deprived it of its clerical character. After all, by depriving the Emperor of the investiture of the bishops he was accelerating the secularization of the State, and this secularization was intensified after his death. What if the Empire had been triumphant? The theocracy would have held the power; the priests would have governed in the name of the prince. Gregory, on the other hand, withdrew the priests from the government. What he really did was to launch the State on the path of secularization.

He did it without realizing what he was doing; or perhaps we may say that he did it in contempt of the laymen whom he did not wish to meddle in the affairs of the Church. But he knew very well that these laymen were in the Church and wished to remain there. Henry IV himself was a convinced Catholic. And it was precisely this that constituted the strength of the Pope and the weakness of his adversary. Against the Pope the Emperor could employ no means but those of the Church. It did not and could not occur to him to oppose the Pope face to face, in the name of the rights which he held—from whom?—From God. But the Pope was God's representative on earth. He was this so completely that the Emperor could not dispense with the Pope at his coronation. There was only one way of resisting the Pope within the Church, and that was to get the Church to declare that the Pope was unworthy of his office.

And this is what Henry did. He had at last defeated the rebellious Saxons. He was free. There were still enough bishops in Germany who were devoted to the sovereign, and discontented, to make it possible for him to act. He assembled them at Worms, and on January 24th, 1076, he induced them to declare that Gregory was unworthy of the

Papacy. Only twenty years earlier Henry III had still appointed the Popes; but what a radical transformation in the situation of the two powers had been effected since then!

Conservators, when they are not men of genius, imagine that it is enough to restore the past without taking account of the present. To attempt the deposition of a Pope by a few German bishops after a Nicholas II and an Alexander II testified to a complete ignorance of the spirit of the age. Nothing could have served the cause of Gregory better than this pretension on the part of the King of Germany to dispose, as the master, of the head of Catholic Christendom. He replied by excommunicating Henry, and absolving from their oath all who had sworn fidelity to him. It then became evident that the decision of the Synod of Worms was not accepted even by the princes of Germany. For if they had considered it valid they need have paid no attention to the excommunication of the king. But the response of one and all to the sentence of Rome was to abandon Henry. In order to avoid a general revolt the king did not hesitate to repudiate the judgement of his own bishops and to humiliate himself before the Pope whom he had just had declared unworthy. On January 28th, 1077, he appeared before the Pope, in the garb of a penitent, at the fortress of Canossa, and obtained his pardon. But Gregory reserved to himself the right to intervene between the Emperor and the princes. As Henry had resumed the royal title without waiting for their agreement, a number of them had given the crown to Rudolph of Swabia. A civil war broke out. Henry, feeling that he was stronger than his adversary, recovered confidence, and with incorrigible obstinacy treated Gregory with flat defiance, reverting to the means which had already served him so ill. At Brixen a synod convoked in obedience to his orders gave the Papacy to the archbishop Guibert of Ravenna. A second and more solemn excommunication was the reply to this fresh proclamation. But Rudolph had just been killed in battle near Merseburg (Grona), and Henry, taking his Pope with him, marched on Rome. This, before his day, had been a means that had never failed to subdue the feudal and turbulent Popes of the old dispensation. But this time the Germans entered Rome only to suffer a fresh humiliation. Gregory, having withdrawn to Castel Sant'Angelo, was impregnable. All that Henry could do was hastily to consecrate Guibert, who, taking the name of Clement III, placed the Imperial crown upon his head. And then the successor of Charlemagne beat a hasty retreat, for Robert Guiscard and the Normans were approaching the city. Gregory accepted their hospitality and withdrew to Salerno. There he died on May 25th, 1085, uttering the famous words which have since then comforted so many exiles: *Dilexi justiciam et odivi iniquitatem, propterea quod morior in exilio.*

Clement III occupied the Lateran palace. But what did men care for this intruder, who was acknowledged, as a matter of duty, only by a few German bishops? For the Church, Rome was wherever the true Pope was: the elect of the Cardinals, the successor of Gregory. Never was the Papacy so powerful as during these years of exile: powerful not by reason of its acknowledged authority, an authority accepted and feared as under an Innocent III, but in the enthusiastic veneration and devotion of the faithful. It was a wandering Pope, far from his capital—Urban II—who in 1095 sent forth a Europe tremulous with the love of Christ to the conquest of Jerusalem. And while the Pope thus gathered Europe about him, the Emperor, now in Italy, now in Germany, dragged out a reign that was troubled by rebellion, treason, flight, and the vicissitudes of fortune; wearing himself out and destroying what little prestige remained to the Imperial power in the civil war which his son Conrad, and then his son Henry V, waged against him: a war which doomed him also to die in exile, at Liége, in 1106, where Bishop Otbert, one of the last to be faithful to him, watched over the last days of his tragic career. But his death did not settle the question of the investitures which had provoked the conflict. Henry V no longer claimed to dispose of the tiara, and no longer ventured to appoint Antipopes. At last a clear-cut question came up for discussion, and since the Emperor now acknowledged the Pope as head of the Church—and how could he have done otherwise in the time of the Crusades?—it was finally solved by the first of those concordats which the Papacy concluded with the secular power: the Concordat of Worms (1122). The Emperor renounced the right of investiture by crozier and ring, and accepted the liberty of ecclesiastical elections. In Germany the bishop-elect was to receive the investiture of his fiefs (*régales*) from the sceptre before consecration; in other parts of the Empire (Italy and Burgundy) after consecration. There was thus a distinction between the spiritual power, in respect of which the Emperor could no longer interfere, and the temporal power, which he continued to confer, but which he could not refuse without a conflict. As for the election of bishops by the chapters, these would now be influenced not by the Emperor but by the neighbouring princes. In reality, the Imperial Church was in ruins; there remained only a feudal Church. The Empire suffered thereby; the Papacy gained in prestige; but the discipline of the Church was not improved; on the contrary. Every election was bound to be a conflict of influences, and while there was no longer simony on the part of the Emperor there was still pressure and intimidation on the part of the magnates. The true solution would have been that of Pascal II, according to which the bishops would have abandoned their fiefs; but to this the Emperor would not give his consent, for the vast territorial wealth of the Church would have passed into the hands of the princes. In the last resort, the quarrel of the investitures ended in the triumph of the feudality over the Church. There were no more such learned and cultured bishops of the Empire as Notger, Wazon, and Bernhard of Worms. Elected by chapters in which the younger sons of the nobles predominated, they were now entirely feudal, and with them the dominating influence was the temporal. In seeking to liberate the clergy from secular influences the Church had made it more than ever subordinate to them.

CHAPTER III

The Crusade

1. Causes and Conditions

The conquest of Sicily in the 9th century, completed in 902 by the capture of Taormina, was the last advance of Islam in the West. From this time forward it made no further conquests. Spain, like the States which had sprung up on the African coast—Morocco, Algiers, Kairouan, Barka, and even Egypt—had lost its primitive power of expansion. The Musulmans no longer attacked the Christians; they dwelt beside them, in a civilization that was more advanced and refined, and had now become less vigorous. They asked only one thing: to be left in peace, and, of course, in possession of the Mediterranean, the whole of whose southern and eastern shores they now occupied.

Unfortunately for them, this was impossible. If they wished to live in security, they should have done what the Romans had done of old: they should have provided themselves with defensible frontiers. Spain was theirs, but they did not hold it up to the Pyrenees. All the islands of the Tyrrhenian Sea were theirs, but neither Provence nor Italy. And how could they retain Sicily without Italy? One might say that they stopped too soon, as though in fatigue. There was something incomplete about the present state of their domain. Nothing could have been more difficult to defend than their advanced positions in Europe. It was inevitable that their neighbours should attack them, being poorer than they, and inspired, since the 10th century, by an ever-increasing religious enthusiasm.

It was in Spain that the counter-attack began. The petty Christian principalities of the North, whose soil was poor and infertile, naturally tended to enlarge their territory in the absence of natural frontiers. The ancient march of Spain had achieved independence during the Carolingian dislocation, as the county of Barcelona, and later, Catalonia. In the mountains various little kingdoms had been constituted: Navarre, the Asturias, Leon, and finally Castile and Aragon. Portugal, a dependency of Castile, established itself as an independent kingdom at the period of the First Crusade, under the rule of the Burgundian prince Henry († 1112). Between these petty states and the Musulmans there were continual frontier wars, in which the Christians were not always victorious. At the end of the 10th century, under the Caliph Hischam II, Barcelona was destroyed (984), and also Santiago, whose Christian inhabitants were forced to remove their bells to Cordova. But after the extinction of the dynasty of the Omayyads (1031) the 11th century was marked by Christian successes. In 1057 Ferdinand of Castile advanced as far as Coimbra and forced several of the Emirs, including even the Emir of Seville, to pay him tribute. His son Alfonso VI (1072–1109) captured Toledo and Valencia and besieged Saragossa. Defeated by the Almoravides of Morocco, whom the Emir of Seville had called to the rescue in 1086, he was checked in his victorious progress, after having advanced with his army as far as the Straits of Gibraltar. But already the progress of the Christians was very appreciable; once it was no longer possible to dislodge them from the mountains they would make their way to Gibraltar.

In Italy events were more decisive. The Byzantines, who had not defended Sicily, were still holding the south of the peninsula when the arrival of the Normans replaced their domination, and that of Islam, by a new, vigorous and warlike State. The conquest of Sicily, and presently that of Malta, meant that the Christians possessed two strongholds in the midst of the Musulman Mediterranean. Moreover, the Pisans had taken part in the war. For some time they had been fighting on the sea against the Moors of Sardinia, whom they expelled in 1016. They played an active part in the conquest of Sicily. The Duomo of Pisa is a sort of *Arc de Triomphe* in honour of the forcing of Palermo Harbour in 1067. Genoa too was beginning to send out expeditions and was harassing the coast of Africa. There was no commerce as yet, but rather privateering, piracy, warfare; the Christian ideal, in the minds of these sailors, being combined with the notion of profit.

Generally speaking, then, from the middle of the 11th century, the Christian Occident was assuming, in a series of detached efforts, the offensive against Islam. But this offensive had nothing in common with a religious war. These wars of conquest would have taken place even between peoples of the same religion if the circumstances and the geographical situation had tended to provoke them. For that matter, the Normans quite impartially attacked both Byzantines and Musulmans.

If we take a general view of the matter, the Crusade, as an episode of world history, was evidently connected with these happenings, being a continuation of the offensive against Islam. But it had only one feature in common with them: the fact that it was directed against Islam. In all other respects—in its origins, its purpose, its tendencies and its organization—it was completely different.

To begin with, it was purely and exclusively religious. In this respect it was intimately related, in respect of the spirit that inspired it, to the great wave of Christian fervour of which the War of Investitures was another manifestation. It was further related to this movement by the fact that the Pope, who had instigated and waged this war, was also the instigator and organizer of the Crusade.

Its objective, to be exact, was not Islam. If the Crusaders had merely wished to repel the Mohammedans they would have had to help the Spaniards and the Normans. Their objective was the Holy Places and Sepulchre of Christ in Jerusalem. This had been in the hands of the Musulmans ever since the 9th century, but no one had paid much attention to the fact. At this period, under the Arab government, the Christians were not molested, and their piety was not as yet unduly susceptible. But just as it was becoming susceptible, towards the end of the 11th century, Syria was seized by the Seldjukid Turks, and they, in their fanaticism, did molest the pilgrims, who broadcast everywhere their indignation at the insult offered to Christ. Now, among the pilgrims there were many princes: for example, Robert the Frisian. It was not, of course, the tales of the humble pilgrims (and of these not many can have reached Jerusalem) but those of the knights and the princes that roused public opinion.

And while the pilgrims complained, the Emperor of Byzantium made certain proposals. The situation of the Empire, since the Seldjuks had appeared in the Near East, was most precarious. In the 10th century the Macedonian Emperors, Nicephorus Phocas, John Tzimisces and Basil II, had largely repulsed Islam, advancing the frontier to the Tigris. But the Seldjuks, in the 11th century, reconquered Armenia and Asia Minor. When Alexius Comnenus ascended the throne (1081) only the coasts were still Greek. There was no fleet, and the army was inadequate. Alexius thought of the Occident. To whom should he address himself, if not to the Pope? The Pope alone could influence the whole of the Western world. But he could be moved only by a religious motive. In 1095 Alexius sent an embassy to Urban II, and the Council of Piacenza, hinting at the possibility of a return to the Catholic communion. Some months later, on November 27th, 1095, at Clermont, the Crusade was enthusiastically proclaimed by the crowd that had flocked about the sovereign pontiff.

The Crusade was essentially the work of the Papacy; as regards both its universal character and its religious nature. It was undertaken not by the States, nor yet by the people, but by the Papacy; its motive was wholly spiritual, divorced from any temporal preoccupation: the conquest of the Holy Places. Only those who set forth without the spirit of lucre in their hearts could share in the indulgences granted by the Pope. Not until the first wars of the French Revolution did history again show combatants so completely careless of any other consideration than devotion to an ideal.

But religious enthusiasm, and the authority of the Pope,

could not of themselves have promoted so vast an under-
taking if the social condition of Europe had not rendered
it possible. The coincidence of these three factors was
necessary: an ardent religious faith, the preponderant
power of the Papacy, and favouring social conditions. A
century earlier the thing would have been impossible, as
it would have been a century later. The ideal realized in
the 11th century persisted, as an ideal motive, under very
different conditions, becoming less and less effective. It survived even into the Renaissance, for the Popes, in the 16th
century, still dreamed of a Crusade against the Turks. But
the true Crusade, the parent of all the others, was the First,
and this was essentially the child of the age.

To begin with, there were as yet no States. The nations
had no governments which could command them. Christianity was not yet politically divided, but could group itself as a whole around the Pope.

Further, there was a military class which was ready to
set forth at any moment: the Order of Chivalry. The army
was in being; it had only to be mustered. What it could
accomplish it had already shown, by the conquests of the
Normans in Italy and England. And it was an army that
cost nothing, since it was endowed, from father to son, by
the fiefs. There was no need to collect money for the Holy
War. It was enough to appoint the leaders and lay down
the routes to be followed. Regarded from this point of view,
the Crusade was essentially the one great feudal war, in
which the Western feudality acted in a body, and, so to
speak, of its own accord. No king took part in this Crusade.
The curious thing is that nobody gave any thought to the
kings, to say nothing of the Emperor, who was the enemy
of the Pope.

It is therefore not surprising that the Crusade recruited
its troops mainly from those countries in which the feudal
system was most advanced—from France, England, the
Low Countries, and Norman Italy. Considered from this
point of view it was above all an expedition, we will not
say of the Roman peoples, but of the Roman chivalry.

Without that chivalry the Crusade would have been impossible, for it was above all the enterprise of the knights

and the nobles. It must not be envisaged as a sort of migration of the Christian masses to Jerusalem. It was before all things an expedition of warriors, and otherwise it would merely have provided the Turks with victims to massacre. Consequently the Crusaders were by no means as numerous as is generally supposed. At the very most they numbered some tens of thousands: a comparatively enormous figure, but in no way comparable with the numbers of a mass migration.

2. *The Conquest of Jerusalem*

The expedition was carefully prepared under the direction of the Pope. Monkish propagandists were sent out in all directions; but the more worldly expedients were not neglected. However great the love of Christ, it was with men that the Papacy had to deal, and it did not hesitate, in order to "excite" them, to appeal to other than the mystical passions. The *excitatoria* who were then despatched throughout Christendom vaunted, in one breath, the quantity of relics to be found in Asia Minor, the charm and luxury of its customs, and the beauty of its women. Measures were taken on behalf of those who were setting forth: their possessions were under the guardianship of the Church; they were certain of finding them intact on their return. As for the plan of campaign, this should not present any great difficulty in view of the large numbers of Western pilgrims who had made the journey to Jerusalem. In the absence of a sufficient fleet they would have to follow the overland route. Only the Normans from Italy and the contingents from the north of the peninsula would cross the Adriatic, to disembark at Durazzo, whence they would march to Constantinople, which was the general rendezvous. There were three armies: the Lotharingians under Godfrey, who marched by way of Germany and Hungary; the Frenchmen of the North, with Robert of Normandy, brother of William II of England, Stephen of Blois and Hugues de Vermandois, brother of Philip I, the King of France, and Robert of Flanders, who went southwards by way of Italy, where they joined the Normans under

Bohemund of Tarento, the son of Robert Guiscard, and his nephew Tancred; and lastly, the Frenchmen of the South, under Raymond of Toulouse, accompanied by the legate, Bishop Adhémar of Puy, who passed through northern Italy and along the Adriatic coast. All assembled at Constantinople, where they arrived in successive groups, in the year 1096.

Bands of enthusiasts, excited by the preaching of Peter the Hermit, without leaders, without discipline, had already set forth, at the beginning of 1096, pillaging and massacring the Jews. Those of them who reached Constantinople were hurried across the Bosphorus by the Greeks and cut to pieces by the Turks.

If the Pope had hoped to bring the Greek Church into the Roman fold by means of the Crusade he was assuredly disillusioned. When the Westerners and the Greeks came into contact the antipathy between them was increased, and the gulf widened, but the mystical purpose which had made the Crusaders take up arms was achieved. After battles and fatigues and perils which are comparable to those of the retreat from Moscow, and must have been equally murderous, what was left of the army appeared at last before the walls of Jerusalem on June 7th, 1099. On July 15th the city was taken by assault, and rivers of blood were shed in the name of the God of peace and love whose sepulchre had at last been recaptured.

The result of the conquest was the establishment of petty Christian States: the kingdom of Jerusalem, of which Godfrey of Bouillon was elected sovereign under the name of Advocate of the Holy Sepulchre; the principality of Edessa, whose inhabitants had given the title of count to Baldwin, brother of Godfrey, as he marched through; and the principality of Antioch, of which Bohemund of Tarento made himself the prince after taking the city in 1098. All these were organized in accordance with feudal law, far from Europe as they were, and threatened on every side by an almost undamaged Islam. They were colonies which did not answer to any of the requirements of colonies. There was no need to establish a surplus population so far from home, no need to organize trading-posts. While the spirit of lucre was far from absent from the minds of all those who took part in the Crusade, not a single Crusader had any thought of commerce. They were actuated only by the religious ideal. But the immediate result was a commercial one. The Christians' military base, which had thus been established in the East, had of course to be revictualled. Venice, Pisa and Genoa at once undertook the task. The Crusader principalities became the objective of their fleets. The eastern Mediterranean was now in communication with the West. From this time forward Christian navigation underwent an incessant development. Those who finally derived the greatest profits from the Crusades were the middle classes of the Italian seaports. But their purpose had not been commercial. Their truest manifestation was the alliance of the military with the religious spirit in the Orders of the Templars and the Hospitallers.

As Christian establishments, the possessions of the Crusaders were extremely difficult to defend. Edessa fell no later than 1143, and a new Crusade had to be undertaken —the Second, which failed in its object. In 1187 Saladin, Sultan of Egypt, conquered Jerusalem, and it was not again recaptured.

And so the great movement of the Crusades had hardly any final result, beyond the greater activity and more rapid movement of trade on the Mediterranean. They did nothing, or very little, to make the West better acquainted with the economic and scientific progress of Islam. These became known through the intermediary of Sicily and Spain. The Crusades might at least have opened up the Greek world; but they did nothing of the kind. It was too early for the West to take an interest in the treasures that lay dormant in the Byzantine libraries. The Western world would have to wait for the moment when the refugees of the 15th century brought them to Italy. It was with the East as it was with America, discovered by the Norsemen and then forgotten, because, in the 11th century, the world had as yet no need of it.

On the whole, then, the immense effort of the Crusades had but few direct results. They did not repulse Islam, they did not recover the Greek Church, they could not even retain Jerusalem or Constantinople. On the other hand, they were of considerable importance in a domain which was totally opposed to the spirit which had inspired them: for their true result was the development of Italian maritime commerce, and, from the time of the Fourth Crusade, the establishment of the colonial empire of Venice and Genoa in the Levant. It is highly characteristic that the whole formation of Europe can be explained without a single reference to the Crusades, but for this one exception of Italy.

The Crusades, however, had yet one more consequence of a religious order. From the time of the First Crusade the Holy War was substituted for the evangelization of the non-Christian world. Henceforth it would be employed against heretics also. The heresy of the Albigenses, and later, that of the Hussites, were extirpated by means of the Holy War. As for the pagans, the methods employed against the Wends, the Prussians and the Lithuanians were characteristic of the age: the infidel had no longer to be converted, but exterminated.

BOOK FIVE

The Formation of the Bourgeoisie

CHAPTER I

The Revival of Commerce

1. *The Trade of the Mediterranean*

The economic organization which imposed itself upon
Western Europe in the course of the Carolingian epoch,
and which was preserved, in its essential features, until the
close of the 11th century, was, as we have seen, purely
agricultural. Not only did it know nothing of commerce,
but one may say that by regulating production in accordance with the needs of the producers it excluded the very
possibility of any professional commercial activity. Profit-
seeking, and indeed the very idea of profit, were foreign to
it. The cultivation of the soil assured the existence of the
family, and no one attempted to make the soil yield him a
surplus, for he would not have known what to do with it.

This does not mean that there was not in those days any
species of exchange. It was impossible for each domain to
produce every imaginable necessity; it was impossible to
dispense entirely with any sort of importation. In the
northern countries wine had necessarily to be brought from
the southern regions. Moreover, local famines were frequent, and in case of dearth the affected province did its
best to obtain help from its neighbours. Again, at reasonable
intervals there were small weekly markets which provided
for the current needs of the surrounding population. But
the importance of all these matters was purely accessory.
People traded their goods as occasion required; they did

not become traders by profession. There was no such thing as a class of merchants, nor was there a class of industrial workers. Industry was restricted to a few indispensable artisans—serfs working at the domainal "court" to supply the needs of the domain, wheelwrights dispersed about the villages, and weavers of linen or woollen stuffs for family consumption. In certain regions, as on the coast of Flanders, the quality of the wool and the conservation of the old Roman technique gave a higher quality to the products of the peasant weavers, so that there was a demand for them in the neighbouring countries. This was a speciality, just as the production of good building-stone or timber was a speciality. There was consequently a certain amount of traffic on the rivers, and this was a convenience to travellers and pilgrims. Small seaports in northern France and the Low Countries served the needs of the few travellers going to or returning from England. But if all these things had never existed the economic order would have been essentially the same. The rudiments of commercial life in the Carolingian epoch did not respond to any permanent need, or any primordial necessity. The best evidence that this was the case is the history of the unification of weights, measures and currency established by Charlemagne. By the end of the 9th century this unity had been replaced by diversity. Each territory had its own weights and measures and currency. This regression could not have taken place if there had been any appreciable amount of trade. But while these conditions obtained in the Carolingian Empire, matters were very different in the two portions of Western Europe which still belonged to the Byzantine Empire: Venice and Southern Italy. The seaports of Campania, Apulia, Calabria and Sicily continued to maintain regular relations with Constantinople. Even thus far afield the attractive power of the great city still made itself felt. Bari, Tarento, Amalfi—and until Sicily was conquered by the Musulman, Messina, Palermo and Syracuse—were regularly despatching to the Golden Horn their vessels laden with grain and wine, which returned to them with the products of Oriental manufactures. But the volume of their trade was soon exceeded by that of Venice. Founded in the lagoons by fugitives

at the time of the Lombard invasion, the refuge of the
patriarchs of Aquileia, the city was at first no more than
an agglomeration of little islands, divided one from another
by arms from the sea, the principal island being the Rialto.
The agglomeration was given the name of Venetia, which
had hitherto been applied to the coast. The arrival of the
relics of St. Mark from Alexandria, in 826, gave it a national patron. Fishing and the refining of sea-salt were at
first the principal resources of the inhabitants. For these,
of course, the market was not Italy, lying close at hand, for
Italy, congealed in the agricultural and domainal organization, had no needs; the market was the remote and vora-
cious city of Byzantium. And nothing more clearly illustrates the contrast between the two civilizations than this
orientation of Venice toward the East. The advance of
Islam in the Mediterranean, by restricting the number of
ports which fed the great city, was advantageous to the
sailors of the lagoons. On the shores of the Bosphorus the
Venetian traders were soon pre-eminent over all their competitors. This city without territory, entirely dependent on
the sea, was in some ways reminiscent of ancient Tyre. With
wealth it gained independence, and without any violent
rupture it shook off the Byzantine domination, and constituted itself, under a Doge (Duke), a merchant republic,
such as the world had never seen. From the 10th century
onwards its policy was directed exclusively by commercial
interest. We can get some idea of the wealth of Venice by
considering her strength. For the sake of her navigation she
was obliged to exercise dominion over the Adriatic, which
was troubled by the Dalmation pirates. In 1000 Doge
Pietro II Urseolo (991–1009) conquered the coast from
Venice to Ragusa, and assumed the title of Duke of Dalmatia. Venice could not allow the Normans, after the conquest of Southern Italy, to establish themselves on the
Greek coast. The Venetian fleet therefore co-operated with
the Emperor Alexis to drive Robert Guiscard out of
Durazzo. For that matter, Venice contrived to get well paid
for her collaboration. In 1082 the Venetians received the
privilege of buying and selling throughout the Byzantine
Empire without the payment of duties, and they obtained,

for residential purposes, a special quarter of Constantinople. Purely commercial, they did not hesitate to enter into
relations with their enemies. But already their vessels were
encountering new competitors in the eastern Mediterranean. In the course of the 10th century the Pisans and the
Genoese had begun to fight the Musulman pirates in the
Tyrrhenean Sea. They ended by taking possession of
Corsica and Sardinia, and the Pisans, after giving battle
on the Sicilian coast, were making bold, by the middle of
the 11th century, to harry the coast of Africa. While the
Venetians were merchants from the very beginning, the
Pisans and the Genoese remind one rather of the Christians
of Spain. Like them, they made war upon the infidel with a
passionate religious enthusiasm; a Holy War, but a very
profitable one, for the infidel was wealthy and yielded
much booty. In them religious passion and the appetite
for lucre were merged in a spirit of enterprise which we find
expressed in curiously vivid language in their ancient
chronicles. Success attending their efforts, they grew bolder,
and finally, passing the Straits of Messina, scoured the
waters of the Archipelago. But the Venetians took very
little interest in the conflict between the Cross and the
Crescent. Their object was to reserve for themselves the
market of Constantinople and the navigation of the Levant.
And their fleets did not hesitate to attack the Pisan vessels
engaged in revictualling the Crusaders.

Once the Christians were established in Palestine it was
impossible to persist in such an attitude. However un-
willingly, the Venetians had to allow the Pisan and Genoese
ships to take part in the maritime traffic between the Crusader States of the Syrian coast and the West. The continual transport of pilgrims, of military reinforcements, of
foodstuffs and munitions of all sorts, made this navigation
such an abundant source of profit that the religious spirit
which had at first inspired the seamen of the two cities
was subordinated to the commercial spirit. Before long
their ships were sailing not only to Christian ports but also
to Musulman harbours. From the 12th century onwards
there was a busy trade with Kairouan, Tunis, and Alexandria. The Pisans, in 1111, and the Genoese in 1115, ob-

tained commercial privileges in Constantinople. Venetian, Pisan and Genoese colonies were established in the commercial centres of the Levant, grouped under the jurisdiction of their national consuls. And presently the movement began to spread farther afield. Marseilles and Barcelona got busy in their turn; the Provençaux and the Catalans utilized the routes which had been opened up by the Italians. By the end of the 11th century one may say that the Mediterranean had been reconquered for Christian navigation. While the Musulmans and the Byzantines undertook their own coasting trade, the commerce between distant parts was entirely in the hands of the Westerners. Their ships were to be seen everywhere in the seaports of Asia and Africa, while in the Italian, Catalonian or Provençal harbours only Greek or Musulman vessels were to be found. The Second Crusade, like the First, took the overland route, but the Third, and all the rest, crossed the sea. They were thus the occasion of much profitable traffic. The Fourth Crusade was quite different from all the rest: for Venice contrived to divert it to her own advantage, and to that of the other maritime cities.

The plan of this Crusade was as follows: the Crusaders proposed to attack the Musulmans in Egypt, and thence to march along the coast of Palestine. The Crusaders had made arrangements with the Doge, Enrico Dandolo. The Venetian fleet was to transport the 30,000 men of the crusading army in return for a payment of 85,000 marks of silver. But the Crusaders were unable to pay the agreed sum. Venice then proposed that they should acquit themselves of their debt by taking possession of Zara for her, a Christian port but a rival of Venice. Zara was captured, and the fleet was making ready to set sail for Egypt, when the Greek prince Alexis, whose father, the Emperor Isaac, had been dethroned not long before (1195), proposed that the Crusaders should restore him to the throne of Constantinople. Despite Pope Innocent III, who went to the length of excommunicating the Venetians, the Crusaders accepted the proposal. On July 6th, 1203, the fleet forced the harbour, the Crusaders occupied Constantinople, and Alexis was crowned. Then, disputes with the new Emperor having arisen, the city was captured anew, on April 12th, 1204, and the Latin Empire was founded. Venice received, as her share, everything that could favour her maritime commerce: part of Constantinople, Adrianople, Gallipoli, the Island of Euboea, with a host of other islands, the southern and western shores of the Peloponnesus, and the whole of the coast from the Gulf of Corinth to Durazzo. The Black Sea was opened up to Italian trade, and immediately Venetian, Genoese and Pisan establishments were founded on its shores.

One cannot say that the Mediterranean had again become what it was in antiquity, a European lake. But it no longer constituted a barrier to Europe. It was once more the great highway between Europe and the East. All its trade routes ran to the Levant. The caravans which came from Baghdad and from China, bringing spices and silk to the Syrian coast, now made for the Christian vessels which awaited them in the Levantine ports.

2. *The Northern Trade*

The cause for this vigorous expansion, whose effects upon European civilization were incalculable, was external to Europe, or at all events to Western Europe. Without the attraction exercised by Byzantium, without the necessity of fighting the Musulmans, Europe would doubtless have continued for centuries in a state of purely agricultural civilization. There was no internal necessity which might have compelled her to venture forth into the outer world. Her commerce was not a spontaneous manifestation of the natural development of her economic life. It may be said that owing to stimuli arriving from the outer world it anticipated the moment when it must have come into being as a natural development.

And singular though it may appear at first sight, this was true not only in the Mediterranean, but also in the North Sea and the Baltic. In antiquity the waters of these seas had enclosed the Roman world as definitely as the waters of the Atlantic. Beyond the Channel, across which plied the vessels that maintained a connection between Gaul and

Britain, there was no navigation at all, or at all events no commercial navigation, and this situation remained unchanged until the 9th century. Apart from Quentovic (which took the place of Boulogne) and Duurstede, which maintained occasional relations with the Anglo-Saxons of Britain, the entire coast of the Frankish Empire, until the mouth of the Elbe was reached, was lifeless, almost deserted. Beyond the Elbe, in the Baltic, one came to the unknown regions of pagan barbarism. Here the situation was exactly the contrary of that which obtained on the shores of the Mediterranean. Instead of being neighboured by more advanced civilizations, the Christian Occident was in contact with peoples who were still in their infancy. Yet it was under the influence of such peoples that these northern waters were awakened to commercial activity. Strangely enough, the centre of this activity was not, as one might have supposed, on the coasts of Flanders and England, but in the Gulf of Bothnia and the Gulf of Finland. And this is explained by the fact that the attraction of the East, and of Byzantium, made itself felt even in these distant lands, so that the same external stimulus that provoked the rise of Italian navigation was also responsible for the beginnings of the northern trade.

We have already referred to this fact, in the chapter on the Scandinavian invasion; we have seen that the Swedes, half conquerors and half merchants, began to make their appearance, from the middle of the 9th century, on the waters of the Dnieper, and that they established there the first political centres round which crystallized the still amorphous mass of those eastern Slavs who borrowed from the Swedes their name of "Russians." Until the close of the 11th century these establishments remained in touch with the mother-country, and continued to receive reinforcements. They maintained commercial relations—very active relations—with Byzantium and the Musulman countries on the shores of the Caspian; at all events, until the invasion of the Petchenegs.[1] Constantinople was the great

[1] This explains how it is that 20,000 Arab coins have been found in Sweden, and very many in Russia.

commercial centre. There slaves were sold, furs, honey, and wax. Constantine Porphyrogenitus gives a curious description of the Russian trade about the year 950. He tells us how in the month of June the boats from Novgorod, Smolensk, Lubetch, Tchernigov, and Vychegrad assembled at Kiev. Armed, and setting out in a body, the traders descended the river, towing their boats where the stream was interrupted by rapids, and defending themselves against the Petchenegs, and then skirted the coast as far as the mouths of the Danube, and so on to Constantinople. These trading expeditions, armed and directed by the prince, were very like the expeditions of the modern African slave-traders. But even as early as the 10th century merchants, properly so-called, were taking part in these expeditions. At this time the Russians were still pagans. They had as yet no notion of landed property, and already, on account of this trade with Constantinople, they had merchants, and were founding towns. These were palisaded towns (*gorod*) or *pagost:* that is, places inhabited by foreigners (*gostj*).

Kiev, by the beginning of the 11th century, was unrivalled in importance by any other town in the North of Europe. Thietmar of Merseburg describes it as it was in 1018, with its forty churches (the text says 400, but that is doubtless an error) and its eight markets. The population still consisted largely of Scandinavians. They were even more numerous at Novgorod, where the men of Gothland, in the 12th century, had a *Gildhalle*. The movement that had its beginning in these centres naturally spread into the Baltic. The island of Bornholm (Denmark), in the words of Adam of Bremen, was *celeberrimus Daniae portus et fida statia navium, quae a barbaris in Graeciam dirigi solent.* But even in the 10th century the Scandinavians, who had been initiated into commerce by Byzantium, were pushing westward. The Flemish coins of the 10th and 11th centuries found in the country show that they frequented the shores of the North Sea. This navigation must have been intensified by the Danish dominion in England. In the 10th century a new port, Kiel, on the Waal, took the place of Duurstede in Holland, and Bruges began to develop. The conquest of England by the Normans, by attaching this country to the Continent, was a further stimulus to navigation on the North Sea and the Channel.

The impulse, then, came from Byzantium, through the intermediary of the Swedes, but the Scandinavian navigation began to decline in the 11th century: on the one hand, the invasion of the Kumans, in the south of Russia, cut the route to Constantinople, and on the other hand, the competition of the Venetian and Italian trade in the South was too much for it. And just at this time the Germans were beginning to spread along the Baltic. The volume of trade had now become so great that it was beginning to expand northwards.

From Venice, by way of the Brenner Pass, it gradually made its way into Southern Germany; or perhaps we should say that Venice attracted this trade to herself, for the Venetians did not travel overland. But the movement was much more active in the direction of France. Under the stimulus of the coastal trade both commerce and industry were becoming established in the Lombard plain, which from the middle of the 11th century was transformed by their influence. Through the passes of Saint Gothard or Mont Cenis the Lombard merchants ventured northwards. The magnet that drew them northwards was Flanders, the centre of the North Sea trade. From the beginning of the 12th century these Lombard merchants frequented the fairs of Ypres, Lille, Messines, Bruges, and Thourout. Then the centre of commercial exchanges shifted southwards, and the great markets of the 12th and 13th centuries were the famous fairs of Champagne: Troyes, Bar, Provins, Lagny, Bar-sur-Aube.

There, through the intermediary of the Flemings and the Lombards, the two commercial worlds, the northern and the southern, touched and intermingled. Of the two, the southern was the more advanced, the more complete and progressive. And this is not surprising. In constant relations with highly developed civilizations, the Italians were early initiated into their commercial practices, and all the complexities of a trade more intensive and more complicated than that of the North. This explains why the first means of exchange, which made their appearance at the close of the 12th century, were Italian. One may say that the organization of European credit is entirely Romanic. Banks, bills of exchange, the lending of money at interest, and commercial companies were exclusively of Italian origin, and probably became generalized through the medium of the great fairs of Champagne. The most striking result of the renaissance of trade was the revival of money, the return to circulation of currency. The stock of precious metals was not actually increased, but money began to circulate again. As exchange became more general money made its appearance wherever man traded. Things which had never been valued in terms of money were now beginning to be so valued. The notion of wealth was undergoing transformation.

3. *The Merchants*

Now we have to consider—and this is an essential question—how the mercantile class which was the instrument of this commerce came into being. The question is very difficult to answer, because of the paucity of documents, and it is probable that it will never be completely elucidated.

To begin with, we note that the merchants (*mercatores*) were "new men." They made their appearance as the creators of a new kind of wealth, side by side with the possessors of the old territorial wealth, and they did not emerge from the class of landowners.

They were so far from originating from the class of landowners that the contrast between the idea of nobility and the mercantile life subsisted for centuries, and has never been completely dissipated. Here were two separate and impermeable worlds. There can be even less question of their ecclesiastical origin. The Church was hostile to commercial life. It saw in commerce a spiritual danger. *Homo mercator nunquam aut vix potest Deo placere.* The clergy were forbidden to engage in trade. The ascetic ideal of the Church was in flagrant opposition to the ideals of commerce. The Church did not condemn wealth, but it condemned the love of riches and striving after wealth. Not the slightest encouragement, therefore, could be expected on the part of the Church.

Did the merchants emerge from the class of villeins, these men who had their definite place in the great domains, living on their *mansus* and leading an assured and sheltered existence? There is no evidence that they did so, and everything seems to point to the contrary.

Strange as it may seem, then, only one solution remains: the ancestors of the merchants must have been the poor men, the landless men, the nomadic folk who wandered about the country, working for hire at harvest time, living from hand to mouth and going on pilgrimages. An exception must be made in the case of the Venetians, since their lagoons made them, from the first, fishers and refiners of salt, which they carried to Byzantium.

Landless men are men who have nothing to lose, and men who have nothing to lose have everything to gain. They are adventurers, relying only on themselves; they have given no hostages to fortune. They are resourceful people, who know their way about; they have seen many countries, can speak many languages, are acquainted with many different customs, and their poverty makes them ingenious. It was from this floating scum, we may be sure, that the crews of the first Pisan and Genoese corsairs were recruited. And in the north of Europe, what were the Scandinavians who set out for Constantinople but men without possessions who were seeking their fortune?

"Seeking their fortune": that is the current expression. How many never found it, but disappeared in battle, or were dogged by poverty? But others succeeded. Starting with nothing but their courage, their intelligence, and their hardihood, they made their fortune. . . .

It seems a simple matter to-day. An intelligent man, with nothing but his wits to rely on, may find capital to back him. But we must consider that the men of whom we are speaking had no hope of capital. They had to make their capital out of nothing. It was the heroic age of commercial origins, and it is worth our while to give a thought to these poor devils, who were the creators of personal property.

Here is a very simple case, which must often have been

repeated. A man takes part in a successful privateering expedition; a Musulman fort is pillaged; a tight vessel with a rich cargo is captured. The privateers return to their port of origin, and now they can recruit a few poor fellows on their own account, and begin over again, or they can buy corn cheap somewhere, and carry it to some country where there is a famine, where they can sell it very dear. For this was one of the prime causes of the creation of mercantile wealth. Everything was local. At the distance of a few leagues you would find the contrast of poverty and abundance, and consequently, the most astonishing fluctuations of price. In this way a man with very little wealth can make a great deal.

On the Rhine, the Scheldt or the Rhone a wide-awake boatman could make considerable profits in time of famine. More than one who began by carrying small parcels of goods to the markets, or selling candles to pilgrims, may suddenly have acquired a useful liquid capital which would enable him to put to sea.

And we must not forget that in the beginning there would have been a great deal of dishonesty and a great deal of violence. Commercial honesty is a virtue of very late growth.

Thus, in this agricultural society, whose capital wealth was dormant, a group of outlaws, vagabonds, and poverty-stricken wretches furnished the first artisans of the new wealth, which was detached from the soil. Having gained a little, they wanted to gain more. The spirit of profit-making did not exist in established society; those whom it inspired were outside the social system; they bought and sold, not in order to live, not because they had vital need of their purchases, but for the sake of gain. They did not produce anything; they were merely carriers. They were wanderers, guests, *gostj,* wherever they went. They were also tempters; offering jewellery for the women, ornaments for the altar, cloth of gold for the churches. They were not specialists; they were one and all brokers, carriers, sharpers, chevaliers of industry. They were not yet professional merchants, but they were on the way to becoming merchants.

They became merchants when commerce had definitely become a specific way of life, detached from the hazardous and hand-to-mouth existence of the carrier. And then they settled down. As soon as they had really entered upon the normal exercise of trade they found that a place of residence was necessary. They established themselves at some point which was favourable to their way of life: a landing-place for river-craft, or a favourably-situated episcopal city where they found themselves in the company of their fellows, and as their numbers increased still others arrived. And then, quite naturally, they began to form mutual associations. If they wanted to enjoy any security they had to travel in companies, in caravans. They banded together in guilds, religious associations, confraternities. All the trade of the Middle Ages, until nearly the end of the 12th century, was undertaken by armed caravans (*hanses*). This not only increased the security of trade, but also its efficiency, for while the companions protected one another on the highways and caravan routes they also bought goods in common in the markets. Thanks to the accumulation of their petty capitals, they were able to undertake transactions of considerable importance. From the beginning of the 12th century there were attempts to corner grain. About this period many merchants had already realized fortunes which enabled them to purchase valuable real estate.[2] Moreover, it was the merchants' guilds that attended to the fortification of the town in which they resided.

Of one thing we may be absolutely sure, that these men were inspired by a greedy spirit of profit-seeking. We must not think of them simply as respectable folk doing their best to make both ends meet. Their one object was the accumulation of wealth. In this sense, they were animated by the capitalist spirit, which the rudimentary psychology of our modern economists would have us regard as something highly mysterious, born in penury or Calvinism. They calculated and they speculated; to their contemporaries they appeared so formidable that no one would have

[2] To understand what great commercial profits could be made in an age when wars and famines were of continual occurrence, we have only to remember what happened in the recent war.

been surprised to learn that they had made a pact with the devil. No doubt the majority were unable to read or write. Many great fortunes have been made by illiterates. To deny that they were actuated by a commercial spirit would be as absurd as to deny that the princes who were their contemporaries were actuated by the political spirit. In actual fact, the capitalist spirit made its appearance simultaneously with commerce.

To be brief: the history of European commerce does not present us, as many would like to believe, with a spectacle of a beautiful organic growth of the kind that delights the amateur of evolution. It did not begin with petty local transactions which gradually developed in importance and in range. On the contrary, it began, in conformity with the stimulus which it received from the outer world, with long-range trading and the spirit of big business—big in the relative sense. It was dominated by the capitalist spirit, and this spirit was even more potent in the beginning than later on. Those who initiated and directed and expanded the commerce of Europe were a class of merchant-adventurers.[3] This class was responsible for reviving urban life, and in this sense we must refer to this class the origin of the bourgeoisie, very much as we refer the origin of the modern proletariat to the great industrialists.

[3] I think the description of merchant-adventurers is that which best fits these precursors, who could not as yet be described as great merchants.

The Formation of the Cities

CHAPTER II

The Formation of the Cities

1. *The Episcopal "Cities" and Fortresses*

A society in which the population lives by the soil which it exploits, and whose produce it consumes on the spot, cannot give rise to important agglomerations of human beings; each inhabitant being tied, by the necessities of life, to the soil which he cultivates. Commerce, on the other hand, necessarily involves the formation of centres in which it obtains its supplies and from which it sends them forth into the outer world. The natural result of importation and exportation is the formation in the social body of what might be called nodes of transit. In Western Europe, in the 10th and 11th centuries, their appearance was contemporaneous with the renewal of urban life.

Naturally, such factors as geographical conditions, the contours of the soil, the direction and navigability of watercourses, and the configuration of sea-coasts, by the direction which they imposed on the circulation of men and goods, at the same time determined the situation of the first commercial settlements. But almost invariably these sites were already inhabited when the afflux of merchants restored them to renewed activity. Some—and this was the case in Italy, Spain, and Gaul—were already occupied by an episcopal "city"; others—for example, in the Low Countries, and the regions to the east of the Rhine and the north of the Danube—were already the site of a *bourg*—that is, a fortress. The reason for this is easily understood.

In the territory of the ancient Roman Empire the episcopal "cities" were built at the most favourably situated points, since the diocesan centres were established, from the beginning, in the principal towns, and these towns owed their importance to the advantages of their position. As for the *bourgs*, which were constructed in the North and the East in order to shelter the populations in time of war, or to check the incursions of the Barbarians, the majority were situated at points which were indicated by facility of access as places of refuge or defence.[1] But neither the "cities" nor the *bourgs* presented the faintest trace of urban life. Those, for example, which were built, like the castles constructed by the Counts of Flanders to hold back the Normans, or like the fortresses erected by Charlemagne and Henry the Fowler along the Elbe and the Saale to check the Slavs, were essentially military posts, occupied by a garrison of men-at-arms and the people necessary for their upkeep, the whole being under the command and supervision of a châtelain.[1] The "cities," on the contrary, were distinguished by their wholly ecclesiastical character. Besides the Cathedral and the canons' close there were usually several monasteries, and the residences of the principal lay-vassals of the bishop. If to these we add the schoolmasters and the scholars, the pleaders cited to appear before the local tribunal, and the host of worshippers flocking from all directions to take part in the numerous religious festivals, we shall be able to form some idea of the activity that must have prevailed in these small religious capitals. They were incontestably more populous and more lively than the *bourgs*, but like the latter, they contained nothing that resembled a bourgeoisie. In the "city," as in the *bourg*, beyond the priests, knights, and monks, there were practically only the serfs employed in the service of the ruling class, and cultivating, for the benefit of that class, the adjacent soil. "Cities" and *bourgs* were merely the administrative centres of a society which was still wholly agricultural.

---

[1] There were naturally exceptions: for example, Thérouanne.

It was in the "cities" of Northern Italy and Provence, on the one hand, and on the other in the *bourgs* of the Flemish region, that the first merchant colonies were established. By the very fact that they had outstripped the rest of Europe in the history of commerce, these two territories were those in which the first manifestations of urban life occurred. Here and there, in these "cities" and *bourgs*, the merchants founded, in the 10th century, settlements concerning which, as a matter of fact, very little is known; in the 11th century these settlements were multiplied, enlarged, and consolidated. Already, in the "city" as in the *bourg*, the merchant colony was beginning to play the leading part. The immigrants dominated the old inhabitants just as the commercial life of the place dominated the old agricultural life, and the opposition of these two interests gave rise to conflicts and necessitated expedients by force of which, amidst innumerable local experiments, a new order of things was elaborated.

If we are to understand this phenomenon of the formation of the middle classes, a development so pregnant with consequences, we must try to realize clearly the full extent of the contrast which existed, from the beginning, between the old population and the new. The old population, consisting of clergy, knights, and serfs, lived by the soil, the lower class working for the upper classes, who, from the economic point of view, were consumers who produced nothing. It is of no real consequence that there existed in most of the "cities" a few artisans who provided for the needs of local customers, and a small weekly market, attended by the peasants of the countryside. These artisans, and this market, had no real importance of themselves; they were strictly subordinated to the needs of the agglomeration which contained them, and it was only for its sake that they existed. They could not possibly undergo development, since this agglomeration itself, whose means of support were limited by the yield of the land which surrounded it, could not by any means increase.

In this tiny, changeless world the arrival of the merchants suddenly disarranged all the habits of life, and produced, in every domain, a veritable revolution. To tell the truth, they were intruders, and the traditional order could find no place for them. In the midst of these people who lived by the soil, and whose families were maintained by labours which were always the same, and revenues that did not vary, they seemed in some way scandalous, being as they were without roots in the soil, and because of the strange and restless nature of their way of life. With them came not only the spirit of gain and of enterprise, but also the free labourer, the man of independent trade, detached alike from the soil and from the authority of the seigneur: and above all, the circulation of money.

It was not only the work of the merchant that was free: by a no less astonishing innovation, his person also was free. But what could anyone really know concerning the legal status of these newcomers, whom no one had ever seen before? Very probably the majority of them were the children of serfs, but no one knew this for certain, and as their condition of servage could not be presumed, they had of necessity to be treated as free men. It was a curious result of their social condition that these forebears of the future bourgeoisie did not have to demand their liberty. It came to them quite naturally; it existed as a fact even before it was recognized as a right.

To these characteristics of the merchant colony, surprising enough in themselves, another must be added: the rapidity of its growth. It presently exercised, upon the surrounding region, an attraction comparable to that which the modern factory exercises over the rural population. By the lure of gain, it awakened the spirit of enterprise and adventure that lay dormant in the hearts of the domainal serfs, and it attracted fresh recruits from all directions. For that matter, the merchant colony was essentially open and extensible. In proportion as its commercial activity developed it provided employment for a host of workers—boatmen, carters, lumpers, etc. At the same time, artisans of every kind came to settle in the town. Some of them—bakers, brewers, shoemakers—found an assured livelihood there, thanks to the constant increase of the population. Others worked up the raw materials imported by the merchants, and the wares which they produced swelled the export trade. In this way industry took its place beside commerce. By the end of the 11th century, in Flanders, the weavers of woollen stuffs were beginning to flock from the country into the towns, and the Flemish cloth trade, being thus centralized under the direction of the merchants, became what it was to remain until the end of the Middle Ages, the most flourishing industry in Europe.

Naturally, neither the ancient "cities" nor the ancient *bourgs* could contain within the narrow circumference of their walls the increasing influx of these newcomers. They were forced to settle outside the gates, and presently their houses surrounded on every side, and submerged by their numbers, the ancient nucleus around which they were assembled. For the rest, the first care of the new town was to surround itself with a moat and a palisade to protect itself from pillagers, and these were replaced later by a stone rampart. Like the original "city" or *bourg*, the new town was itself a fortress: it was called *"nouveau-bourg"* or *"faubourg"*—that is to say, outer fortress; for which reason its inhabitants were known, from the beginning of the 11th century, by the name of *bourgeois*. The bourgeoisie underwent the same development as the nobility in this mediaeval society, which enjoyed, thanks to the abstention of the State, the advantage of complete plasticity. Before long its social function had transformed it into a juridical class. It is obvious that the law and administrative measures then in force, which had come into existence in the heart of a purely agricultural society, could no longer suffice for the needs of a merchant population. The formalistic apparatus of legal procedure, with its primitive means of proof, bailment, and seizure, had to give way to simpler and more expeditious rules. The judicial duel, that *ultima ratio* of the litigants, appeared to the merchants the very negation of justice. To ensure the maintenance of order in their faubourg, which was swarming with adventurers and jailbirds of every kind, such as had hitherto been unknown in the tranquil environment of the ancient *bourg* or "city," they demanded that the ancient system of fines and compositions should be replaced by punishments capable of inspiring a salutary terror: hanging, mutilation of every kind, and the putting out of the eyes. They protested against the prestations in kind which the collectors of tolls demanded before they would pass the merchandise that the merchants were exporting or importing. If it happened that one of their number was recognized as a serf, they would not suffer his seigneur to reclaim him. As for their children, whose mothers were necessarily almost always of servile condition, they refused to admit that such offspring should be regarded as servile. Thus the encounter of these new men with the ancient society resulted in all sorts of clashes and conflicts, due to the opposition of the domainal law and the commercial law, of exchange in kind and exchange for monetary payment, of servitude and liberty.

Naturally, the social authorities did not accept the claims of the nascent bourgeoisie without resistance. As always, they endeavoured first of all to conserve the established order of things: that is to say, to impose it upon these merchants, although it was in absolute opposition to their condition of life; and as always, their conduct was inspired as much by good faith as by personal interest. It is evident that it took the princes a long time to understand the necessity of modifying, for the merchant population, the authoritarian and patriarchial régime which they had hitherto applied to their serfs. The ecclesiastical princes especially displayed, in the beginning, a very marked hostility. To them it seemed that commerce endangered the salvation of the soul, and they regarded with mistrust, as a criminal derogation from obedience, all these innovations whose contagion was spreading from day to day. Their resistance inevitably led to revolts. In Italy and the Low Countries, and on the banks of the Rhine, the War of Investitures provided the bourgeois with an occasion or a pretext for rebelling against their bishops: here in the name of the Pope, and there in that of the Emperor. The first commune of which history makes mention, that of Cambrai, in 1077, was sworn by the people, led by the merchants, against the Imperialist prelate of the city.

2. The Cities

The princes, by their resistance, were able to impede the movement, but they could not check it. Towards the close of the 11th century it became more precipitate and more widespread and imposed itself upon the authorities. The princes began to realize that they had more to lose than to gain by persisting in their opposition to the movement. For while it undermined their local authority and imperilled certain of their domainal revenues, it more than made up for these drawbacks by the supplementary payments received in the shape of market tolls, and the inestimable advantage of a constant influx of corn and wares of every kind, and of money. By the beginning of the 12th century certain princes had frankly adopted a progressive policy, and were seeking to attract the merchants by the promise of immunities and privileges. In short, whether by agreement or by force, the claims of the bourgeoisie were everywhere triumphant, just as the parliamentary system was everywhere triumphant in the Europe of the 19th century. And great as were the differences between these two transformations in other respects, they offer a really striking similarity in respect of the character of their diffusion. Just as continental parliamentarianism was an adaptation of English and Belgian institutions to the special conditions of each country, so the urban institutions, although they exhibited, from town to town, peculiarities resulting from the nature of the local environment, might none the less be referred, on the whole, to two dominant types: on the one hand, that of the cities of Northern Italy, and on the other hand, that of the cities of the Low Countries and Northern France. Here, as in respect of the domainal régime, the feudal system, the Cluniac reformation, and chivalry, Germany and the other regions of central Europe merely followed the impulse that reached them from the West.

In spite of innumerable differences of detail, the towns of the Middle Ages presented everywhere the same essential features, and the same definition may be applied to one and all. We may formulate this definition by saying that the mediaeval city was a fortified agglomeration inhabited by a free population engaged in trade and industry, possessing a special law, and provided with a more or less highly developed jurisdiction and communal autonomy. The city enjoyed immunities which did not exist in the surrounding country; which amounts to saying that it had a morally privileged personality. It was constituted, indeed, on the basis of privilege. The bourgeois or burgess, like the noble, possessed a special juridical status: bourgeois and noble, in different directions, were equally removed from the villein, the peasant, who until the end of the *ancien régime* remained, in the majority of European countries, outside political society.

However, the privileged condition of the bourgeois was very different in its nature from that of the noble. The noble was, in reality, the old landowning freeman. His privilege, in some sort negative, arose from the fact that the mass of the people had lapsed into servitude under him. He had not ascended; he merely belonged to a minority which had kept its place amidst a general social decline. The privileges of the bourgeois, on the contrary, were very definitely positive. The bourgeois was a *parvenu,* who, of necessity, had made for himself a place in society which was finally recognized and guaranteed by the law. The domainal régime, which set the noble over the head of the peasant, at the same time bound them together by so strong a mutual tie that even to this day, after so many centuries, traces of it survive. The bourgeois, on the other hand, was a stranger both to the noble and to the peasant; both distrusted him and regarded him with hostility, and of this also the traces have not entirely disappeared. The bourgeois moved and had his being in a wholly different sphere. The contrast between him and them was the contrast between the agricultural and the commercial and industrial life. Compared with the noble and the peasant, the direct producers of the indispensable necessities of life, he was a mobile and active element; the traffic of the country was in his hands, and he was an agent of transformation. He was not indispensable to human existence; it was possible to live without him. He was essentially an agent of social progress and civilization.

There was yet another point of difference that divided the bourgeoisie of the Middle Ages from the nobility and the clergy. The nobility and the clergy constituted homogeneous classes, all of whose members participated in the same *esprit de corps*, and were conscious of their mutual solidarity. The case of the bourgeois was very different. Living in segregated groups in the various cities, in them the spirit of class was replaced by the local spirit, or was at all events subordinated to it. Each city was a little separate world in itself; there were no limits to its exclusivism and its protectionism. Each did its utmost to favour its own trade and industry at the expense of the other cities. Each endeavoured to become self-sufficient and to produce all that it needed. Each endeavoured to extend its authority over the surrounding countryside, in order to assure itself of sufficient supplies of food. If it occurred to the cities to act in concert, to conclude temporary or permanent leagues, like the London *Hansa*, and at a later date, the German *Hansa*, they did so in order to take action against a common enemy, or for the sake of a common utility, but within its own walls each had room only for its own burgesses; the foreigner could trade there only through the medium of his brokers, and was always liable to expulsion. In order to live there he had to acquire burgess rights. And all this is readily comprehensible. It was merely a question of local mercantilism. Are not our States, to-day, in the same situation? Do they not raise customs barriers in order to favour within their frontiers the birth of industries which they do not possess? Urban exclusivism came to an end only when the towns were united in the superior unity of the State, just as the exclusivism of the State will perhaps one day disappear in the unity of human society.

The moral result of this exclusivism was an extraordinary solidarity among the burgesses. Body and soul, they belonged to their little local *patrie*, and with them there reappeared, for the first time, since antiquity, in the history of Europe, a civic sentiment. Each burgess was obliged, and knew that he was obliged, to take part in the defence of the city: to take up arms for it, to give his life to it. The knights of Frederick Barbarossa were astounded to find that the shopkeepers and merchants of the Lombard cities were able to hold their own against them. In that campaign there were examples of civic virtue which remind one of ancient Greece. Other burgesses gave their fortune to their city, commuted the market tolls, or founded hospitals. The wealthy gave without stint or reckoning, and no doubt they were inspired by charity as much as by pride.

For the rich men were the rulers. The burgesses of the cities enjoyed civil equality and liberty, but not social equality, not political equality. The bourgeoisie, deriving from commerce, remained under the influence and the leadership of the wealthiest. Under the name of "*grands*" or "patricians," they kept the administration and jurisdiction of the city in their own hands. The urban government was a plutocratic government, and it actually ended, in the 13th century, by becoming oligarchic, the same families holding power in perpetuity. Yet nothing could have been more remarkable than these governments. They were responsible for the creation of urban administration: that is, the first civil and secular administration known in Europe. It was their work from top to bottom. This has not been sufficiently considered: it should be realized that they had no model, and had to invent everything: financial system, systems of book-keeping, schools, commercial and industrial regulations, the first rudiments of a health service, public works, market-places, canals, posts, urban boundaries, water supply—all this was their work. And it was they too who erected the buildings which even to-day are the glory of so many cities.

Beneath them, the rest of the urban population consisted of artisans, and it was they who formed the majority in every city. As a rule they were foremen or small employers, masters, with one or two journeymen under them, who constituted an active and independent bourgeoisie. While wholesale trade was free, there developed, for the protection of the artisans, a social policy which was a masterpiece no less interesting, in its way, than the Gothic cathedrals; and of which the last traces have only recently disappeared. Its object was the maintenance of all these petty lives which constituted the strength of the city, and to secure its regular revictualling. Each citizen was a producer and a consumer, and regulation intervened in respect of both production and consumption. The municipal authority undertook to protect the consumer. To this end it revived the old municipal regulations of which some traces had perhaps survived in Italy. Nothing could have been more admirable than the precautions taken against "dishonest" products, fraud, and falsification. The consumer was protected in the twofold interest of the local bourgeoisie and of the city's good repute in the outer world.

As for the producer, he protected himself by the trade corporations or guilds which made their appearance as early as the 12th century. Their essential purpose was to prevent competition, and it was this that rendered them so odious to the liberal economy of the 19th century. Every producer had to earn his living; therefore he had to retain his customers. He must accordingly sell his wares at the same price as his comrades, and he must make them in the same way. The trade or handicraft was originally a voluntary association, like our syndicates or trade unions. But it boycotted the "yellow" workers who did not apply for membership, and it was finally recognized by the public authority. Let us note that this organization had nothing in common with the association of workers whose purpose is negotiation with the employer. It was an obligatory syndicate of petty burgesses. It was created essentially for the benefit of the small independent producer. In most of the cities of the Middle Ages there was no proletariat. The craftsmen worked for the local market and reserved it for themselves. Their numbers were maintained in proportion to the number of their customers. They had complete control of the situation. In this sense, they had solved the social problem. But they had solved it only where the city was a "closed State," a situation which was not so general as one might suppose. For there was one industry at least—the cloth industry in Flanders and in Florence—whose products supplied not the local, but the European market. In this industry there could be no limitation of production, nor was it possible for the small employer to acquire his raw material for himself. Here he was in the power of the great

merchant, so that in this industry there was a division between capital and labour which we do not find elsewhere.
The industrial system was the system of the small work-
shop. But in the cloth industry the "master" was not an
independent producer; he worked for wages, so that here
we find something closely resembling the "cottage industry" of our own age. Trade organization existed, but in this
case it was far from protecting the artisan efficiently, as it
could not affect the conditions of marketing or of capital in-
vestment. Hence there were strikes, conflicts of salaried
workers, an exodus of the weavers from Ghent, and industrial crises. Hence the uneasy, unruly, turbulent, Utopian
spirit that characterized the weavers from the 12th century onwards, and made them the adepts of a naïve com-
munism which was allied with mystical or heretical ideals.
It is therefore incorrect to say that the Middle Ages knew
only small, independent, and corporative industries. In the
more advanced environments there was no lack of labour
troubles and social conflicts. The influence of these conflicts
was again perceptible in the 14th century.

With the rise of the towns and the constitution of the
bourgeoisie the formation of European society was completed; such as it was it remained until the end of the
ancien régime. Clergy, noblesse, bourgeoisie—these made
the trinity that ruled human destinies and played its part
in political life. The agricultural people, below the privileged classes, were restricted to their function of food
producers until the day when civil equality, and to some
extent political equality, should become the common possession of all. For one cannot too strongly insist on the fact
that the bourgeoisie was an exclusive and privileged class.
It was in this respect that the cities of the Middle Ages
differed essentially from the cities of the Roman Empire,
whose inhabitants, whatever the standard of their social
life, were all in enjoyment of the same rights. The Roman
world never knew anything analogous to the European
bourgeoisie; nor has the New World seen its like. When the
American cities were founded the moment had passed
when each social profession had its peculiar law; there were
merely free human beings. In our days the word bourgeoi-

sie, which we continue to employ, is completely diverted from its original sense. It denotes a social class of heterogeneous origin which has no common quality except that it is the class which possesses wealth. Of the bourgeoisie of the Middle Ages nothing remains, just as nothing remains of the nobility of the Middle Ages.

CHAPTER III

The Growth of the Cities
and Its Consequences

1. *The Growth of the Cities*

While in its remotest origins the renaissance of urban life in the West dates back to the first merchant settlements of the 10th century, it was not until the end of the 11th and the beginning of the 12th century that it reached its full development: only then did the first cities, in the full acceptation of the word, make their appearance in history. As we have already seen, the first fully-developed examples came into existence in the two regions whose commercial activity was most intense: in the south of Europe, in Northern Italy; in the north of Europe, in the Low Countries. There were striking parallels in the situation of these two regions. In Italy, as in Flanders, the maritime commerce, and the inland commerce which was its continuation, resulted in the activity of the seaports: Venice, Pisa, and Genoa in the South; Bruges in the North. Then, behind the seaports, the industrial cities developed: on the one hand, the Lombard communes and Florence; on the other, Ghent, Ypres and Lille, Douai, and further inland, Valenciennes and Brussels. It was evidently the proximity of the seaports that gave such an extraordinary impetus to the industry of the cities—an impetus unique in Europe. The Italian and Flemish ports, with their hinterland, acquired an international importance, and in this way they were unique.

For this very reason they necessarily entered into mutual relations. Here the initiative proceeded from the more developed of these two centres: that is, from Italy. The Italian merchants visited Flanders from the beginning of the 12th century. But presently the fairs of Champagne became the point of contact, and, so to speak, the Bourse of Italo-Flemish commerce. Situated on the route which joined the South to the North, running from Lombardy by way of the Gothard Pass, the Lake of Geneva, and the Jura, they kept the merchants of the two countries in touch throughout the year. But these were merely business rendezvous, and no really important cities were founded on the sites of these fairs. Even Troies never developed into a very large city, while Lagny, Provins and Bar-sur-Aube remained places of secondary importance.

The south of France was not far behind Italy. Marseilles, Montpellier, and Aigues-Mortes played their part in Mediterranean commerce. And behind them were Albi, Cahors, and Toulouse, which gravitated toward them, and prospered without interruption until the Albigensian War. In Spain the port of Barcelona likewise acquired great importance, though it did not produce any very active urban centres in the hinterland.

The Rhone is the only Mediterranean river in France, and the only river which by virtue of this fact gave rise at an early date to important cities: Avignon and Lyons. The other rivers flow into the Atlantic and the Channel, and on them there were only coasting and fishing ports, of which the most important is Bayonne, or ports engaged in local traffic with England, such as Rouen and Bordeaux. In the same way, in England navigation was restricted to the opposite coast, and the towns had acquired no importance. Even London did not attain any great importance until the 13th century. One single city in the interior of France developed until it was the peer of the greatest, but this was for political reasons: Paris. It was the only city of the kind in Europe, a true capital, growing larger with every forward movement of the monarchy. With these exceptions there were hardly any but local centres, none of which was comparable with those of Languedoc or Flanders.

Germany had no centre of international trade. She was in touch with Italy through the Rhine and the Danube; on the one river Cologne and Strasbourg made their appearance; on the other, Ratisbon and Vienna. The most important of these centres was Cologne, where the Germany of the West and South came into contact with the Germany of the North, and both were in touch with the Low Countries. The Germany of the North had no other direct communication with the South; it was oriented toward the two inland seas. It had Hamburg and Bremen on the North Sea, and above all, Lubeck, founded by Henry the Lion, on the Baltic. And here we are entering upon colonial territory, and new cities, which had never been subject to the Roman influence. The coastal ports were new settlements, favoured by the princes of the region. They were strung along the coast as far as Lithuanian territory: Danzig, Reval, Memel, Riga, Dorpat. The Baltic had been a German lake since the Russian route had been deserted—on the one hand, because commerce had gravitated to Italy, and on the other hand, because since the middle of the 12th century the advance-guard of the Mongols—the Kumans—made the neighbourhood of Kiev too dangerous. When this happened the Scandinavians lost their commercial significance, which was inherited by the Germans. Visby, in the island of Gothland, was a Teutonic station, and the "Niemetz"[1] made their way as far as Novgorod, where they had a market in the 12th century. Denmark alone attempted to hold her own with them, but was defeated at Bornhöved under Waldemar II (1227), and made way for Germany.

In the interior of Germany, between the Rhine and the Danube, there was no large town. Munster and Magdeburg were places of secondary importance; so were Frankfort and Nuremburg. Berlin was quite insignificant, and so were Munich and Leipzig. As far as urban life was concerned, the country was obviously backward. Frederick Barbarossa had no understanding of the bourgeoisie. Urban life existed

---

[1] The name which the Russians gave to the Germans.

only on the periphery, and except on the banks of the
Rhine it did not begin to assume any importance until the
13th century. Thus the general picture is that of two great
centres, Italy and the Low Countries—that is, Belgium—in
which the largest cities existed, and with which all the other
important centres were in communication. The commercial
movement of the Baltic gravitated toward Bruges, while
that of Southern Germany gravitated towards Italy.

But between the great commercial centres, whether these
were of local or of general importance, a host of small secondary towns arose, of the same character as the large
cities, and living under the same law. It had now become
indispensable that each region should have its little urban
centre. The disorganization of the domainal system, and the
appearance of free peasants, necessarily called into existence—to replace the "courts" from which the servile population had supplied their needs—little *bourgs*, which offered
an asylum to the artisans, and served as commercial centres
for the neighbourhood. Their urban life was a spontaneous
gift from the great cities. New towns were founded. In Germany the two Fribourgs became important centres. A host
of others led a quiet, semi-urban, semi-agricultural existence; Kreuzburg, where I am writing these lines, received
its charter in 1213. These were towns of secondary formation, belonging to a period when the bourgeoisie had
established itself, and when the princes, impelled by the
advantages which they derived from these towns, were
establishing them in all directions. Formerly the traveller
passed from monastery to monastery; now he journeyed
from town to town; there were towns on all the roads, at
intervals of a few leagues, constituting a transition between
the great cities, like the little beads of a rosary between the
dizaines.

The rise of the towns provoked an increase of population,
relatively comparable to that which occurred in the 19th
century. And even more remarkable than the increase of the
urban population were the effects of this multiplication of
urban centres on the population of the countryside. Compared with the Carolingian population, we may estimate,
roughly, that its strength was doubled. The maximum in-

crease was attained at the beginning of the 14th century. From that time, until the 18th century, there was no essential change.

It would be of the greatest importance to obtain some idea of the relative strength of the urban as compared with the rural population. But this is unfortunately impossible. Of this, however, we may be certain, that in all the centres favoured by commerce the bourgeois population continued to increase until about the middle of the 14th century. Everywhere the walled enclosures which had become too restricted had to be enlarged, and faubourgs which had been built outside the gates had to be enclosed by walls. There were now large towns in Europe—relatively speaking, very large towns. But what was a large town at the beginning of the 13th century? The area enclosed by the walls was still—relatively speaking—quite small. The figures provided by contemporaries are of no value, because they are not based on actual enumeration, and the oldest statistics that we have date only from the 15th century. Moreover, they are so contradictory that we cannot admit their validity. At an interval of only ten years, the population of Ypres was estimated respectively at 50,000 and at 200,000 inhabitants. All that we can affirm is that until the end of the Middle Ages no European city attained a population of 100,000. The largest cities—Milan, Paris, Gand—must have contained about 50,000 inhabitants, more or less. The cities of medium size would have contained from 20,000 to 50,000 inhabitants; the small towns from 2,000 to 5,000. But this need not prevent us from speaking of great cities, for size is entirely relative. If we take into account the very low density of the rural population, an agglomeration of 50,000 human beings must appear something very different from what it is to-day.

2. The Consequences for the Rural Population

Moreover, we must be very careful not to envisage the relation between the cities and the countryside in the Middle Ages as in any way resembling what it is to-day. In our days the town is not sharply divided from the coun-

try. There are industries in the villages, and some part of
the urban population lives in the country, and returns to it
every evening. The case was very different in the Middle
Ages. Then the town was absolutely distinct from the open
country. It was divided from it even materially, sheltering
behind its moat and walls and its gates. Juridically, it was
another world. Directly one entered the gates one became
subject to a different law, just as one does to-day on passing
from one State to another. Economically the contrast was as
great. Not only was the city a centre of commerce and
industry, but there was no commerce and no industry elsewhere. In the country they were everywhere prohibited.
Every city endeavoured to dominate the surrounding countryside, to subjugate it. The country had to provide it with
a market, and, at the same time, to guarantee its supplies
of foodstuffs. There was not, as there is to-day, constant
exchange and interpenetration; there was a contrast, and
the subordination of the one element to the other.

This subordination was more or less complete according
to the number and the power of the cities. It attained its
maximum in Italy, and its minimum in the Scandinavian
and Slav countries. The result of this subordination was
everywhere a more or less profound disturbance of the
rural economic system and a corresponding transformation
of the condition of the agricultural classes.

The rise of the towns, in fact, made it impossible to preserve the domainal system. This, as we have seen, may be
described as essentially an economy without outlet. Having
no market in which to sell its products, the domain restricted its production to the needs of its own consumption,
and its whole internal structure—methods of agriculture,
forms of tenure, prestations, and relations between the inhabitants and the seigneur—is explained by this special
situation. Now, from the moment the towns made their appearance this special situation ceased to exist wherever
their influence was felt. For apart from its merchants and
artisans, the urban population was a sterile population—to
employ a favourite formula of the 18th-century physio-
crats. It could live only by sending out of the city for its
means of subsistence—that is, by purchasing them from the

cultivators of the soil. It therefore provided them with the outlet for their products which they had hitherto lacked. Consequently it awakened in their minds the idea of profit, since henceforth production was remunerative. And so the moral and the economic conditions to which the domainal organization corresponded both disappeared simultaneously. The peasant, whose activity was now solicited by the outer world, no longer regarded his work as a mere burden. Further, as a necessary consequence of the new state of affairs, the seigneur himself was even more conscious of the need of a reformation. For since the prestations of his tenants were fixed by custom, he soon discovered that his resources were dwindling unpleasantly. His revenues were still the same, while his expenses were constantly increasing. The towns, in fact, by their purchases, were putting money into circulation throughout the countryside; and as money became more and more abundant its value diminished in proportion. The cost of living was continually rising, and the landowners, restricted to fixed revenues, found themselves launched on the road to ruin. For the petty military noblesse, who, as a general thing, possessed only small fiefs which just provided them with a living, the crisis was a veritable catastrophe. A large proportion of the chivalry, so numerous in the 11th century, was overwhelmed by poverty at the close of the 12th century.

It is difficult to say whether the increase of the population of the rural districts, which manifested itself at the very time when the conditions of rural life were undergoing such a profound modification, should also be referred to the appearance of the towns. After the devastations of the Normans, the Saracens and the Hungarians, Europe had known a period of relative tranquillity, during which the natural excess of births over deaths must insensibly have increased the numbers of the inhabitants. But it is only in the second half of the 11th century that we perceive, in certain parts of Europe, the traces of a malaise due to the excessive density of the population, and we are almost bound to believe that in affording the peasants new means of livelihood, the towns, by that very fact, had contributed, not, of course, to increase the fecundity of marriages,[2] but to increase their number. However this may be, it is certain that in the Low Countries, for example, the cultivated land, about 1050, was beginning to prove insufficient for the needs of the inhabitants. Moreover, events like the conquest of England in 1066, and the Crusade, evidently justify the supposition that the population was somewhat excessive, at all events in the north of France.

This excess of population was due also to the rapid increase in the numbers of the inhabitants of the towns, and to the bands of mercenary adventurers which were being formed about this time in Italy—at Genoa, for example—and, under the name of Brabançons and Cotereaux, in France. From the beginning of the 11th century we have something more than presumption to go upon. The peopling of the regions beyond the Elbe by immigrants from the banks of the Rhine, Holland, and Flanders, evidently cannot be explained save by the superabundance of the rural population of these countries.

Thus, at the moment when the ancient domainal system had had its day, and no longer responded to the needs of a more economically advanced society, there were numbers of men who offered themselves to whomsoever would give them land. The great landowners, and above all the territorial princes, did not fail to profit by so favourable a situation. They possessed plenty of uncultivated land, for it seems that to the west of the Rhine and to the south of the Danube, at all events, the great domains had hardly spread beyond the fertile soil already cultivated in the days of the Roman Empire. The rest of the land was untouched forest, heath, and marshland. The time had come to bring this land into cultivation. This great task, which, for the first time since the disappearance of the Roman Empire, increased the territorial wealth of Europe, was begun about the middle of the 11th century, reached its apogee during

[2] The fecundity of marriages was very great, both among the peasants, as may be seen from the Polyptych of Irminion and the monastic charters, and the nobility (on this subject see Gislebert). It is only among the princes that we find any traces of pre-Malthusianism.

the course of the 12th century, and was completed, at a
gradually relaxing pace, towards the end of the 13th century. From that period until the end of the 18th century the
area of cultivable soil was not sensibly increased in the Occident, and this fact alone shows the importance of the
progress effected by internal colonization in the Middle
Ages. No doubt the intakes would have been less extensive
had agriculture been more advanced. The great areas which
it occupied, in order to increase its production, were the
consequence of the rudimentary methods of an agriculture
which was still wholly of the extensive type. The crisis of
the domanial organization could have been avoided had it
been possible to increase the fertility of the soil by more
rational methods.

The system followed in the peopling and cultivation of
virgin soil differed greatly, in what might be called its liberal character, from the practices of the preceding epoch.
The peasant's relations to the landowner were now merely
such as necessarily arose from his quality of tenant. He
paid a rent for the land which he occupied, but his person
remained free. One of the means most frequently employed
by the seigneurs in order to attract colonists was the foundation of "new towns," which were regular agricultural
colonies. The area of the "new town" was divided into a
certain number of equal units, and these, on payment of a
quit-rent, could be secured under a hereditary title. A charter, usually an imitation of the charter of the neighbouring
town, recognized the personal liberty of the inhabitants,
and determined the powers and the competence of the
mayor and the court who were charged with the affairs of
the colony and the administration of justice, and defined
the respective rights of the seigneur and the peasants as to
forestal usages, etc. Thus a new type of village appeared,
the *village à loi*. It no longer had anything in common with
the old domanial organization, except for the fact that, like
the latter, it presupposed a great property and a small-scale
exploitation. For the rest, everything was new. Not only was
the peasant a free man, but the prestations which he had to
pay the seigneur, instead of consisting of natural products,
were usually payable in money. It is not surprising that the

demand for land, which became more and more pressing as the population increased, brought the colonists flocking to the new settlements. In all directions they thrust back the frontier of the untamed wilderness, colonizing the great forests, uprooting the heath, and draining the marshes. All over Europe there was a new growth of villages, and the very form of their names, ending in *sart* in the French-speaking countries, and in *kerk, kirche, rode, rath,* in countries where German was spoken, still enable us to distinguish them from their neighbours in the long-settled regions.

The Church played a considerable part in this great cultural task of the 12th century. She entrusted the work to the new orders of Cistercians and Premonstrants. The extraordinary vitality manifested by the monks at the time of the Clunisian reformation had not survived the triumph of the latter. The object once achieved, the enthusiasm waned. The crisis was succeeded by a decline, and from the close of the 11th century the Benedictine monasteries, whose fortune, by the singular but inevitable irony of things, had been still further increased by the donations of the faithful, which came to them despite their disdain of worldly wealth, were beginning to lapse into a period of lethargy from which they did not emerge until their renaissance in the 17th century. Their religious and social rôle was ended, and they were now little more than great landowners. The Cistercians and the Premonstrants—the former founded by St. Bernard in 1113,[3] and the latter by St. Norbert in 1119—resumed the ascetic propaganda which the Benedictines had abandoned. In order that the prescription of manual labour might be applied in all its rigour they established themselves, by preference, in uncultivated regions where there was land to be cleared or drained. The princes made haste to help on the pious work by ceding tracts of moor and marshland to the monks. The two Orders played a great part in draining the Flemish polders and bringing the soil of Eastern Germany into cultivation. The domains

[3] Cîteaux (not far from Dijon) was founded in 1098 by Robert de Molesnes, but it did not become the centre of a movement until St. Bernard entered it in 1113.

which they constituted there were of a completely novel type, in which we see, for the first time in the Middle Ages, the principle of large-scale agricultural exploitation. Instead of being parcelled out in family holdings, the newly-cleared areas were organized into great farms, which were worked by "convert brothers" or free peasants under the direction of a monk. The cultivation of cereals or the breeding of cattle was practised, not as formerly, with a view to immediate consumption by the convent, but for the purpose of sale in the markets. The worker was not burdened with *corvées*, and the only prestation he had to pay was the tithe. The profits realized enabled the monks to acquire more land, and to continue the work of bringing it into cultivation. The proprietors of the old domains, unable to dispose of their land, on account of the hereditary rights of their tenants, did not find it easy to liberate themselves from tradition. Burdened with debts, and driven to extremities by the uninterrupted dwindling of their revenues, they were obliged, from the end of the 11th century, to take decisive measures. The domainal "courts," formerly cultivated by the serfs, were divided into parcels and ceded in return for a quit-rent, or leased *à metayage*, or transformed into large farms. The peasants were permitted to free themselves, in return for money payments, not only from the *corvées*, but also from the capital tax, the marriage fee, and mortmain—in short, from all those survivals of a bygone age which had lost their utility. Hardly anywhere, save in regions which were difficult of access, or very remote from the great commercial movements, did serfdom retain its primitive form. Everywhere else, if it did not actually disappear, it was at least mitigated. One may say that from the beginning of the 13th century the rural population, in Western and Central Europe, had become or was in process of becoming a population of free peasants. And this great transformation was accomplished without violence, without the co-operation of principles and theories, as an inevitable consequence of the revival of trade and the appearance of the towns, which, by providing agriculture with the outlets of which it had hitherto been deprived, had compelled it to modify its traditional organization and to adopt freer and more flexible forms of exploitation. Economic progress had destroyed the social patronage which the seigneur had hitherto exercised over his men. In proportion as liberty was substituted for serfdom the landowner put off his old paternal character, and material interest tended to become the sole criterion of his relations with his tenants.

3. Other Consequences

The appearance of the towns in the course of the 11th century, which so profoundly modified the social condition of Europe, naturally influenced its political and religious life also. By depriving the State of its essentially agricultural character, and subjecting the rural population to the attraction and the influence of the urban centres, the towns restored it to the condition from which the invasions of the Barbarians had deposed it. As in the Roman Empire, although under very different circumstances, the city resumed its position in political society. Thanks to the city, the administration, which had wandered from place to place, was again becoming sedentary. Moreover—and this was the most considerable advance which had been accomplished in civil life since the Carolingian epoch—it was beginning to employ a secular and literate personnel. Hitherto the State had been obliged to borrow from the Church all those of its agents in whom a certain degree of learning was indispensable. Henceforth it was able to borrow them, more and more extensively, from the bourgeoisie. For unlike the noble, whose military profession called for no other apprenticeship than that of arms, the bourgeoisie, in consequence of the needs of commerce, found it necessary to acquire at least a rudimentary education. The ability to read and write was indispensable to the merchant, and from the 12th century onwards there was no city of any importance without its school. At first the education provided was still entirely Latin, and it was in Latin that the most ancient administrative and commercial documents which we possess were written. But this was only an intermediate stage, through which it was necessary to pass, as at first it was impossible to find masters outside the Church. It was obvious that the bourgeois population could not long continue to employ, in its ordinary business affairs, a tongue that was not the language which it spoke. From the beginning of the 12th century the inevitable development took place: the vulgar tongue began to be employed by the urban scribes, and it is characteristic that this innovation made its first appearance in the country whose municipal life was most highly developed: namely, in Flanders. The first document of this kind in our possession is a charter of the corporation (*échevinage*) of Douai, dated 1204, which is written in the Picard dialect. In proportion as the urban administration became more complex, when the magistrates had to undertake a more extensive correspondence, and had to pronounce judgement in more important disputes, while the keeping of the communal accounts demanded more care and greater knowledge, the clerks employed by the city, and the notaries and advocates to whom the private person applied for assistance, had naturally to become more highly educated, and in this way there was formed, in the heart of the bourgeoisie, a class of lay practitioners who were much better qualified, by their knowledge of the world and of business matters, to satisfy the requirements of the civil administration than were the ecclesiastics whom it had hitherto been necessary to employ. From the end of the 12th century an increasing number of such experts entered into the employ of the princes or kings and applied their skill and experience in the service of the State. We may say that the first lay personnel in Europe since the disappearance of the Imperial Roman bureaucracy was furnished by the bourgeoisie.

And even while the cities were thus so effectively secularizing the State, they were influencing its very constitution, and this influence constantly increased in the course of the centuries. Everywhere they began to play a greater and greater part in political life, whether, as in France, they helped the king to oppose the pretensions of the great feudal nobles, or whether, as in England, they united with the barons, in order to wrest the first national liberties from the Crown, or whether, as in Italy or Germany, they constituted themselves independent republics. The absence of the bourgeoisie in the Slav States shows what the West owed to it.

Neither the Church nor civil society could escape its influence. With the renaissance of urban life a period began for the Church in which piety and charity received a fresh stimulus, but at the same time formidable problems presented themselves, and it was an age of bloody conflict. Nothing could have been more ardent or more deep-rooted than the religion of the bourgeoisie. Of this we need no other evidence than the extraordinary number of confraternities and guilds and associations of all kinds, which in every city devoted themselves to prayer, or to the care of the sick, the poor, the aged, and the widows and orphans. From the end of the 12th century the *béguines* and *bégards*, who practised asceticism in secular life, were beginning to spread from city to city. But for the bourgeoisie, the foundation of the new Orders—the Franciscans (1208) and Dominicans (1215)—whose spirit inspired the orthodox mysticism of the 13th century, would have been impossible. With these mendicant monks monasticism, for the first time, deserted the country for an urban environment. They lived on the alms of the bourgeoisie; they recruited their ranks from the bourgeoisie; and it was for the sake of the bourgeoisie that they exercised their apostolate, and the success of this was sufficiently proved by the multitude of brothers of the tertiary order, among both the merchants and the artisans, who were associated with the Franciscans.

Urban piety, as we see, was an active piety. The laymen—and this was still a novel phenomenon—collaborated directly in the religious life, claiming their right to play their part in it beside the clergy. This represented a twofold peril to the Church. The first and the most dangerous of these was the threat to orthodoxy. The greater the interest of the bourgeois in the things of religion, the more liable they were to adopt the Manichaean doctrines which, in the 12th century, were spreading into Europe from the East; or to be impressed by the mystical dreams of the "Apostolics" or the "Brothers of the Free Spirit." It is highly characteristic that the West was not troubled with heresy before the renaissance of the cities. The first and most formidable heresy known to Europe before the advent of Protestantism, that of the Cathars, began to propagate itself in the 11th century, and was therefore precisely contemporaneous with the urban movement. And we must not forget that the sect of the Vaudois (Waldenses) was founded by a merchant of Lyons. Even after the terrible massacres of the Albigenses the urban populations continued, now in this part of Europe, now in that, to harbour their suspect sects, in which the aspirations of the proletariat tended to orientate mysticism toward confused visions of social transformation, and which dreamed of establishing, on the ruins of Church and State, in some sort of communistic society, the rule of the just.

These instances were doubtless exceptions, but one thing was common to all the cities, and it constituted one of the most striking features of the urban spirit: namely, their attitude toward ecclesiastical power. With the rise of the cities the relations between the secular and the spiritual authority entered upon a new phase. Since the Carolingian epoch the conflicts between the two authorities had been due to the efforts of the kings to subjugate the Church and force it to serve their policy. They were merely the consequence of the alliance of the two powers: the question was, which of the two was to be supreme in society. But neither the one nor the other attempted to deprive its rival of its prerogatives or privileges. It was the relation of the two forces, but not their nature, which was at issue. In the cities the case was very different. There the very situation which the Church enjoyed as a privileged corporation was imperilled. The cities openly attacked the tribunals of the Church, its financial exemptions, and the monopoly which it claimed to exercise in respect of education. From the end of the 12th century there were perpetual conflicts between the communal councils and the chapters and monasteries included within the urban precincts, or even between the council and the bishop of the diocese. In vain did the Church blast them with her excommunication or interdict: they still persisted in their attitude. At need, they did not hesitate to compel the priests to sing the mass and administer the sacraments. However religious and orthodox they might be,

they claimed the right to prevent the Church from inter-
fering in the domain of temporal interests. Their spirit was
purely secular, and for this reason the urban spirit must be
regarded as the prime and remote cause of the Renaissance.

We may therefore say that with the appearance of the
cities and the formation of the bourgeoisie a new Europe
had arisen. Every department of social life was transformed; the population was doubled; liberty was becoming
general; trade and industry, the circulation of money, and
the achievements of the intellect were becoming more and
more important, and were providing new possibilities for
the development of the State and of society. Never, until
the end of the 17th century, was there such a profound
social—I do not say intellectual—revolution. Hitherto men
had been mainly restricted to the relations of producer and
consumer. Now they were increasingly ruled by their political relations. The only circulation in Europe had been
that of the Church toward Rome and the religious centres.
Now this was accompanied by a lay circulation. Life began
to flow toward the coasts, the great rivers, the natural highways. Civilization was purely continental; but it was now
becoming maritime.

We must not, of course, exaggerate. The Church continued to dominate the world of ideas, and the soil was still
the foundation which supported the noblesse, and even the
State. But the roots of the tree which had recently planted
itself upon the wall would inevitably, without intention, by
the mere fact of their growth, dislodge the stones. The cities
had no desire to destroy what already existed, but only to
make a place for themselves. And gradually this place became larger and larger, so large that it presently created a
new order of things. In European civilization the cities were
essentially elements of progress, not in the sense that everything emerged from them, but in the sense that they furnished the indispensable conditions of all these renewals.
Since the appearance of the bourgeoisie civilization seemed
to be waking up, to be shaking itself; it was more mobile,
more nervous. From the 7th to the 11th century the movement of history was everywhere analogous. But after the
11th century, what variety! The strength of the bourgeoisie

differed from country to country, giving to each a national character of its own, a character hitherto unknown. The active centres of the world were the centres in which the urban population was concentrating: Paris, Lombardy, Tuscany, Venice, Flanders, the Rhine.

There is a sort of contradiction in the enthusiasm of the cities of the 13th century for the mendicant orders and their capitalistic activities. They were filled with enthusiasm for the ideal of poverty, but they sought riches.

BOOK SIX

The Beginnings of the
Western States

CHAPTER I

England

1. *Before the Conquest*

The Barbarian kingdoms erected on the ruins of the Roman Empire had vainly endeavoured to appropriate, together with the territory, the old system of government. We have seen how and why these efforts were abortive. Pippin the Short and Charlemagne succeeded in restoring the power of the monarchy, with the help of the Church, and they applied themselves, by agreement with the Church, to the institution of a Christian society. The social conditions did not allow them to accomplish their mission. They found it impossible to create a royal administration at a time when the system of great estates subjected men everywhere to the protectorate of the territorial seigneurs. Political unity was replaced by the parcelling out of the State in territorial principalities. The subjects of the king passed under the authority of the feudal princes, and from the end of the 9th century it was really they who acquitted themselves of the onerous task which had proved too heavy for the sovereign's hands. But while the king allowed the princes to govern in his place, he nevertheless continued to reign above their heads, and, faithful to the Carolingian ideal, he awaited the moment when he would be able to exercise the supreme magistrature which he had never renounced. He was therefore the great political force of the future. Without exception, all the European States were the work of royalty, and in all of them the rapidity and the amplitude of their development was in proportion to the royal power.

It was at the end of the 11th century—that is, at the epoch when the appearance of the bourgeoisies was completing the social constitution of Europe—that royalty began to lay the foundations of the first States worthy of the name. Here again progress began in the West: to be exact, in France. Just as feudality and chivalry and the Clunisian reformation spread from France into other countries, it was in France that the forces operated, or it was from France that the forces came which presently created the new States. It was a vassal of the King of France who founded the English State, and the kingdom of France was the earliest of the continental States. For that matter, the vassal preceded the sovereign. So that in this sketch of the political work of the monarchy we must begin with England.

Of all the Roman provinces, Britain was the only one whose inhabitants had refused to accept the domination of the Barbarians at the time of the invasions. After a violent struggle they were driven back into the West, into Cornwall, and Wales—where their Celtic idiom has been preserved to this day—while others emigrated to Armorica, which thereupon took the name of Brittany. The Anglo-Saxons, finding themselves alone in their new country, were able to preserve their national institutions intact. The seven petty kingdoms which they founded there did not reveal the slightest trace of that Romanization which had imposed itself so completely on the Germanic kings on the other side of the Channel. Owing to the restricted area of these kingdoms, they were perfectly adapted to institutions which had been born in the bosom of the tribe, and which would have been unsuitable to a great State. Thus the Germanic States whose conquest by the Franks had checked evolution in Germany continued to develop unhindered in England. The assembly of the people, the *Witenagemot*, existed simultaneously with the king, and the popular magistrate, the ælderman, was found side by side with the royal officials, the sheriffs. The Christianization of the country at the end of the 6th century brought no essential modification to this state of affairs. Of course,

the Church imported its language, Latin, into its new conquest, but the national development was too alien to the
Roman traditions, and the geographical situation rendered
permanent contact with the Frankish Church too difficult,
for it to be possible that this language should become, as
on the Continent, the language of the State. The Latin
Church behaved in England as the Greek Church, for the
same reasons, behaved in the Slav countries in the 10th
century. It accepted the language of its faithful, learned
it immediately for the purposes of evangelization, and
being forced to recruit its clergy from among its new con-
verts, it taught the latter to read and write their national
idiom. There thus developed, beside a scholarly literature
in the Latin language, a popular literature in the Anglo-
Saxon language, and it was naturally this language that was
used in recording laws and regulations, which on the Continent were written exclusively in Latin. Nor did the Church
exercise over the political organization the preponderant influence which the Carolingians had given it; the conversion
of England did not in any way alter the Germanic character
of the country.

The union of all the petty Anglo-Saxon kingdoms under
the King of Mercia, Offa († 796), would undoubtedly have
opened a new phase in their history had not the Norsemen
descended upon their country. From 839 their invasions
continued almost without interruption, and their result was
the establishment, on the eastern coast of the island, of a
numerous population of Danish origin. King Alfred the
Great († 901) successfully checked the invaders, to whom
he ceded the Danelaw—that is to say, the region situated
to the north of a line running from London to Chester. His
successors actually ended by reconquering this area. But
at the close of the 10th century Svend, King of Denmark
(† 1014), came to the aid of his compatriots, conquered
Mercia, East Anglia, and Wessex, and forced King Ethelred
to take refuge in Normandy. England was thus politically
attached to Scandinavia, and the bond was tightened under
Canute (1035), the son of Svend, who, like his father, was
at once a king of England and of Denmark. It was the

Anglo-Saxon missionaries who at this period introduced Christianity into Sweden and Norway.

But this state of things could not last. The forces of Scandinavia were never large enough to enable her to impose herself on the outer world. The Danish expansion in the 11th century suffered the same fate as the Swedish expansion of the 17th century under Gustavus Adolphus, and in the 18th century under Charles XII. The military power on which it depended was quickly exhausted. Under the successors of Canute, Harold and Hardicanute, the Danish dynasty became decadent. An Anglo-Saxon prince, Edward the Confessor, recovered the throne. His death, without issue, in 1066, was the occasion that decided the fate of England, and forced her to enter the European community, in respect of which she had hitherto observed a policy of isolation which could no longer be continued.

For the great island was naturally allied to the Low Countries and Northern France, from which it was divided only by the narrow waters of the Straits of Dover. Civilization had crossed the water with the legions of Caesar, and Christianity with the monks of Gregory the Great. Not until the equilibrium of the world was disturbed by the cataclysm of the Roman Empire could the Anglo-Saxons seize the island and retain possession of it. The economic stagnation of Europe after the period of the invasions, and the almost complete disappearance of commerce, explain very simply why from that time forward their relations with Christian Europe were exclusively religious. Charlemagne never attempted to absorb the Anglo-Saxons into the Empire, and after his death the weakness of his successors was yet another cause of their prolonged isolation. However, at the very time when the Danish invasions were threatening them with the domination of the Scandinavians, the revival of navigation began to re-establish, between them and their neighbours on the adjacent coasts of Flanders and Normandy, the relations that were naturally imposed by their geographical proximity. Bruges and Rouen, from the end of the 10th century, maintained an increasingly active navigation with England. With the return of a more advanced civilization the order of things which had so long been interrupted by the Barbarian invasion once more followed its natural course.

The Norman conquest was merely the consequence and final consecration of what may be called the Europeanization of England. While the incidents that provoked the conquest were due to fortuitous circumstances, and while the orientation of the island toward the Continent might, of course, have been effected in a manner very different from that which we know, this orientation itself responded so profoundly to the natural circumstances that it must have been accomplished sooner or later.

The ducal house of Normandy was closely related to that of Edward the Confessor, whose mother, Bertha, was a Norman princess. Being without children, Edward promised the succession to Duke William, thus himself disposing of the royal power, although, in accordance with Anglo-Saxon custom, only the assembly of the people could decide the matter. The assembly paid no attention to the King's resolve. On his death (1066) it elected Harold, the son of Godwin, who, during the lifetime of the feeble Edward, had played the part of a mayor of the palace. War was inevitable, and its issue was not in doubt.

In reality, the Anglo-Saxon kingdom was very weak. The old Germanic constitution, which had survived in its essential features, guaranteed the rights of free men as against the king, but condemned both the king and his subjects to a like condition of impotence. On the Continent the powerful feudal aristocracy had diminished the status of the king only to increase its own; the power had passed from the sovereign into the hands of the territorial princes. In England, on the contrary, no one had any real power. The aristocracy which constituted the National Assembly prevented the birth of the monarchical government, but was itself powerless to govern. Faithful to the old Germanic customs, it was essentially conservative. It consisted of landowners of mediocre importance, who lived by the labour of their serfs and retainers. The feudal system and the order of chivalry were unknown. The Anglo-Saxon earls and thanes, armed with battle-axe and sword, fought on foot. Both as a political organization and as a military power,

Normandy was superior to England in every respect. In all his territory, from the Canche to the Seine, the Duke had no rival. As the protector of peace he governed the people, and as the associate of the clergy, as the suzerain, he ruled the chivalry and the barons who held their fiefs from him. The domains whose comptrollers delivered their accounts every year to his exchequer were a model of good organization. Two great monasteries which he built at Caen, the Abbaye aux Hommes and the Abbaye aux Dames, were evidence not only of the prosperity of his finances: their architectural beauty is sufficient proof of a social progress which appears all the more striking if we reflect on the primitive condition of Anglo-Saxon architecture at this period. While in England literary culture had vanished from the Church amidst the turmoil of the Scandinavian invasions, the Norman clergy were distinguished by such writers as St. Anselm and Odericus Vitalis. Lastly, the military power of the Duke was formidable. The Norman chivalry was incontestably the first of the age. To realize its valour, we have only to recall its extraordinary exploits in Italy. It was bound to throw itself with enthusiasm into a conquest which offered it, on the other side of the Channel, prizes and adventures as brilliant as those which Robert Guiscard and his companions had found in Sicily. Moreover, William did not call upon his vassals only. Large numbers of French and Flemish knights and adventurers came to join them. The despatch of a banner by the Pope gave the expedition the semblance of a Holy War, and this tended to increase the ardour of the army.

Having no fleet, the Anglo-Saxons could not oppose its landing. It disembarked at Hastings on October 13th, 1066, and on the following day marched against the enemy. Harold had taken up his position on the hill of Senlac, behind a defence of palisades which compelled the Normans to fight on foot. After a violent hand-to-hand encounter their victory was complete. Harold was among the dead; those who had not fallen in the battle understood that further resistance was useless. The day had given England to William. A few weeks later he had himself crowned in Westminster Abbey, and in order to take possession of the rest of the kingdom he had only to make his progress through it. The Anglo-Saxons, who had so long struggled against the Scandinavian invasion, submitted at once to the Norman invasion.

2. The Invasion

The invasion was really the consequence of the conquest; it could not have been otherwise. In order to retain his kingdom, to which he was a complete stranger, and of whose very language he was ignorant, William was obliged to keep a permanent garrison of Normans in the country, and the only means of doing this, under the economic circumstances of the time, was to distribute them amidst the conquered population as so many gendarmes of the Crown. This distribution of the conquerors in the midst of the conquered has a very close resemblance to the colonization of Southern Gaul, Spain, and the Valley of the Rhone by the Visigoths and the Burgundians of the 5th century. But the result was very different. While the Barbarians, brought into contact with a population infinitely more civilized than themselves, became Romanized immediately, it was only with the greatest difficulty that the Normans were absorbed into the mass of the surrounding Anglo-Saxon population. The principal cause of this difficulty was evidently their superior civilization. To this may be added the constant influx of reinforcements, which continued to come, until the end of the 12th century, not only from Normandy, but also, after the advent of the Plantagenet dynasty, from Poitou and Guyenne. The influence of the court, which, until the end of the 15th century, was entirely French in language, if not in manners, must also have been considerable. For the immigrants Anglo-Saxon was merely a barbarous patois which they did not take the trouble to learn. As on the Continent, the native idiom was replaced, as an administrative language, by Latin, and then by French. People left off writing it, and its literature fell into oblivion. But it did not disappear before the language of the conquerors as the idioms of the provinces conquered by Rome had formerly disappeared before Latin, or as in Normandy the Scandinavian tongue itself had given way to the French language. The people continued to make use of it. But nothing could be more erroneous than to explain their fidelity to the national language by their antipathy for the tongue of the conqueror. On the contrary, they borrowed from the latter as freely as they could. Insensibly, Anglo-Saxon became transformed into English; that is to say, into a language whose vocabulary is half Romanic while its grammar and its syntax have remained Germanic.

But at the period which we are considering—the close of the 11th century—the time when this idiom, in the formation of which the conquered collaborated with the conquerors, was to become the language of both, was still far distant. Long centuries were necessary to weld the conquering and the conquered people into a single body, and to make the constitution of England the most national constitution in the world. In the beginning, under William the Conqueror and his more immediate successors, the political system which was installed in England was a system of foreign occupation.

Never was the conquest of the country accompanied by a more complete upheaval of its political institutions, and of the whole organization of the State.[1] Since he held his kingdom only by the sword, since he ruled his new subjects only by force, how could William dream of preserving a system of government which allowed the assembly of the people to reign in conjunction with the king? The indispensable condition of success was to subject everything to the royal power, to make it so strong that nothing could shake it. The constitution had to be, and was in fact, essentially monarchical. It was reserved for a great vassal of the King of France to create the most vigorous monarchy in Europe.

And the first thing to be noted is, that it was precisely because he conceived his monarchy as a feudal prince that he was able to make it so powerful. All the Continental kings were elected by their great vassals, but the great vas-

[1] Of course, I am speaking only of the conquest of one Christian State by another Christian State. Obviously the Musulman invasion gave rise to far more profound upheavals.

sals themselves were hereditary. William was the hereditary
Duke of Normandy, and he remained a hereditary prince
as King of England, so that while the other kings were given
their crowns, and could not dispose of them, he was from
the first the true possessor of his own crown. At the same
time, by virtue of the Conquest, he was the proprietor of
his kingdom. The entire territory of England was his property; he exercised over it a right analogous to that which
the seigneur of a great domain exercises over his estate;
in their relation to him, all the private occupiers of land
were merely his tenants, so that one of his first cares was to
obtain an exact account of these occupiers. It is to him that
we owe the Domesday Book, which was compiled between
1080 and 1086, and which may be justly likened to a
polyptych, but to a polyptych containing the territorial
statistics of the whole State.[2] His enormous territorial
wealth enabled him to create a feudal organization, imported from the Continent, but infinitely more systematic,
and above all, devoid of alien elements. The feudal system
in itself, as we have already seen, was by no means incompatible with the sovereignty of the State. That it rapidly
became incompatible with the sovereignty of the State was
due to the fact that the great vassals, having usurped the
rights of the Crown, attached them to their fiefs, so that
they obtained the investiture of these rights simultaneously
with that of their land. William took good care to avoid the
introduction into England of this confusion of the political
and feudal elements. The fiefs which he distributed to his
Norman knights gave them no financial or judicial authority. In conformity with the very principle of feudality,
they were simply military tenures conferred by the sovereign. The great vassals, who themselves had large numbers of subordinate vassals, constituted the army of the
Crown, but to none of them did the Crown surrender the
least of its prerogatives. The rights of the monarch were
not frittered away into the hands of the great nobles. William, as Duke of Normandy, knew what the establishment

[2] In the state in which it has come down to us, the Domesday
Book does not contain a complete return of all the occupiers of
land in the kingdom. A certain number of counties are missing.

of territorial princes all around him must cost a monarch. He took good care to ensure that no one should become, in his kingdom, what he himself was in the kingdom of France, and neither under him, nor at any other time, was the English feudality more than what may be called a purely feudal feudality. It had lands, but no principalities; it had tenants, but no subjects.

Thus, by a unique exception, the power of the King of England was an intact monarchical power; it was not necessary for him, as it was for the King of France, to wage a long and difficult war against his vassals in order to reconquer his prerogatives. From the very beginning the State was entirely his property, which explains the different course of political evolution to the north and to the south of the Channel. In France, the king, who was originally very weak, and who had to deal only with individual princes, gradually built up his power from the ruins of theirs, making his own all that he took from them, and adding to his own strength as he restored the unity of the kingdom, so that in proportion as this unity was accomplished the king's government approached the condition of pure monarchy. In England, on the contrary, where from the very first the political unity of the country was as complete as the royal authority was firmly founded, the nation confronted the king as a single body, and when at last it felt the monarchical power pressing upon it too heavily it would find that it was able, by uniting its forces, to insist upon its right to participate in the government, and to wrest guarantees from him.

3. The Great Charter

Neither under William the Conqueror († 1087) nor under his two successors of the House of Normandy, William II († 1100) and Henry I († 1135), had the nation any grievance to complain of. Faithful to the feudal tradition, the kings took counsel with their great vassals, and were careful to avoid any conflict with them. The first difficulties arose on the death of Henry I, for he left no children. Stephen of Blois, the son of a daughter of the Conqueror, claimed the crown and seized it. His reign was merely the turbulent transition to a new epoch. This opened with the advent, in 1154, of the first Plantagenet, Henry II (1154–1189).

The first kings of England had had no Continental possessions beyond their Duchy of Normandy. Henry Plantagenet added to this the Duchy of Anjou, which he received from his ancestors, and the Duchy of Guyenne, of which he had become possessed, by a stroke of "realistic" policy, through his marriage with the heiress, Eleanor of Aquitaine: whom the King of France, Louis VII, a less complaisant and less practical husband, had just repudiated. Thus all the coasts of France, with the exception of wild Brittany, belonged to the King of England. The territories which he possessed on the Continent were more extensive than his island kingdom. But his power enabled him to undertake, on the frontier of that kingdom, conquests which the geographical situation made inevitable, sooner or later. In 1171 he took possession of a portion of Ireland. And in 1174 he forced the King of Scotland to swear fealty to him. From his reign the first beginnings of English expansion may be dated. But to his reign also must be referred the origin of that conflict with France which, from then until the beginning of the 19th century, recurred, under many forms and with varying amplitude, throughout the history of Europe. As a matter of fact, even under the Norman dynasty a more or less overt hostility had always characterized the relations between the King of France and his Norman vassal, become a king in his turn. But Philip I and Louis VI, conscious of their weakness, were too prudent to risk open warfare against their neighbours. They confined themselves to wrangling with them, and giving proof, on every possible occasion, of their insuperable malevolence. Louis VII was able to act more vigorously. The Continental domain of Henry II represented too serious a menace: it was inevitable that henceforth the French monarchy should make use of all its resources in its effort to contain an adversary who seemed destined to crush it. The war which presently broke out was the first of the political wars of Europe. Hitherto the kings had fought only to make conquests. Here the origin of the conflict was the necessity of maintaining the rights and the sovereignty of the State against the encroachments of the foreigner. The contest seemed unequal. Neither in power, intelligence nor energy was Louis VII comparable to his adversary. Fortunately for him, Henry II's government provided Louis with unexpected auxiliaries in England itself.

With the first Plantagenet the monarchical power, already so strong, tended plainly to absolutism. The feudal forms with which the Norman kings had impregnated their government were disappearing. An excellent administrator, an excellent financier, the new prince made his kingdom a model of organization. But the condition of his reforms, and their result, was the omnipotence of the Crown. He irritated the nobles by subjecting them to a tax which was to provide payment for bands of Brabançon mercenaries. He irritated the Church by forcing upon it the Constitutions of Clarendon, which subordinated the ecclesiastical jurisdiction to the control of royal agents. The Archbishop of Canterbury, Thomas Becket, who had sought refuge in France, where Louis VII had taken him under his protection, had fomented a spirit of discontent which was all the more formidable in that he justified it by religious motives. And presently the very sons of the King, supported by a party of knights and barons, rebelled against their father, and, reinforced by French auxiliaries, waged war against him in Guyenne and Normandy. Henry was able to hold his own against the rebels and abandoned none of his claims. In order to suppress the discontent which these claims had excited, it was necessary that his successors should be worthy of him. Richard Cœur-de-Lion (1189–1199), by his rash and quarrelsome incapacity, and John Lackland (1200–1216), by his baseness and cowardice, ruined their father's work all the more rapidly in that they had to fight, in Philip Augustus, the first politician of his age and the first great king that France had known. The conflict of the two Western States became more involved, and as it grew more embittered the area of hostilities was extended. Each of the parties sought allies in the outer world. The kings of England allied themselves with the Guelphs of Germany, while the kings of France supported the Hohenstaufens. The victory of Bouvines, the first of the great European battles, was as terrible a blow to Otto IV as it was to John Lackland. At the same time, it decided the issue of the political conflict which, since the death of Henry II, had been pending in England.

The feudal opposition which had been excited by the absolutist tendencies of Henry II, and which had been assuaged for a time during the purely military reign of Richard I, broke out more vigorously than ever under John Lackland. In order to carry on the war against Philip Augustus the King had imposed fresh taxes, and had contracted crushing debts. These might have been overlooked had he won overwhelming victories. The confiscation and then the occupation of Normandy and Poitou by France, and the crowning humiliation of Bouvines, finally unchained the rebellion. The barons led the revolt, but the clergy and the burgesses supported the barons' cause, which was one with their own. Equally oppressed by the king's despotism, the three privileged classes, from one end of the country to the other, acted in common accord. The stronger and the more centralized the English monarchy, the more general and the more unanimous was the resistance which it excited. The royal government had made a nation of this people, which spoke two different languages; but to-day this nation, with a common impulse, had turned against the King, and the unity which the government had given it left him isolated as he confronted it. The struggle was brief. Defeated, John capitulated, and submitted to the terms of the Great Charter (1215).

Magna Carta might be called the first Declaration of Rights of the English nation; for it was as truly national as the rebellion from which it emerged. The barons who imposed it upon the King did not forget their allies; they made stipulations not only for themselves, but also for the clergy and the bourgeoisie. At first sight, nothing would appear more incoherent than this charter, which proclaims, without order, entirely at random, the confirmation of feudal usages, clerical franchises, and urban liberties. And it is precisely in this that its strength and its novelty reside. For by wresting pell-mell from the king so many different rights, and by confounding, in a single text, the claims of all the classes, it established between them a solidarity which would endure, and which, of itself, rendered possible the development of the English Constitution. The nobility, the clergy, and the bourgeoisie were not, as on the Continent, separate bodies, acting each on its own account, and pursuing only its own advantage. The common danger, and the common oppression, had here allied and united a solid complex of interests, which were doubtless, at many points, mutually opposed, but which were forced, by the strength of their adversary, to effect a reconciliation and make common cause. Elsewhere the kings had been confronted by different "Estates," deliberating with each separately, and reaching some accommodation. In England, the Crown had to deal directly with the nation, had to treat with the whole country.

A remarkable feature of this episode was that the barons of 1215 did not attempt to dismember the royal power. The monarchical State founded by the Conquest remained intact. The victors did not dream of dismembering it, or of depriving it of the rights of sovereignty in order to exercise them in its place. What they wanted, and what they obtained, was not so much a limitation of these rights as the guarantee that they could collaborate in their exercise when it should be necessary, for the welfare of the kingdom, to levy on the wealth of the king's subjects. The principle that taxes should be voted by the nation constituted the essential basis of the Great Charter, and for this reason it was the basis of the first free government that Europe had known. However, this principle was not definitely recognized until the reign of Edward I after the Battle of Falkirk (against Scotland) in 1298.

John understood very well all that the Charter imposed upon him, and he had hardly sworn to observe it when he broke his oath and obtained absolution from Innocent III. The barons took up arms again, and Philip Augustus hastened to send his son Louis to fight beside them. The struggle continued until the death of the king in 1216. The son, Henry III, on ascending the throne, ratified the Charter for the sake of peace. From that time onward it was part of the public law of England.

CHAPTER II

France

1. *The King and the Great Vassals*

From Hugh Capet to Philip I, the French monarchy was contented to exist. It was so modest that it was hardly perceptible in the midst of the great vassals. The names of this epoch whose memory posterity has preserved are not those of the kings; they are the names of feudal princes, like the Count of Flanders, Robert the Frisian; the Duke of Normandy, William the Conqueror; or of the heroes of the first Crusade—Godfrey of Bouillon, Robert of Flanders, Robert of Normandy, Raymond of Toulouse. In the midst of the epic of the Crusade, when the princes were covering themselves with glory, the king, who had remained at home, made a very poor show. The *chansons de geste,* which were then becoming the vogue, had barons for their heroes, and often depicted the monarchy as playing a very secondary part.

Towards the end of the 11th century three-fourths of the kingdom were occupied by a few great fiefs which were really principalities, their dependence on their sovereign being merely nominal. In the north, between the Scheldt and the sea, was the County of Flanders; below this, running along the coast as far as Brittany, was the Duchy of Normandy; still further south, on the other side of Brittany, was the County of Anjou, and beyond it, stretching to the Pyrenees, the Duchy of Guyenne (Aquitaine). The County of Toulouse occupied the plain of Languedoc; the Duchy of Burgundy lay in the basin of the Saône, and marched with the County of Champagne, which was watered by the Marne and the upper Seine. In the midst of these territories, and hemmed in by them, was the royal domain, the Île de France, the region surrounding Paris, which did not at any point touch the sea-coast or reach the external frontiers of the kingdom. Though equal in area to most of the principalities of the great vassals, it was inferior to many of them in point of wealth. The cities of the Midi, and the valley of the Rhone, which were roused to activity by the Mediterranean trade, and the cities of Flanders, which constituted the terminus of the great route that joined the North to Italy, and along which were strung the fairs of Champagne, enjoyed incontestable advantages over the cities of the king's domain. Laon, Orleans and Senlis were engaged only in local trade, and even in Paris the most important merchants were merely wholesale shippers, who obtained their cargoes in the Norman port of Rouen. Thus, neither its geographical position nor its economic resources gave the Île de France a privileged situation. On the other hand, its position was admirably calculated to assist the monarchical policy. Thanks to its central position it was in touch with the different regions of the country, both with the semi-Germanic Flanders in the north and with Languedoc in the south. Interposed between contrasting nationalities and feudal principalities, it enabled the king to keep in touch with the whole of France, and to embark, at the fitting moment, upon his secular task of unification and centralization.

He began this task at the beginning of the 12th century, and it is characteristic that at about the same time the predominance of the dialect of the Île de France over the provincial idioms became increasingly perceptible, so that the French language developed harmoniously and contemporaneously with the progress of the royal power, and, by a piece of good fortune unique in history, the formation of the State in France went hand in hand with the formation of the nation. Who knows but that we should look to this fortunate phenomenon for the fundamental explanation of those qualities of lucidity, simplicity and logic which are generally accepted as qualities of the French genius?

Feeble as the monarchy had become, surrounded by its great vassals, and vegetating in their shadow, it none the less harboured within it the principle of its future power. For while in point of fact the feudality had paralysed the royal power, in point of law it had left it intact. The princes who nominated the king, and who, each in his principality, had usurped his authority, had not replaced the old Carolingian monarchical conception by any other. The idea never occurred to them that the king held his power from them, and that his competence was limited by their will. Of the election of the king, as of the election of the Pope and the bishops, it might be said that it merely selected a particular person; it could not confer upon him an authority which it was not within human power to confer, since it came from God. As to this, all the world was agreed. The king was the servant, the minister of God, and the ceremony of consecration, piously retained by the Capets, both attested and confirmed its semi-sacerdotal character. He derived from this ceremony a moral ascendancy which set him beyond all rivalry, which made him a unique personage, whose like was not to be found. Nothing could be more erroneous than to liken the king in the midst of his vassals to a sort of president, *primus inter pares*. Between them and himself there was no common measure. He was above them, out of reach.

It must be admitted that this special situation did not endow him with any clearly defined authority. It inspired in the king the obligation to reign in accordance with Christian morality, although it conferred upon him no formal title, save that of the Defender of the Church. But even this meant a great deal, for the Church helped to maintain his ascendancy throughout the kingdom. In the heart of the great fiefs, even the most distant of them, the monasteries applied to the king for the ratification of their possessions, and it was to him that the bishops appealed in their disputes with their vassals or their baronial neighbours. It mattered little that he was unable to help them; these priests and monks, by invoking him, prevented the world from forgetting him, and reserved a future for him.

Safeguarded by the Carolingian tradition, the king's pre-eminence over the great vassals was preserved. However independent they were in reality, they none the less held their fiefs from the Crown, and they had to swear an oath of fidelity to the Crown, and this involved very definite obliga-tions: military service and counsel. They were "the king's men," and although they hardly thought of him save when they wanted to meddle in his affairs, and give him, at his court, advice which, often enough, he would have preferred not to receive, they none the less recognized that he ex-ercised over them a right of overlordship, which was one day to become a right of sovereignty.

In order to exploit the advantages of his position, and to proceed from theory to practice, the king must have power, and he secretly applied himself to acquiring it. The first condition of a firmly established monarchy is its heredi-tary character. It was out of the question that the Capets should impose this condition upon their electors, who were more powerful than they. They contented themselves with appointing their successors during their own lifetime. By good fortune, every one of them had a son, so that from the time of Hugh Capet to that of Philip Augustus the kingdom was spared the dangers of an interregnum. For some two hundred years the kings passed the crown from hand to hand, and by virtue of prolonged possession the State at last became their property. Even by the 12th cen-tury the election by the great vassals had become little more than a ceremony. Philip Augustus felt that he was strong enough to do without it. His son Louis VIII suc-ceeded him, and was universally acknowledged without any intervention on the part of the princes. By its persistent patience, the dynasty had achieved the end which it had so obstinately pursued. The French monarchy had become hereditary, without commotion, without a *coup d'état;* hereditary by simple prescription.

At the same time, it had carefully and wisely adminis-tered its domain. This domain was neither very wealthy nor very extensive, but thanks to the specific policy of the king it enjoyed, from the reign of Hugh Capet to that of Louis

VII, a period of unbroken tranquillity. Paris, where the
dynasty led a sedentary existence, which contrasted so
strongly with the wandering life of the Emperors, always
on the move through Germany and Italy, or that of the
kings of England, continually leaving their island for Normandy, was gradually becoming the administrative centre
of the Île de France, and preparing for its future rôle as
the capital of the kingdom. The Archbishop of Sens came
to reside in the city. The provosts of all the king's domains
rendered their accounts to Paris. The permanent presence
of the court maintained a political and administrative activity whose like was not to be found in Europe. As Rome
was the city of the Pope, so Paris was the city of the king,
and for that reason its life was more varied and its character less bourgeois than that of other cities. Even in the
12th century the attractive power of the city conferred an
ever-increasing importance on the schools attached to its
monasteries. Under Philip Augustus the corporation of their
masters and scholars gave birth to the first "university"
in Europe. It is not surprising that art should have vigorously developed in so active an environment. Abbé Suger
de St. Denis, the minister of Louis VII, attracted to his
abbey the artisans of the adjacent regions, and Notre-
Dame de Paris, begun in 1163, is the first in date of the
great Gothic cathedrals. The prestige of Paris contributed
greatly to the unity of the kingdom, and from the 12th
century onwards, as the one increased, so did the other.
The social influence of the capital and the political influence
of the monarchy contributed in equal measure to the creation of the nation.

2. *The Progress of the Monarchy*

Since the accession of Hugh Capet the monarchy had
had no foreign policy. The only neighbour with whom
France might have entered into conflict was the Empire,
her neighbour along the whole extent of her eastern frontier: on the Scheldt and the Meuse in Lotharingia, and on
the Rhone in the kingdom of Burgundy. But on succeeding
to the last Carolingians, the new dynasty had abandoned

their claims to Lotharingia; and the Emperors having nothing to fear from its weakness and prudence, and being moreover engrossed in their Italian expedition, had given it no cause for uneasiness. The situation was suddenly altered when in 1066 the Duke of Normandy became King of England. A formidable power had now arisen on the western frontier, which, being washed by the sea, had seemed, since the last of the Scandinavian invasions, to be protected from all danger by Nature herself. It was impossible to maintain the same relations of indifference and security with this new power as with the Empire. For being a vassal of the king of France in respect of his Norman duchy, the new king was bound to his sovereign, and his feudal subordination was in too extreme contrast with the power which he wielded on the further side of the Channel to be other than a permanent cause of misunderstanding, suspicion, and hostility. Henceforth the Capets could not persist in the attitude of abstention to which they had hitherto restricted themselves. Anxiety, and the dignity of the Crown, compelled them to confront the external danger, and since they would henceforth find it necessary to pursue a foreign policy, this would give them the opportunity of at last pursuing a monarchical policy in France itself.

This policy was inaugurated by Louis VI (1108–1137), and it naturally began in a very modest fashion. Too weak to act alone, the king sought as an ally the Count of Flanders, an old enemy of Normandy. In connection with his English policy, he conceived the project, in 1127, of profiting by the assassination of Count Charles the Good to invest with the crown of Flanders a Norman prince who was a mortal enemy of the king of England. The project was abortive, but is none the less worth noting: and it was actually the first attempt on the part of the Crown to draw a great fief into the sphere of its influence. The external danger which the king had to face compelled him to exercise his sovereignty over his great vassals in order to absorb their forces into his own.

Louis VII (1137–1180) continued the struggle which his father had begun. His adversary, Henry Plantagenet, was far more formidable than the Norman king. We have seen already how it happened that Louis was able to hold his own against him. The long-drawn war which he fought upon the frontiers of Anjou was merely a succession of small and obscure actions, and meanwhile the great vassals maintained an indifferent neutrality. There was nothing remarkable about Louis, whether as a soldier or as a politician. The manner in which the royal prestige was increased under such a prince is therefore all the more characteristic. It was in his reign that the royal historiographer made his first appearance, and the first minister of the Crown to be remembered in French history: the Abbé of St. Denis, Suger. He was also the last minister whom the monarchy borrowed from the Church. After him, the State felt itself so strong, was so clearly conscious of its task, and was confronted with problems so difficult and so numerous, that it was obliged to require, in its councillors, a kind of training in direct correspondence with their mission. Its progress compelled it to break with the Carolingian tradition, and it could no longer content itself with collaborators drawn from the clergy. It needed men of affairs, jurists, men of action, whom it would recruit from among the laymen trained in its service, who were drawn from the ranks of those educated bourgeois whose numbers were constantly increasing. Suger appeared at a turning-point of the political evolution of the nation. Before his time the State had been so simple, or rather, so primitive, that a prelate could be entrusted with its direction without previous apprenticeship; after his time its increasing complexity called for specialists, and its personnel would no longer belong to the Church, or would belong to it only in name.[1]

From the reign of Louis VII to that of Philip Augustus the royal power made such progress as cannot be explained merely by the genius of the king. It was due very largely to the economic and social transformations occasioned by the

---

[1] This reservation is indispensable, since from Suger to Talleyrand and Fouché the Church constantly furnished the State with ministers and councillors. But these were no longer ecclesiastics in the true and full sense of the word; they were politicians who had retained little of the clerical profession beyond the robe and the benefices.

development of the bourgeoisies. During the second half of the 12th century all the cities of Northern France had constituted themselves as sworn communes. Almost everywhere, in the episcopal cities—at Arras, Noyon, Senlis, Laon, Reims, etc.—they had to struggle against the resistance or the ill-will of their bishops, imploring the king to support them, a request which he hastened to grant. In this way an understanding was established between the Crown and the bourgeoisies which assured the royal policy of the co-operation of the youngest, most active, and wealthiest class of society.

We may distinguish under Louis VII the first signs of this alliance, the full importance of which was recognized by the clairvoyance of Philip Augustus, who systematically strengthened and extended it. The rapid increase of monetary circulation, a consequence of urban trade, was none the less profitable to the Crown. By permitting the transformation of such prestations and feudal dues as had hitherto been paid in kind into dues payable in money, and by improving the minting of money, and consequently increasing the profits of the mints, it enabled the Crown to procure the indispensable instrument of all political power: financial resources. The royal treasury, hitherto merged in the total private fortune of the king, became a special branch of the administration. The oldest treasury accounts that we possess date from the reign of Philip Augustus. Not only was the king henceforth able to hire bands of mercenaries in time of war, but he was able, above all, to attach to his service men who were true functionaries: that is to say, paid agents who could at need be dismissed. Such were the bailiffs, first mentioned in the year 1173, and presently to be found throughout the royal domain. Capable henceforth of paying his servitors, the prince was no longer obliged to entrust their offices to hereditary incumbents whom he could not dismiss if he chose. The replacement of the old agricultural economy by a monetary economy removed the obstacle which, since the Frankish epoch, had invincibly hindered the development of the State.

The reforms introduced under Philip Augustus in the

organization of the royal court adapted it to the necessities of the central government. The assembly of lay magnates and ecclesiastics which, ever since the Carolingian epoch, had assembled at definite intervals round the king, constituting at once a council and a court of justice, without precise attributions, without specified competence—and which more often than not did little more than hamper the activities of the Crown in the interests of the great vassals— was divided into two permanent bodies: the Consel du Roi on the one hand, for political affairs, and the Parlement on the other hand, for judicial business. Both bodies were still composed, for the greater part, of members of the *haute noblesse* and the superior clergy. But already the king was introducing his own men into these bodies, and his influence was steadily increasing, while that of the feudal element was waning. The great officers of the Crown, all chosen from the *grande noblesse* who had hitherto exercised a real tutelage over the king, disappeared, or were reduced to purely honorific functions. The administration of the chancellery broke with the antiquated usages and superfluous phraseology of the Carolingian age, and adopted more practical methods. A record office was established in the Louvre, and in the measures adopted for submitting the annual accounts of the bailiffs we find something like an embryo form of the future *Chambre des comptes*.

Philip Augustus may therefore be regarded as the veritable creator of monarchical power, not only in France, but on the Continent.[2] The surname of Augustus was bestowed upon him by Rigord: *Quia rem publicam augmentabat*.[3]

Before his time the most powerful kings, the Emperors, and even Charlemagne himself, were able to govern only by virtue of the prestige and power which they derived from their victories, or from the support of the Church. Their power depended essentially on themselves, and was merged, so to speak, in their person. Without finances and

---

[2] Except in Sicily, where the foundations of the State were Byzantine.

[3] Cf. the title of the Emperor: *Mehrer des Reiches*.

without functionaries, their activities depended upon the extent to which they were supported by the Church and obeyed by the aristocracy, the latter becoming more and more independent and the former more and more hostile. Henceforth, on the contrary, the king had at his disposal a permanent administration whose activities he himself inspired, and which was independent both of the Church and of the feudality. The rights which tradition recognized as his could now become a reality, and in so becoming real they constituted the State. The young monarchy retained the fundamental principle of the old Carolingian monarchy: the religious character of the royal power. Since the end of the 9th century it had been as though embalmed, preserved intact despite its feebleness, and despite all the feudal usurpations. We have just seen how it acquired a new vigour, and how, as the neighbour of the English State, it had constituted in France, under very different and much more difficult conditions, a rival State.

The Counts of Flanders, who under Louis VI had fought beside the monarchy against England, under Philip Augustus sided with England against the monarchy. It was very natural that being threatened by the increasing power of their suzerain they should seek support in the great island whose next-door neighbours they were, and on which the industrial cities of their country were dependent for their wool. The cities, which in France supported the Crown, took the side of their prince in Flanders; not, as a superficial view of the case might lead one to suppose, by reason of a pretended sense of racial solidarity, but simply on account of their economic interests. No difference of attitude is perceptible, whether they were Walloon-speaking cities like Lille and Douai, or cities of Germanic language like Bruges and Gand. The policy of the Flemish princes thus assumed, from the beginning of the 13th century, an amplitude which no longer permits us to regard it as a mere policy of feudal resistance. On the one hand, it inaugurated an alliance with England, which, being based on mutual interest, was perpetuated through the centuries, finally becoming one of the most important factors of the future independence of the Low Countries (Holland and Belgium); on the other hand, by relying on the support of the bourgeoisies it assumed the appearance of a national policy, which identified the cause of the bourgeoisies with that of the dynasties.

The protracted war between Philip Augustus and Philip of Alsace (1180–1185) had involved as yet only the king and the Count of Flanders, and was concluded, after alternate victories and defeats, by a treaty to the advantage of the former. But no later than 1196 Baldwin IX formed an alliance with Richard Cœur-de-Lion, and four years later was able to obtain from the king the restitution of the northern region of Artois, ceded by his predecessor. The Crusade, which periodically interrupted the course of European policy, and in which Philip Augustus, Richard, and Philip of Alsace had taken part together some years earlier, drew Count Baldwin to the East in 1202. In the following year he received in St. Sophia the crown of the ephemeral Latin Empire of Constantinople, and died mysteriously shortly afterwards (1205), during an expedition against the Bulgars. He left two young daughters, whom their uncle Philip of Namur delivered, at the king's request, to Philip Augustus. The king gave the elder, Jeanne, in marriage to a husband of his own selection, Ferrand of Portugal, having taken the precaution of making him swear a special oath of fidelity, which was ratified by the cities and the barons of Flanders. He counted on being able to take any liberties with this new vassal, who owed him his good fortune. He sent his troops to occupy Aire and St. Omer, and by the bestowal of fiefs and pensions he secured the connivance of most of the members of the Flemish nobility. Driven to extremities, it was not long before Ferrand gave ear to the advances of the King of England, John Lackland. In 1213 he concluded a treaty of alliance with him.

The conflict in which Flanders was once more involved was this time a European conflict. The policy of Philip Augustus, developed by success and the genius of the king, now embraced the whole Occident, and the war became a general war, which was to decide the fate of the French monarchy.

The war between France and England, interrupted during the last years of Henry II's reign, was resumed as soon as Richard had returned from the captivity in which the Duke of Austria had held him, into whose hands he had fallen on his return from the Third Crusade (1194). It had no decisive result. But no sooner was Richard dead, and his brother John Lackland on the throne, than Philip resolved upon a decisive action. Profiting by the discontent which the new king had provoked, he summoned John to appear before him in his quality of Duke of Normandy, in order to clear himself of the charge of murdering Arthur of Brittany.[4] Since John did not deign to reply, the King of France, acting in the full rigour of his rights as suzerain, confiscated all the fiefs held in France by the Crown of England, and occupied them all, with the exception of Guyenne, thus at a single stroke doubling the extent of the Crown lands and acquiring the whole of the sea-coast from Bordeaux to Boulogne. The many offences of his rival, already at war with the English barons, which had drawn upon him, in 1209, the excommunication of the Pope, gave gratuitous support to this audacious policy. Philip, having got Innocent III to entrust him with the execution of the sentence pronounced upon John, made active preparations for an expedition against England. These preparations were already completed when John, humiliating himself before the Pope, and acknowledging that his kingdom was a fief of the Holy See, obtained his reconciliation with the Church. Philip employed his army and his fleet against Flanders, advancing as far as Damme, where the English surprised his ships and burned them; he then returned to France, while Ferrand of Portugal resumed possession of his territories.

Meanwhile, the conflict of the Western States had spread to Germany. Of the two parties at war there, Guelfs and Ghibellines, the first had been allied with England since the marriage of Henry the Lion with Matilda, daughter of Henry II. The natural rapprochement followed between the Ghibellines and France. Philip Augustus exploited the situation with brilliant success. The Emperor Otto of Bruns-

[4] Son of Godfrey, the eldest son of Henry II, who was acknowledged by Brittany in place of John.

wick, the head of the Guelfs, who had been completely won over by John Lackland, was excommunicated in 1210 by Innocent III. The King of France seized this opportunity to exhort young Frederick of Hohenstaufen, then confined in Sicily under the tutelage of the Pope, to take the bold step of entering Germany and placing himself at the head of the partisans of his house. The adventure had a romantic look; in reality nothing could have been more prosaic. The king's treasury had come to the help of his policy, and he had bought the German princes who were necessary to its success. On November 9th, 1212, they elected Frederick King of the Romans.[5] Thus the conflict between France and England divided the whole of Europe into two camps, and its issue was to decide the fate of the West. The enemies of Philip Augustus resolved, in 1214, upon a decisive effort. While John was to attack him through Guyenne, Otto of Brunswick marched upon Paris through the Low Countries, rallying, as he did so, the troops of Ferrand of Portugal. The army with which Philip went to meet him illustrated, by its composition, the progress of the royal power. Twenty years earlier it would have consisted entirely of the feudal militia. But now, beside the chivalry of the Crown vassals, there were bands of mercenaries and companies of bourgeois despatched by the cities. The clash took place at Bouvines, near Tournai, on July 27th, and the result was a brilliant triumph for Philip Augustus. This was the first of the great European battles, and if we except Waterloo, where six hundred years later the same adversaries were to confront one another, no other battle had such vast and immediate consequences. In Germany, Otto of Brunswick was replaced by Frederick II. In England John Lackland, humiliated, saw the barons rise against him and enforce his acceptance of the Great Charter. In France the territorial conquests were assured (Treaty of Chinon); the feudality was vanquished in the person of Ferrand of Portugal; and the royal power, which had just proved its strength by defeating the external enemy, was invested in the eyes of the people with a national prestige that endowed it with twofold vigour.

[5] On this subject see the following chapter.

CHAPTER III

The Empire

1. *Frederick Barbarossa*

The Concordat of Worms did not end the struggle between the Empire and the Papacy. Under Gregory VII the problem of the relation of the two universal powers had presented itself in all its amplitude, but afterwards, owing to the exhaustion of the two parties, it was restricted to the dispute relating to investitures, and even this had ended in a compromise. By this settlement the Emperor lost as much as the Pope had gained, but neither could be content with a state of affairs that provided no solution of the conflict of principles which had evoked the quarrel.

It was necessary to determine whether the Carolingian conception was to continue in force: that is to say, whether the Church, regarded as the whole body of the faithful, and also as a political society, should continue to have at its head two principals, mutually independent, the first governing men's souls and the second their bodies: or whether, on the contrary, it was the duty of the Pope to dispose of the Imperial crown—whether, in the language of the time, both the spiritual and the temporal swords were his, the Emperor receiving the latter from him as a vassal receives a fief from his sovereign. Only a new war could furnish the reply to this question, for no compromise was possible between the contradictory affirmations of the two adversaries.

This war, which broke out under Frederick Barbarossa,

was lost in advance by the Empire. While European society acknowledged the universal authority of the Pope in the Church, it could not concede an authority of equal amplitude to the Emperor. This would have been, in effect, to subordinate all the Western States to the Emperor in the temporal order, reducing them to the status of clients. Since the reign of Otto I the Imperialist theory no longer corresponded with the reality, for the Empire no longer comprised, as in the days of Charlemagne, all the Christians of the Western world. No formal protest had hitherto been made against it, because no prince was powerful enough to break with the German sovereigns. But what likelihood was there that in the middle of the 12th century the young and vigorous monarchies of France and England should amiably accept the Imperial tutelage? Just as the rising feudality had worked for Gregory VII against Henry IV, so the national States in process of formation were to work for Adrian IV and Alexander III against Frederick Barbarossa. It was the misfortune of the Imperial policy that whenever it attempted to impose itself upon the Papacy it merely provoked the opposition of the most active powers in Europe, and oriented them toward Rome.

To this must be added the fact that the Emperor's power within the Empire itself was constantly diminishing. After the Concordat of Worms he no longer appointed the bishops, and the right which he retained of investing them with their principalities was more often than not illusory. In actual fact, the episcopal elections were most frequently determined by the secular princes, who forced the Chapters to accept relatives or allies of their houses. Thus, the Imperial Church on which the German sovereigns had lavished privileges and territories ever since the reign of Otto I was now escaping from their control, and, one might almost say, was becoming feudalized. The great vassals whose power it had hitherto balanced had no longer anything to fear from it, and the ecclesiastical principalities, being no longer at the disposal of the Emperor, were merely fresh elements of political disintegration. At the very moment when in France the king was beginning to get the upper hand over the feudality, in Germany the feudality was getting the upper hand over the Crown. Nothing could be more striking than the comparison of the influence of the princes over the royal power in the two different countries. While in the 12th century the King of France was elective only in theory, and from the reign of Philip Augustus became the hereditary sovereign, the German princes continued to insist on their right to dispose of the throne. On the death of Henry V they refused the crown to his nearest relative, Duke Frederick of Swabia, and gave it to Lothair of Saxony (1125); then, on the death of Lothair, they reverted to the house of Swabia, and appointed Conrad III (1137). Of course, what determined their selection was the promises and concessions of the candidates, so that the royal power grew weaker in the very act of transmission.

Under such circumstances, how could the Emperor dream of resuming the quarrel with Rome? Instead of treating the Pope as an equal, Lothair obtained the Imperial crown only by a damaging revision of the Concordat of Worms, and by his acquiescence in the Pope's claim to the right of refusing to crown the Emperor if he did not approve of his election. Conrad III was weaker still. His nomination was opposed by the Duke of Bavaria, who took up arms against him, thus inaugurating the quarrel of the Guelfs and the Ghibellines which was so long to trouble Germany and Italy. The struggle was continued after his death by his son Henry the Lion, who in 1142 had to be given the Duchy of Saxony in the place of that of Bavaria, which had become a fief of the house of Babenberg. Poor Conrad had no time to cross the Alps for his coronation; he hoped to increase his prestige by taking part in the Second Crusade, only to suffer the mortification of defeat. He died in 1152, and his nephew Frederick, after previous arrangement with the enemy of his house, Henry the Lion, obtained the suffrage of the princes.

With Frederick Barbarossa a reign began whose brilliance appeared all the greater because of the obscurity of the reigns which had preceded it. The young king, eager and ambitious, had resolved to restore the prestige of the Imperial dignity in the eyes of the world, and with fiery energy he devoted himself to attaining this inaccessible goal, the final result being merely a notorious defeat and the wasting of the remaining forces and the last resources of the German monarchy. At first sight, Frederick's policy seems a continuation of the Carolingian tradition, and the canonization of Charlemagne in 1165 by a German synod appears to confirm this filiation. In reality, there was nothing in common between the Carolingians and the Hohenstaufens but their tendency to universality. As Barbarossa conceived it, the Empire was no longer the Christian Empire which was born in St. Peter's, in the year 800, so intimately allied with the government of the Church, and so closely united to the Papacy, that they were indissoluble. As he conceived it, the Empire was in the full sense of the word the Roman Empire—but the Roman Empire of Augustus, as it was before the invasions. It was from this that he derived his right to govern the world, and since its origin dated back before the birth of Christ, how could it have anything in common with the Papacy? More ancient than the Papacy, it was as independent of the Pope as was the Emperor of Byzantium. The Empire was not contained in the Church, but the Church in the Empire, and notwithstanding his sacred character, the Pope, in the last resort, was merely a subject of the Emperor. The religious mysticism at the root of the Carolingian conception was here replaced by a sort of political mysticism, boldly harking back through the centuries to that eternal Rome who was mistress of the world, and deriving the Imperial claims from her, as the unique source of all temporal power. As early as the 11th century Otto III had flattered himself with the hope of restoring to its pristine magnificence that golden Rome (*aurea Roma*) whose ancient glory still shone in men's minds as the ideal of all terrestrial splendour. But what in Otto were only vague dreams and sentimental aspirations became in Frederick a precise theory. At the beginning of the 12th century the study of Roman law had made considerable strides in Italy, particularly in Bologna, where Irnerius was teaching. For Irnerius and his pupils the Code of Justinian was a sort of Holy Scripture, the revelation of law and civil order. Hence the veneration of these jurists for the Imperial power, which they regarded as the first condition of the maintenance of temporal society. It can hardly be doubted that the doctrines of this school had influenced Barbarossa. According to them, his political conception, unlike that of the Carolingians and their successors, had a secular base; those who were entrusted with its defence were no longer the theologians, but the jurists. For the first time, in the conflict between the Emperor and the Pope, the opposition between the temporal power and the spiritual power revealed itself.

Many bishops, no doubt, remained faithful to Frederick, and he did his utmost to obtain "good elections" in the Chapters. However, he could no longer lean on the German Church, whose situation, since the Concordat of Worms, had undergone such a profound transformation. He looked for compensation to the lay feudality. Until the reign of Henry V, the Emperors, who could then rely on the bishops, had regarded the feudal nobility with more or less suspicion. Moreover, the nobility had sided with the Pope against the Emperors; since the reign of Lothair the Saxon it had constantly increased its influence by this means, and had even succeeded in imposing its will upon the episcopal principalities.

Frederick frankly accepted this new condition of affairs. In singular contradiction to the unlimited power which he dreamed of possessing as Emperor, as King of Germany he allowed the secular princes to enjoy almost complete independence. Instead of attempting to impose his will upon them as their sovereign, he sought rather to obtain a personal following among them by intervening in their quarrels and flattering their ambitions. To them he seemed rather the leader of a party than a king, and his monarchical policy consisted, at bottom, in creating a Ghibelline faction, which the malcontents and those of contrary views opposed by forming a Guelf faction. However, he did not confine himself to influencing the princes; he endeavoured also to rally the lesser nobility, and to make of it at once a political instrument and a military force. At this period the customs of chivalry were beginning to spread from France and Lotharingia to the right bank of the Rhine. Frederick did his utmost to encourage this diffusion, and to impress the knights with his own prestige, and also to attract them to his court by brilliant feasts and tourneys. He promoted many *ministeriales* to knightly rank, and he utilized what was left of the Imperial domain in creating fiefs for these military retainers. It was under his reign that the mountains of Swabia, Franconia and Thuringia began to bristle with the "feudal castles" of which so many are still to be seen in a state of ruin.

It may thus be said that in Germany Frederick sacrificed the political rights of the monarchy to the necessity of creating a strong feudal army. However, he could not have done otherwise. The social development of the Germanic countries, which were backward as compared with the Western States, did not allow him to create the financial resources which would have enabled him to raise bands of mercenaries. The economic system of Germany, apart from the valley of the Rhine, was still that of the old domainal constitution, and the circulation of money was still extremely restricted. There was hardly any city of real importance, except Cologne, the only commercial centre comparable to those of Flanders; the ports of the Baltic were barely beginning to make themselves felt; and in the south Augsburg, Vienna, and Nuremberg were still only third-rate towns.

Moreover, in Frederick's plans Germany played quite a secondary part; he regarded her merely as an instrument which would enable him to open up the path to Italy and empire. Essentially German as regards his manners, feelings and character, in politics he was as little of a German as it was possible for him to be. His mind was entirely filled with the Imperial ideal. At the very moment when the French and English monarchies were laying the foundations of stable national States he was about to reopen a conflict which was finally to hurl his country into the anarchy of the great interregnum, and leave it for long centuries cut up into feudal subdivisions.

Of the conflict which he was about to provoke he appreciated neither the difficulties nor the extent. It was not the Pope alone whom he would have to fight. Since the end of the 11th century the Lombard plain had become covered with a dense vegetation of urban communes, through which he would have to make his way in order to reach Rome. In all the cities of the Po basin the bourgeoisie, enriched by trade and industry, had wrested the government from the bishops, and had founded municipal republics, which no longer had any regard for the rights of the Empire, and considered themselves to be independent of it. But Frederick, in his ignorance of urban civilization, felt the same disdain for these bourgeois as was felt by the German nobles, and for their republican constitutions he felt the contempt of the successor of Constantine and Justinian. He had made this very clear in 1154, when he crossed the Alps for the first time. Having convoked the princes and the cities of Upper Italy in the Plain of Roncaglia (near Piacenza), he attempted to impose upon them an oath of fealty, and to inform them of their duties toward himself. There was some resistance. Frederick saw fit to crush this by means of terror; he besieged Tortona and razed it to the ground. Then, having crowned himself at Pavia with the crown of the King of the Lombards, he marched upon Rome, where the Imperial crown awaited him.

The city was then in a state of rebellion. However, there was nothing in common between the insurrection of the Roman people, which was supported by the Church, as it had formerly been supported by the Emperors, and the revolts of the active and vigorous Lombard bourgeoisie. The traces which antiquity had left upon Rome were so profound that the inhabitants of the city could not free themselves from the memories and the splendours which surrounded them, and by which they lived. Periodically, the Roman people have lost their heads, intoxicated by the idea that they were still the masters of the world and the descendants of the sovereign people. The only municipal organization that Rome had ever had was that which conquered the world and perished of the conquest. Having become the centre of world politics, and then of the universal Church, the city could not belong to itself: it belonged too completely to Christian Europe. A mere communal council could not take the place of the Senate, yet at every one of these crises of their turbulent history the Romans really believed that they had re-established the Senate, the ancient Senate, the supreme legislator and administrator of human affairs.

Rome was at the height of one of these crises at the moment when Barbarossa approached the Tiber. The Pope had fled; Arnold of Brescia was ruling the city, and dreaming of reforming both the Church and the Empire. In him religious and political mysticism were allied. He wanted to restore the Church to evangelical purity and poverty, while the Emperor, on whom the Roman people had conferred the government of the world, would be the organizer of temporal society and would reduce the Pope to the rank of a simple priest. Thus, by a curious coincidence, antiquity had inspired both the King of Germany and the Italian revolutionary. But how could they have understood each other? The king considered that the Imperial rights were derived from the people, and looked to the people for a renovation of the world. The revolutionary regarded the Imperial power merely as dominion over the world as it was, or rather, as it appeared in the eyes of the feudal warrior. For Frederick, as for the Pope, Arnold was simply a dangerous heretic. Frederick handed him over to Adrian IV, who had him burnt at the stake.

Returning to Rome in the midst of the German knights, the Pope appeared to be under an obligation to Frederick, and Frederick might well have believed, when he received the Imperial crown in St. Peter's (June 18th, 1155), that he would henceforth be safe from the attacks of the Papacy. But Adrian had surrendered none of the claims of the Holy See. Frederick realized this, to his indignation, almost immediately upon his return to Germany. The legate Rolandi went so far as to describe the Empire, in his presence, as a "benefice" (fief) of the Holy Father. At the same time, the Lombard communes asserted their independence, and under the leadership of Milan, were openly preparing for war. This time the Emperor was resolved to strike one great blow, and annihilate his adversaries. In 1158 he was once more in Lombardy: he then and there made the most solemn proclamation of his sovereign rights (regalia), condemned the liberty of the cities as a frivolous and criminal rebellion, ordered the demolition of their walls, and subjected them to the jurisdiction of podestàs appointed by himself. The disdainful arrogance of his language and his attitude merely embittered the resistance. The German knights, with surprise as great as their anger, saw that mere townsfolk dared to oppose them in the open country, and were infuriated to discover that they could not carry by assault the ramparts which these vulgar citizens victoriously defended. The contrast of nationalities increased the mutual hatred of the combatants, but the real issue was the opposition of two incompatible forms of society: on the one hand, absolutism supported by a military aristocracy; on the other hand, political autonomy and municipal liberty; and those who proclaimed them were ready to die for them. At a distance of six hundred years, and in a more restricted setting, the resistance of the Lombard burghers to Frederick Barbarossa resembles the resistance of the French Revolution in 1792 to the armies of Prussia and Austria. Cremona was destroyed by fire after a seven months' siege (1160). Milan defended itself for nine months, and was at last forced to surrender (March 1162) only by famine and pestilence. It could not hope for pardon. Frederick understood nothing of the superior civilization of his enemies. In his naïve brutality he inflicted upon them the punishment which he would have inflicted upon a feudal "bourg" that had dared to hold out against him. He had the city razed to the ground, as though the destruction of a city could prevent its rebirth.

To him this victory must have seemed all the more decisive, as he believed that he had just won another victory over the Papacy. Adrian IV was dead (September 1st, 1159), and the Cardinals being unable to agree on the election of his successor, Alexander III and Victor III each assumed the tiara and excommunicated the other. This was an excellent opportunity for the Emperor to impose his will upon the Church, by deciding, as Henry III had formerly done, between the rivals. He assembled a Synod at Pavia, and the German and Italian bishops who attended it naturally voted for Victor, since Alexander was none other than the insolent Rolandi, and the majority of the Conclave, in electing him (February 1160), had been deliberately af-

firming its anti-Imperialist policy. But Frederick was immediately forced to realize that Europe was no more inclined
than the Lombard cities to surrender to his will. The whole
Catholic world ranked itself behind Alexander, and despite
the prayers which the Emperor deigned to address to them,
the kings of France and England remained immovable.
However, the Emperor persisted. Victor IV being dead, he
procured the election of Pascal III (April 20th, 1164), thus
prolonging, by his pride, a schism from which he no longer
had anything to hope.

He had at least the satisfaction of escorting his Pope to
Rome, while Alexander took refuge in France (1167), and
of proclaiming the sovereignty of the Empire over the city.
He was then obliged to recross the Alps with all possible
speed, the plague having broken out in the army.

The state of Italy was more threatening than ever. The
terror employed against the Lombard cities had merely
fired them to more passionate resistance. They were closely
allied with the Pope and had given his name to Alexandria.
Milan rose from its ruins and rebuilt its walls. The whole
process was beginning over again. A new campaign was
opened in 1174, which at first went slowly, a war of sieges,
and was suddenly terminated, on May 29th, 1176, by the
battle of Legnano, when the Imperial army was cut to
pieces and dispersed by the Milanese and their allies. The
catastrophe was irremediable, as was the humiliation. At
one stroke, Alexander III and the Lombard cities had tri-
umphed over this Emperor, whose arrogance had been so
intolerable as long as he had believed in his own strength.
From brutality he suddenly passed to deference and humility. He sacrificed the new Pope, Calixtus III, whom he
had caused to be elected on the death of Pascal; he acknowledged Alexander, and at Venice, where the reconciliation with the Pope took place, the Emperor dropped the
trappings of Augustus, prostrating himself and kissing the
Pontiff's feet. The deputies of the Lombard cities, whom
the Pope had promised to reconcile with the Emperor, were
present at this ceremony. A truce of six years, transformed
later, at Constance (June 1183), into a definitive treaty,
was concluded: for form's sake, it defined the rights of the

Empire to their subsidies and their military contingents, which were never furnished.

Frederick returned to Germany only to find Henry the Lion and his Guelf partisans in open revolt. He succeeded in overcoming the revolt, but his victory did nothing to establish the monarchical power on a stronger basis. Being obliged to conciliate the princes, he found himself compelled to distribute among them what he had taken from Henry. The Duchy of Bavaria was given to Otto of Wittelsbach; the Duchy of Saxony was divided between the Archbishop of Cologne, who was given Westphalia, and Bernard of Anhalt. The fall of Henry the Lion rid the Emperor of a dangerous enemy, but it was a misfortune for Germany. Ruling the country from the Alps to the Baltic, and having conquered and colonized vast Slavish territories beyond the Elbe, Henry wielded a power which, if it had endured, could have imposed its will upon the country as a whole, amalgamating the very different regions into which it was divided. He was overthrown by the coalition of dynastic interests with those of the feudality, and the triumph of his enemies had no other result than still further to increase the feudal subdivision which in Germany was becoming more extreme from reign to reign. It had already gone so far by the end of the 12th century that Frederick realized that if he was to assure the future of his dynasty he would have to find a territorial base outside the country. Hence the marriage of his son Henry, in 1186, with Constance, the heiress to the kingdom of Sicily. In order to survive, the House of Hohenstaufen was obliged to denationalize itself, turning from Germany to Italy.

This was the only lasting result—but obtained at what a price!—of the turbulent and sterile career of Frederick Barbarossa. Did the Third Crusade seem to offer him some hope of consolation for his misfortunes, and did his chimerical spirit see in it a good opportunity of refurbishing the Imperial majesty, by placing it at the head of a Christendom going forth to reconquer the tomb of Christ? He took the Cross in 1183. On June 10th, 1190, he met his death as the result of a trivial accident, falling from the saddle into the waters of the Cydnus.

2. Before Bouvines

To his son Henry VI, Frederick Barbarossa bequeathed an ungovernable Germany. Instead of improving the situation of the dynasty the defeat of Henry the Lion had aggravated it. Henry, having retired into England, had directed the attention and the ambition of the Plantagenets to German affairs, and had obtained their support for his partisans. Thus the new reign was greeted by a revolt of the Guelfs, who had to be appeased by concessions and promises. Even more than his father, Henry VI neglected Germany for Italy. Since the universality of the Imperial policy did not ally it to any one nation, it naturally had to make its headquarters wherever it found forces to support it. The heritage of the kingdom of Sicily, which Henry had received in 1189 on the death of his father-in-law William the Good, anchored him to the south of the peninsula and determined his career.

Raised to the rank of kingdom for the benefit of Roger II by Pope Innocent II, in 1130, the Norman State of Sicily was incontestably the wealthiest, and, in point of economic development, the most advanced of all the Western States. Byzantine as to its continental portion, Musulman as regards the island, favoured by the enormous extent of its coast line, and by the active navigation which it maintained with the Mohammedans of the coast of Africa, the island Greeks of the Aegean Sea, the Greeks of the Bosphorus, and the Crusader settlements in Syria, it was as remarkable for its absence of national characteristics as for the diversity of its civilization, in which the culture of Byzantium was mingled and confounded with that of Islam. Above this hybrid mixture of peoples, the Norman sovereigns had established a constitution which was feudal in its forms but absolutist in reality, and which had adopted the methods of the Byzantine administration. Despite their devotion to the Papacy, these Norman princes, in their political lucidity of thought, allowed both their Musulman and their Orthodox subjects to practise their respective religions. Their financial system was admirable. The culture of rice and cotton, which the Musulmans had introduced into Sicily, and the Oriental industries carried on in the great cities of Palermo, Messina and Syracuse, furnished the treasury with revenues more abundant than those of any other State, and collected in the most scientific manner. Having always been accustomed to the most improved methods of administration, whether those of Byzantium or of Islam, the population allowed itself to be governed with docility; the Norman nobles constituted the only element to be feared. While they had quickly lost their pristine vigour, and were softened by the luxuries of their semi-Oriental life, they were none the less greedy and seditious.

The acquisition of such a kingdom placed Henry VI in possession of resources which, compared with the miserable revenues that Germany still furnished for the monarchy, might well seem inexhaustible. He hastened to get himself crowned by the Pope, after which he broke with the pontiff, cast off the bonds of suzerainty which tethered Sicily to the Holy See, and revived the claims of Frederick to the city of Rome and the States of St. Peter. But his plans were far from ending here. They envisaged nothing less than the reconstitution of the Roman Empire; but this time in the Mediterranean basin, formerly conquered by Rome, and now shared between Byzantium and Islam. Byzantium, especially at this particular juncture, was in a state of anarchy, what with dynastic intrigues, palace revolutions, and military revolts, and in this condition it seems to have appealed to the Emperor's ambition. Even before his time, it had excited the covetousness of the Norman princes. Had not King Roger II taken advantage of the Second Crusade to ravage Dalmatia, Epirus, and Greece, and to seize the islands of Zante and Corfu? As enterprising and as chimerical as his father, Henry had entered into relations with the Crusader States in Syria and the Musulman princes of the African coast, and was preparing a great expedition against Constantinople when his unexpected death (November 27th, 1198) made an end of all these fine plans, and also spared him the embarrassment of an inevitable war with the Papacy, which, even if he had lived, would have rendered the execution of these plans impossible.

Thanks to his Sicilian riches, he had succeeded in obtaining the election, by the German princes, of his son Frederick II as King of the Romans. The child was then two years of age. The princes immediately forgot his existence and set about choosing another king. But they were no longer able to agree. The two parties into which they were divided, the Guelfs and the Ghibellines, were simply two feudal factions, one as little concerned as the other with the interests of the monarchy, and seeking merely to place in power a sovereign who would allow his electors to enrich themselves at the expense of their adversaries, and of the State itself. Foreign money, which in the time to come would so often determine the issue of the royal elections in Germany, now openly intervened for the first time. The pounds sterling of Richard Cœur-de-Lion were lavished in favour of his candidate, Duke Otto of Brunswick, the son of Henry the Lion, reared in England, and having little of the German in his composition apart from his hatred of the Hohenstaufens. In opposition to him, the partisans of the Hohenstaufens supported the brother of Henry VI, Philip the Swabian, who purchased the alliance of Philip Augustus by the cession of Imperial Flanders. He also gave the royal crown to the Duke of Bohemia in order to attach him to his fortunes. And civil war broke out from the Alps to the North Sea and from the Elbe to the Rhine, all the princes falling upon one another on the pretext of defending the legitimate monarch (1198).

This war was just what the Pope wanted. Basing his action on the old claim that the election of the King of the Romans must be approved by the Holy See, he intervened between the rivals. Philip could not renounce the traditions of his house and sacrifice the rights of the Empire. Weak as he was, he regarded himself as the successor of the Caesars, so that he actually called himself Philip II, having remembered that in the 2nd century Philip the Arabian had governed the Roman Empire. As for Otto IV, he promised all that was required of him: abstention from the episcopal elections, renunciation of all claims to sovereignty over Rome, and the surrender of the kingdom of Sicily. Innocent pronounced in his favour; however, his decision, and the excommunication pronounced against Philip and his supporters, did not weaken their cause to the point of compelling them to lay down their arms (1201). The struggle continued until Philip's assassination in 1208. Once rid of his rival, Otto set out for Rome, and the following year he received the Imperial crown. A few months later he was excommunicated. Hardly was he crowned, indeed, when the Guelf turned Ghibelline, and proceeded to claim, just as the Hohenstaufens had done, all the powers and pretensions which he had renounced a few years earlier.

The weapon destined to lay him low was already in the hands of the Pope. The son of Henry VI, Prince Frederick, whose mother, dying a few months after her husband, had confided him to the guardianship of Innocent III, while acknowledging that Sicily was a fief of the Holy See, had just attained his 14th year, and had taken over the government of the kingdom of Sicily. What more ingenious policy could be conceived than to send him to Germany, to see that he was acknowledged as king there, and in his interests to incite the Ghibellines—who this time would be acting on behalf of the Holy See—to fall upon the Guelfs? But in order to carry out so bold a plan the Pope must have an ally. The question of his identity was solved by the war which had just broken out between France and England: Philip Augustus was the man. Philip, indeed, knew that Otto had promised his support to John Lackland, and nothing could have suited him better than a rising in Germany against his enemy's auxiliaries. Just as the English treasury had formerly bought Otto's electors, so the French treasury now purchased the electors of Frederick II. Almost as soon as the young prince had shown himself in Swabia a number of the princes declared for him (1212). Two years later the crushing blow of Bouvines defeated, in the person of Otto, the last representative of the Imperial policy as conceived by all the German emperors since Barbarossa. On November 19th, 1212, Frederick concluded with France a treaty against Otto and England. On July 12th, 1213, at Eger, he recognized all the possessions of the Pope in Italy, and renounced the right of supervising the episcopal elections, in conformity with the Concordat of Worms. The war was decided, simultaneously, between him and Otto, between the Empire and the Church, and between France and England.

This was the final end of the chimera which these Emperors had pursued as they dreamed of the revival of the Roman Empire. The Pope was triumphant: he could not suspect, in 1214, that his ward would presently become the most persistent of the enemies of the Holy See. But the struggle which was about to begin between the Emperor and the Pope inaugurated an entirely new phase in the relations of Papacy and Empire. In this conflict, however, Germany was to play no part; since Frederick left Germany for Italy, and the former country, left to herself, finished by falling into a state of political decomposition; before foundering in the anarchy of the great interregnum.

INDEX

ANCHOR BOOKS

EUROPEAN HISTORY

DOLPHIN BOOKS

ANCHOR BOOKS